A History of
America's Most Popular Pickups

CarTech ®

FORD F-SERIES *Trucks*

1948–Present

JIMMY DINSMORE AND JAMES HALDERMAN

CarTech®

CarTech®, Inc.
6118 Main Street
North Branch, MN 55056
Phone: 651-277-1200 or 800-551-4754
Fax: 651-277-1203
www.cartechbooks.com

Edit by Bob Wilson
Layout by Connie DeFlorin

ISBN 978-1-61325-512-4
Item No. CT661

Library of Congress Cataloging-in-Publication Data Available

Written, edited, and designed in the U.S.A.
Printed in China
10 9 8 7 6 5 4 3 2 1

All photos are courtesy of authors Jimmy Dinsmore or James Halderman unless otherwise noted.

DISTRIBUTION BY:

Europe
PGUK
63 Hatton Garden
London EC1N 8LE, England
Phone: 020 7061 1980 • Fax: 020 7242 3725
www.pguk.co.uk

Australia
Renniks Publications Ltd.
3/37-39 Green Street
Banksmeadow, NSW 2109, Australia
Phone: 2 9695 7055 • Fax: 2 9695 7355
www.renniks.com

Canada
Login Canada
300 Saulteaux Crescent
Winnipeg, MB, R3J 3T2 Canada
Phone: 800 665 1148 • Fax: 800 665 0103
www.lb.ca

TABLE OF CONTENTS

ABOUT THE AUTHORS

Authors Jimmy Dinsmore and James Halderman teamed up again to offer this unique perspective on the Ford F-Series. Their first book, *Mustang by Design*, gave an insider's look at the creation of the Ford Mustang. In this book, they bring their blend of storytelling with technical information to the iconic pickup truck.

Jimmy Dinsmore is an automotive journalist who has covered the auto industry for more than a decade. *Mustang by Design* was his first published book, although his car review column called Driver's Side is syndicated nationally and runs in several newspapers and weekly in the *Dayton Daily News*.

He specializes in content creation and social media marketing as well.

James Halderman is the author of many automotive books including *Automotive Technology*, *Light Vehicle Diesel Engines*, and *Automotive Chassis Systems*, all published by Pearson. He also holds a US patent for an automotive electronic control device and gives technical seminars to regional and national audiences on automotive topics. James is also the first cousin of Gale Halderman, the well-known designer at Ford who rendered the first original Mustang. Automotive expertise runs in the family.

ACKNOWLEDGMENTS

This book represents our second collaboration together, following the success of *Mustang by Design*. We hope you find this book to be an informative and unique perspective on the Ford F-Series. This book would not have been possible without the help of many people. The authors would like to thank their wives and families for their support throughout this process. A special thanks to the many avid truck enthusiasts who provided photos of their personal trucks, many of which are featured in this book. This is your book as much as it is ours!

Also, this book would not have been possible without the following people who played a role in this project: Tom Birch, Carl Borsani, Jeff Bulin, Josh Conrad of the Early Ford V8 Foundation and Museum, Justin Mitchell and Noah Besvington of the Model T Museum, Tracy Dinsmore, Gale Halderman, Michelle Halderman, John Heitmann, Andy Jacobson, Dr. John Kershaw, Dick Krieger, Bud Magaldi, Bill Moraniec, Dick Nesbitt, Glen Plants, Jeff Rehkopf, Jim Sherritt, Hal Sperlich, Randy Stern, Jeff Trick, Richard Truesdell, Cam Vanderhorst, and Susan Yaeger of the Model T Ford Club of America.

INTRODUCTION

The pickup truck concept can trace its history to the infancy of automobiles in the early part of the 20th century. Henry Ford, who revolutionized the automotive industry with his moving assembly line, soon expanded his young company beyond cars into trucks. Although the Ford F-Series history doesn't technically begin until the first generation in 1948, the genesis of the F-Series started decades before that.

The Model TT

Henry Ford, the visionary pioneer, understood that vehicles had to be all things to all people. His Model T was handy and useful, but it wasn't practical for American farmers. The legendary Model T had a revolutionary manufacturing process that allowed it to be modified in many ways. It was so versatile that it became an agricultural and commercial darling. In fact, Ford produced a commercial version of the Model T called the "commercial chassis." The commercial chassis was basically a Model T without a body so that an individual or a company could create a body to meet their needs. This was the first Ford truck in its rawest, crudest form.

Ford listened and created the Model TT (Model T Ton) in 1917. This was the beginning of the Blue Oval's pickup truck, though that phrase wouldn't be coined until many years later.

Ford Truck Evolution

Throughout this nation's history, the pickup truck has been a constant. As America evolved through a World War (1916–1918), a Great Depression (1929–1941), and a second World War (1939–1945), the pickup truck and Ford's eventual F-Series was there, changing along the way. As America moved from an agricultural society to an industrial society and eventually into today's modern suburban life and urban sprawl, the truck evolved as well. Historians can often look at a truck and tell exactly what was happening in America at that time.

The automotive genius Hal Sperlich, who is rightfully credited with so many vehicles in automotive history and also worked on the Ford F-150 as well as the Dodge Ram, used the phrase, the "civilization of the truck" to describe the truck evolution. That perfectly sums up this book and sums up the Ford F-Series. It has evolved along a continuum of transportation needs and demands to take its rightful place in history.

Since 1981, the market share for trucks has increased. Economically, that's great news for manufacturers such as Ford because the profit margin for trucks often exceeded $10,000 per vehicle while margins on cars were significantly lower. Even in today's automobile industry, sedans are going away. At Ford, the Mustang will be the last remaining car under the Ford

Ford trucks were used on American farms in the early 20th century in the same way that farmers used Model TTs, such as the one pictured here. (Photo Courtesy Ford Motor Company)

nameplate. The rest will be comprised of crossovers, sport utility vehicles (SUVs), and of course, pickup trucks.

In today's era of fuel economy, hybrids, electric vehicles, and autonomous vehicles, Ford has sold more than 35 million F-Series trucks. According to stats provided by Ford, in 2018 the F-Series accounted for $41 billion in the company's annual revenue. Indeed, the F-Series is a force throughout America and even Canada, where it is also the best-selling vehicle. Ford also has a strong foothold in South America and Mexico.

Our Journey

As America became more civilized, more industrialized, and more commercialized, so too did the F-Series. Much the same as its Blue Oval mate, the Mustang, the F-Series has transcended beyond just a vehicle to something of stature and icon. Country singers write songs about it and rap artists shoot music videos in trucks. And the F-150 is the king of the trucks.

We will take you on a journey that illustrates the progress and the evolution of the F-Series throughout American history. Each mechanical and design change happens for a reason. Fourteen generations of F-Series trucks have been manufactured, each significant for different reasons.

Ford has played an integral role in the creation of the daily use truck. Henry Ford was very quotable, and one of his lesser-known sayings fits perfectly with the staying success of the truck: "The only prosperity the people can afford to be satisfied with is the kind that lasts." For more than 100 years, Ford's truck has lasted, and the future continues to look bright.

In the 1930s, Ford's truck began to evolve from the early Model TT and Model A to something that resembled a pickup truck. This is a 1935 Ford truck. (Photo Courtesy Ford Motor Company)

FORD F-SERIES FIRST GENERATION (1948–1952)

enry Ford II carried the burden of his grandfather's legend, his family's wealth, and history. It was a tremendous burden for a young and professionally inexperienced man. First up on his plate, with only a few years under his belt of running the Ford Motor Company, was launching Ford's first official truck, known as the F-Series.

Financially, Ford was just recovering from the effects of World War II. Across the country, a postwar boom was underway. Ford was primed to gain traction in the truck market. The stylish looks and success of the 1940 Ford trucks paved the way for what would become the F-Series in the 1948 model year.

The F-Series, or F-1 as it was sometimes called, was Ford's first postwar investment. It was a bold move to throw significant financial resources into a new vehicle rather than play it safe and invest in the car line. Had Henry Ford II played it safe, there may not be the F-Series as we know it today.

> "The F-Series trucks were called 'bonus built' because they were the first Ford vehicles with their own true truck platform. All the previous trucks were based off car platforms, such as the Model A and Model T."

Many consider the 1950s the golden era of the automobile industry. Styling during this time was outstanding. Automakers produced some all-time classics during this era. This 1950 Ford F-100 demonstrates that even trucks got a lot of exterior styling attention. This mildly modified example has been lowered and includes a custom grille with added driving lights. (Photo Courtesy Bob Spear)

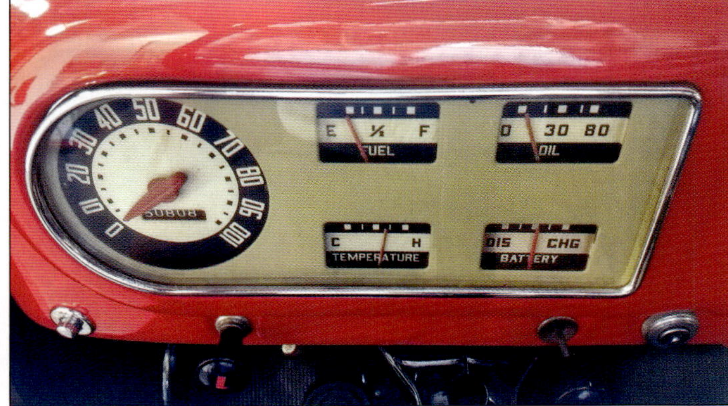

The Ford "Bonus Built" truck era was underway. In 1948, Ford launched the F-1 pickup truck as part of its new F-Series truck line. Pictured here is a 1949, which represented the second year for Ford's F-1 pickup truck. (Photo Courtesy Richard Truesdell)

The 1949 F-1 carried over much of the same looks as the first-year F-1 of 1948. The exception was that the grille took on a different look with silver-painted bars on the grille instead of red-striped chrome. (Photo Courtesy Richard Truesdell)

The instrumentation on this 1949 F-1 is classic. On the left was the speedometer that goes as high as 100 mph, something that the truck would likely never be able to achieve. The fuel gauge was clearly labeled with full (F) on the right and empty (E) on the left. The oil pressure gauge in the upper right is seldom seen on recent vehicles, but this truck shows a reading from 0 to 80 psi. Normal oil pressure is 10 psi for each 1,000 rpm. The temperature gauge in the lower left is showing the temperature of the coolant. Normal engine coolant temperature in 1949 vehicles was about 160°F. The battery gauge is another gauge not found on recent vehicles. This gauge indicates whether the current was flowing into or out of the battery. Everything electrical ran off the battery, and the generator was used to keep the battery charged. To the lower right of the dash is the ignition switch. A key was used to turn on the ignition circuit but was not used to operate the starter motor. To crank the engine, the driver had to push the starter button located at the lower left of the dash below the speedometer. (Photo Courtesy Richard Truesdell)

The back of this 1949 F-1 shows the rear fenders, the tailgate, and the spare tire located under the bed of the truck. The tailgate features a script "Ford" stamped into the sheet metal. A runner covering the chain helped prevent the chain from damaging the paint when the truck was in motion. The tailgate and the pickup bed were single steel panels. This meant that if a load shifted in the bed and struck the side or the tailgate, it could cause a dent that was then visible on the outside. Newer pickups use double-wall construction. Also notice the single taillight located at the left rear. This was before turn signals were required, necessitating a taillight on each side. (Photo Courtesy Richard Truesdell)

The interior of a stock 1949 Ford pickup truck featured the gear shifter on the floor. Also notice the brake and clutch pedals are attached to the linkage under the floor instead of being suspended as in newer vehicles. The center part of the dash shows an Art Deco–type design. (Photo Courtesy Richard Truesdell)

Ford Bonus Built

In January 1948, the F-Series was introduced as a light-duty and medium-duty (Class 1—7) truck. The first F-1 was a 1/2-ton truck meant to expand upon the look and success of prewar and 1947 trucks. The F-2 (3/4 ton) and F-3 (1 ton) soon followed.

In 1948, Ford adopted new promotional nomenclature for its first-generation F-Series trucks. Under this new system, each basic model (exclusive of engine) was designated

Early truck beds were a metal floor over a wood subfloor. Most restorers remove the metal floor and replace the wood with something nicer. In this example, the floor of the bed was replaced with oak with steel strips that fasten the boards to the chassis. (Photo Courtesy Richard Truesdell)

with a particular series, which was marked on the side of the cowl. The range extended from the F-1 or 1/2-ton pickup to the series F-8 truck. The 1948 light-duty trucks were the F-1 1/2-ton pickup, F-2 3/4-ton pickup, F-3 3/4-ton Heavy Duty, and F4 1-ton pickup. Most variations of the early F-Series trucks were true pickup trucks (as we know them today), but there were still chassis-cab trucks and commercially used trucks that Ford produced.

The F-Series trucks were called "bonus built" because they were the first Ford vehicles with their own true truck platform. All the previous trucks were based off car platforms, such as the Model A and Model T. The Bonus Built era was a monumental and expensive shift in Ford's production and its approach to the truck. The Ford Bonus Built trucks represented the largest commercial model expansion in Ford's history.

In addition to the truck-based chassis platform, there were other significant differences on the Bonus Built F-Series. The F-Series had the following features:

- 114-inch wheelbase
- New front sheet metal featuring integrated headlights
- A one-piece windshield
- A wider and longer truck bed

This generation of the F-Series remained in production until 1952. There were 16 different Ford assembly factories for the F-Series trucks. Serial numbers indicate the truck model, engine, year, assembly plant, and unit number.

The most common model was the F-1, which had a 6.5-foot bed. Both the F-2 and F-3 Express models were manufactured with an 8-foot bed. This new truck had all sheet metal for the body, which included a completely redesigned cab. This was the first cab redesign for the F-Series since 1938.

The new cab was used on both conventional and cab-over-engine (COE) models. It was 65 inches wide and suspended using a system of pads and rubber-mounted links. The one-piece windshield (1947 had a split front windshield) had returned, as did the use of side vents. These side vent windows were commonly referred to as "smoker windows" or "smoker vents" because they would allow the smoke from a cigarette or cigar to escape the cab without having to lower the door glass. There was also a new instrument panel layout that had gauges for fuel oil pressure, temperature, and ammeter. There was more of a design focus on driver comfort.

Even though the majority of consumers' needs were still agricultural in nature, the F-Series took interior design cues from Ford's cars at the time. The trucks were still far from the luxurious examples seen today, but they did show the early shift to a broader consumer base.

Engines

The flathead V8 engine was still being used in many of Ford's vehicles during this time, so it was part of the early model years of the F-Series. It wasn't until the last year of the first-generation F-Series (1952) that the flathead was finally replaced by an overhead valve engine (OHV).

There was a 6-cylinder flathead engine used for the 1948–1951 models. This L-Head (flathead) 6-cylinder used aluminum alloy pistons with four piston rings, which helped reduce oil consumption. It had a compression ratio of 6.8:1 and used a high-lift camshaft that provided more power. This engine, known as the 7HT, produced 95 hp and 180 ft-lbs of torque. It was also called the Rouge engine because it was built in the Ford Rouge plant.

An all-new V8 model was used in some trucks starting late in the 1948 model year, although the 6-cylinder was standard. Both the 7HT flathead 6-cylinder and model 59 flathead V8 engine used a new pressure-sealed cooling system and a weatherproof ignition system with vacuum spark advance only for 1948–1955. This design was called the "Load-O-Matic" and was changed to distributors that used both a vacuum and mechanical advance in later model engines.

The first-generation F-Series had a 3-speed manual transmission as standard equipment, although there was an optional 4-speed manual and eventually a 5-speed manual by the end of the model year run. The rear axle was a semifloating axle

The underside of the Ford flathead V8 engine shows the three main bearing caps and the eight cylinder bores. At the top and bottom of the block, there are just three exhaust ports for the four cylinders in each bank. This is because the two center cylinders on each side are routed into a shared exhaust port. This design results in some confusion from younger people who think that the Ford flathead V8 was a V6 because they only see three exhaust ports on each side.

A cutaway of a typical OHV engine shows where the valves are located in the cylinder head and therefore are "overhead" of the cylinders. OHV engines are able to produce more power than a flathead engine because the airflow in and out of the cylinders is more efficient. In an OHV engine, the compression can be increased higher than with a flathead engine. In a flathead engine, when the compression is increased, the amount of airflow into the cylinders is reduced. As a result, there is always a trade-off between the compression and airflow, which is not an issue with an OHV design.

A Ford flathead V8 engine is shown here mounted in a chassis. The most visible Ford flathead identifying aspect are the two upper radiator hoses. The engine uses two water pumps located at the front of the engine and driven by the V-belt that also powers the generator (top). The coolant flows through the engine block to each cylinder head and returns to the radiator through the upper radiator hoses.

that delivered quiet operation with a final drive ratio of 3.73:1 with an optional 4.27:1 axle ratio available. This allowed for a 14-percent increase in towing capacity compared to the trucks offered before 1948. All-wheel drive (AWD) was introduced with the optional Marmon-Herrington on all F-Series trucks until 1959.

By 1952, Ford replaced the ever-popular flathead engine with an OHV V8 engine. As Ford's trucks continued to gain weight, the flathead became obsolete, and the OHV engine replaced it with higher compression ratios and a significant increase in power and performance. The result was a more efficient-running vehicle with more power. The 215-ci 6-cylinder OHV engine produced 101 hp and 185 ft-lbs of torque with an increased compression ratio over the flathead engine. The quest for fuel efficiency and increased power has not stopped throughout the F-Series history. Ironically, the shift in today's truck has swung the opposite way; going from V8s to today's EcoBoost 4-cylinder engines.

GERMAN FORD FLATHEAD

From 1941 to 1947, there was a Ford flathead V8 engine manufactured in Germany. There were some features only found in this German flathead that could not be found in the more common American version. Some of those unique features included:

- 12-volt system with a pre-engaged starter
- Bosch distributor mounted at the rear of the engine (rather than off the front by the camshaft)
- Cylinder heads with larger cooling capacity for the rear two cylinders
- Oil pan made of aluminum
  Only 72,000 of these engines were manufactured and very few survived the war. Today, it would be considered a rare find for any collector.

1948

The 1948 Ford F-1 went on sale January 16, 1948. It had a starting price of $1,144 for the 6-cylinder model and $1,164 for the V8 model. The wheelbase was 114 inches. The standard

The first-generation F-Series trucks were introduced in 1948. This is Jerry Drenzek's 1948 F-1, which was known as the Bonus Built truck. (Photo Courtesy Jerry Drenzek)

Although this 1948 Ford F-1 was highly stylized, it had agricultural roots. (Photo Courtesy Jerry Drenzek)

engine was a 226-inch flathead V6 that made 95 hp. There was an optional 239-ci 100-hp V8 engine.

The standard transmission was a 3-speed manual with an optional 4-speed manual. The 1948 F-1 had a 6.5-foot bed with an all-steel floor, giving it 45 cubic feet of load space. The F-2 and F-3 models had an 8-foot bed.

The wheels were black, although some period brochures showed them in body color. The most drastic change to this model year was the cab design. The 1948 F-1 was referred to as the "Million Dollar Cab" because Ford invested more than $1 million to redesign the cab's interior. The 1948 F-Series' cab was 7 inches wider than the previous models. The door entrance was even wider and there was significantly more headroom and legroom.

Focusing on driver comfort, there was an optional Spiralounge bucket seat that had hydraulic shock absorbers that were adjustable to the driver's height and weight. This is the first adjustable driver setting in any Ford truck. Other first-time features included a passenger-side sun visor, a right-hand windshield wiper, a nylon waterproof seat cover, and a push-button radio.

There were optional leather door armrests, extended exterior mirrors, and front tow hooks. This was the first major effort by Ford, its engineers, and its design executives to invest heavily in a truck. In 1948, Ford produced 194,104 trucks.

F-Series Truck Model Lineup for 1948	
F-1	1/2 ton (4,700 GVWR maximum)
F-2	3/4 ton (5,700 GVWR maximum)
F-3	Heavy Duty 3/4 ton (6,800 GVWR maximum)
F-3	Parcel Delivery (7,000 GVWR maximum) and optional rear spring package (7,800 GVWR maximum)
F-4	1 ton (7,500 GVWR maximum) and optional 1.25-ton package (10,000 GVWR maximum)
F-5	1.5 ton: Conventional, school bus, and COE (10,000–14,500 GVWR)
F-6	2 ton: Conventional, school bus, and COE (14,000–16,000 GVWR)
F-7	Conventional (17,000–19,000 GVWR)
F-8	Conventional (20,000–22,000 GVWR)

1949

In 1949, there were very few design changes. The most significant change was that the wheels were painted to match the body color, whereas the 1948 model had only black wheels. Additionally, the grille took on a slightly different look with silver-painted bars instead of red-striped chrome. The wing-side window molding was painted black instead of chrome as well. This was likely a cost-saving measure.

The trucks were built in Michigan at the Highland Park Ford plant. The 1949 model was available as F-1, F-2, and F-3

Ford introduced the F-Series truck as a light- and medium-duty Class 1–7 truck. The first F-1, pictured here, was a half-ton truck. (Photo Courtesy Ford Motor Company)

The engine compartment of this 1949 F-1 shows a Ford flathead V8. What is unusual about the engine in this truck is that it is equipped with an optional oil filter (black canister at the right next to the oil fill cap and tube). This was used in parallel, and oil could flow though the filter, but all of the oil was not forced to flow through the filter as in recent engine designs. Full-flow oil filters were not used because if the filter became clogged, then the engine would be starved for oil. Modern oil filters feature a bypass valve to prevent that from happening. This oil filter housing design also allowed the vehicle owner to use a roll of toilet paper as the filter media, therefore making an oil filter change easy (no need to drain the oil) and inexpensive. (Photo Courtesy Richard Truesdell)

Pictured here is a "field find" that, although rusted, could be restored to its original state. Apparently, this truck had been used and abused for many years since the hood is a different color from the rest of truck. Also notice that most of the glass is missing and the sideview mirror is broken. (Photo Courtesy Jeff Curtis)

1950

A war was breaking out on the Korean peninsula, and fear shook many in this country, even at Ford headquarters. Would this be another World War? Would it halt the momentum that Ford was gaining in the truck segment? In the end, there was a car-buying frenzy for fear of another war and another vehicle shortage. Ford benefited significantly by selling 345,801 trucks for the model year.

The only significant difference for the 1950 model was that the 3-speed transmission shifter moved from the floor to the steering column (4-speed shifters remained on the floor). Four-wheel drive was introduced, but it was not made by Ford. It was built by the American Coleman Company of Omaha, Nebraska,

versions. Ford also announced a number of new parcel delivery chassis trucks for this model year. Six-cylinder models had a base price of $1,302 and the V8 models were priced at $1,333. In 1949, Ford produced 104,803 F-1 trucks.

The gas filler cap is located on the passenger's side with the fuel tank located behind the seat. (Photo Courtesy Richard Truesdell)

This 1950 barn find shows how stout these trucks were with the body intact, despite some rust and patina.

CANADA'S TRUCK

To say that the Mercury M-100 was just a rebadged F-100 sold in Canada is mostly accurate. It's true the M-100, a truck sold almost exclusively in Canada, shares many similarities to the Ford F-100.

After the war, Ford was ramping up production of the F-Series pickup truck. Just to the north, Ford already had production facilities in Canada and had a facility in Windsor, Ontario, as far back as 1904. The Canadian market was different from the US market, however. With a higher sales tax rate in Canada, vehicle prices had to be controlled to sell well there.

The Mercury brand was heavily pushed in the Canadian market as a high-class Ford. Ford of Canada successfully launched two high-end vehicles known as the Meteor and the Monarch. On the heels of those successful rebadged Fords, the M-100 sprung forth and was first produced in 1946. The M-100 truck would be produced almost exclusively for the Canadian market from 1946 to 1968.

Northern states that bordered Canada saw M-100s on the road regularly, and people often called it the Canadian F-100. The differences were generally slight and mostly cosmetic; most model years just had different badging on the front and the tailgate. The early year M-100s had more chrome on the grille than the F-100.

The Flathead V8 engine continued being used in the Mercury M-100 until 1952, when a new OHV V8 was

The Mercury M-100 was made almost exclusively for the Canadian market. Production started in 1946 and ran until 1968. It's quite similar to the F-100, only with the Mercury badge instead of the Ford. (Photo Courtesy Joel Guevara)

introduced. No 6-cylinder variant was available north of the border until the introduction of the 223-ci 6-cylinder in the 1956 M-100. During the 1961–1965 model years, the M-100 had a distinctive lightning bolt symbol on the horn button. This is one easy way to tell a Canadian truck from a US one. Ford of Canada also produced and sold a rebadged Econoline van as a Mercury, known as the EM-100 or M-Econoline.

When the United States and Canada signed a trade agreement in 1965, it meant a much easier flow of imports across the border and ushered in the demise of the M-100. The F-100 was new and fresh and wildly popular, which helped Ford drive sales of the F-100 across all of North America.

During the tail end of its life cycle, the M-100 was manufactured in Ontario and in the San Jose, California, plant. Still, the M-100 was not sold in the United States and is a rare find for collectors there.

A small script "Ford" was imprinted on the back of the tailgate of the 1950 F-100, as indicated in this photo of a 1950 barn find.

and Littleton, Colorado. The base price for the 1950 F-1 6-cylinder truck was $1,175 and $1,205 for the V8-equipped truck. The maximum gross weight rating of the 1950 F-2 was 5,700 pounds compared to the 4,700-pound GVW of the 1949 F-1.

1951

The 1951 model year Ford trucks got a minor facelift, including a new grille, known as the Dagmar Grille. The truck had a new full-width grille with the headlights and parking lights at each end. In the center of the grille were three bullet-shaped supports. The hood got new side spears and a new three-slot ornamentation embellished the front. The front bumper and front fenders were redesigned.

Other changes for 1951 included a larger rear window, dual windshield wipers as standard equipment, and a new dash with two round instrument dials. New bumpers were fitted to the entire F-Series lineup, and the brakes were revised on both the 3/4- and 1-ton trucks, which included the F-2 and F-3. A number of engine improvements were made to the line, including the use of a waterproof ignition system. The pickup bed was modified with a hardwood floor instead of the previous metal floor. Door panels were added too.

Toward the end of the 1951 model year, metals, including copper, chromium, and zinc, were needed for the mounting war effort overseas,

The bed of this 1950 Ford F-100 has been removed to reveal the suspension is intact. Today, many of these trucks are favorites for restoration projects, and their truck parts are sold at swap meets.

This 1951 F-100 showcases the gorgeous styling of the first generation of the F-Series. The 1951 model year saw an updated grille for the first-generation truck known as the Dagmar Grille. (Photo Courtesy Bob Spear)

and many trucks were built with more painted surfaces instead of bright metal. The base price for the 6-cylinder-equipped F-1 was $1,331, while the V8-equipped truck prices were $1,363. Ford produced 317,252 trucks in the 1951 model year.

1952

This was the last model year for the first-generation Ford F-Series. Only minor cosmetic changes were made to the truck, including hubcaps that were painted instead of plated in bright metal. The hood nose molding was also painted instead of plated, and plastic was used for the headlight surround casing instead of metal. All of these changes were primarily due to the metal shortage due to the Korean conflict. Ford also moved the vehicle identification number (VIN) plate to the rear face of the driver's door.

The biggest change of all was in the addition of a 215-ci OHV 6-cylinder engine. The flathead V8 was still an option; however, the new straight-six OHV was more efficient and made 101 hp and 185 ft-lbs of torque. Ford used this domestically produced OHV engine for many years until the introduction of overhead cam designs.

Ford's overall production was down due to the US's entry into the Korean conflict. Government-imposed sanctions as well as tempered enthusiasm by a war-leery American consumer kept production numbers lower. As such, Ford produced 188,083 of the last model year of the first-generation F-Series. The 1952 F-1 had a starting price of $1,100 for a 6-cylinder and $1,800 for the V8 F-3.

With a war raging in Korea, there was unease at home and a shortage of some materials. As such, the 1952 F-1 reflects some minor cosmetic changes, including a painted hood nose molding and plastic headlight surrounds. This truck features wood stake bed boards that are mounted to the top of the rear sides of the pickup bed. (Photo Courtesy Richard Truesdell)

Note the "Ford" script on the tailgate is highlighted with white paint instead of the body color. With the United States' entry into the Korean conflict, overall production numbers were down for the 1952 Ford F-1. Ford produced only 188,083 of these trucks, which would be the last model year of the first-generation F-Series. (Photo Courtesy Richard Truesdell)

This yellow 1952 F-1 was a restoration project that took two years. There are some mechanical modifications including a 351/358 Windsor and automatic transmission. (Photo Courtesy Tim King)

One of the small but noticeable changes to the 1951 F-100 was a larger rear window. This model year received new bumpers too. (Photo Courtesy Bob Spear)

The grille of the 1951 Ford F-100 is one of the most unique in Ford truck history. This grille style would only run from 1951 to 1952.

MODEL YEARS 1948–1952 ASSEMBLY PLANTS

Chester, Pennsylvania
Dearborn, Michigan
Highland Park, Michigan
Edison, New Jersey
Long Beach, California

Norfolk, Virginia
St. Paul, Minnesota
St. Louis, Missouri
Hapeville, Georgia

Conclusion

Henry Ford II was happy with his company's first investment into trucks. New engines, new designs, and millions of dollars were put into the F-Series. Although its rival, Chevrolet, continued to outpace it in sales during the 1948–1952 time period, Ford was able to make an impact on the truck market. The Bonus Built truck was a success. The automaker had learned a lot about consumer wants and demands, and it also paid close attention to what its rivals were doing.

Ford F-1 Sizes and Prices (1948–1952)									
Year	Model	Wheelbase (inches)	Length (inches)	Bed Length (feet)	Height (inches)	Width (inches)	Gross Vehicle Weight (pounds)	Price	Number Manufactur
1948–1952	Ford F-1 1/2-ton pickup	114	188.78	6.5	75.64	75.94	4,700	$1,175–$1,363	587,185*
1948–1952	Ford F-2 3/4-ton Express pickup	122	206.96	8	76.52	75.94	5,700	$1,295–$1,522	54,085**
Note: Information included in this chart is designed to be inclusive. Dependent upon reference, year, and carryover, information may vary.									
* Is a total of all F-1 1/2-ton pickup body, bed, engine, and cab types.									
** Is a total of all F-2 3/4-ton Express pickup body, bed, engine, and cab types. Number manufactured excludes 1948 because data is not available.									

FORD F-SERIES SECOND GENERATION (1953–1956)

The 1950s are considered by many historians as one of the most influential decades in American culture. A baby boom was in full effect, and the economy grew as did household incomes. It certainly was an influential time for the automotive industry.

Classic cars, such as 1955–1957 Chevrolets, evolved in both styling and engineering. A hiring boom saw great engineers and talented designers make their way through the doors of automakers. That definitely applied to Ford as well, which saw a great boom in its product line and automotive technology during this decade.

Nationwide, two major trends helped change the automotive industry and helped drive the Ford F-Series evolution. Hal Sperlich, a Ford engineer, used the phrase "the civilization of the truck," and the second generation of the F-Series definitely became more civilized. A lot of that was thanks to the development of the interstate highway system, a vision and legacy of President Dwight D. Eisenhower. The interstate highway system became possible from the Federal Aid Highway Act of 1956. With construction underway, cities, towns, and states became connected

Truck enthusiasts and collectors find the second-generation F-Series trucks to be beautiful. They really show how Ford started to find its groove on truck design. (Photo Courtesy Richard Truesdell)

Welcome to the colorful 1950s with this new generation of Ford trucks. For the second-generation F-Series, Ford changed the name, going from F-1, F-2, and F-3 to F-100, F-250, and F-350. This is a similar naming convention to the trucks today. (Photo Courtesy Jeff Curtis)

The side of this 1954 F-100 shows the F-100 emblem. It was only appropriate, and certainly intentional, that a monumental change to the Ford F-Series occurred one year earlier in 1953, since that was the year of Ford's 50th anniversary. The F-1 became known as the F-100 in 1953. (Photo Courtesy Richard Truesdell)

and more accessible. On-road and interstate commerce became more common. With the highways formed, the automobile industry exploded.

Coinciding with the expansion of the highway system was a population explosion and expansion from city dwelling to suburban developments. Thanks to the highways, subdivisions began to spring up all around the country. By the end of the 1950s, one-third of Americans lived in suburbs. This move away from the cramped quarters of urban centers contributed to a change in vehicles, including the Ford F-Series.

Ford invested $30 million to create a world-class truck that would fit into the changing suburban mindset. The automaker accomplished this with the newly named 1953 F-100 (replacing the F-1 name). The other light-duty trucks were named F-250 and F-350 (names that continue today).

It seemed fitting that the new truck would come out in 1953, since that was Ford's 50th anniversary year. Ford went all out celebrating its 50th year in business and culminated with a celebration that aired on CBS and NBC television. The network television special featured musical and dance numbers by some of the biggest names in Hollywood including Ethel Merman, Mary Martin, Frank Sinatra, and Eddie Fisher.

With all the pomp and pageantry, Ford showed the world that it would once again challenge its crosstown rival Chevrolet, which also launched a new truck in 1953. The rest of the decade would see Ford gaining ground on Chevrolet in trucks as well as cars.

The second-generation Ford F-Series trucks are considered some of the most attractive and collectible trucks manufactured by Ford. Increased dimensions, more powerful engines, and more attention to cab and interior comfort were all a direct result of growth of the 1950s culture. The truck was adapting to a growing population and the changing needs of the average American consumer.

Ford-O-Matic

Part of the $30 million investment for trucks was the development of an automatic transmission. The 1953 F-100 was the first Ford truck to have an automatic transmission, known as the Ford-O-Matic. The idea for this started in 1948. Ford realized it was late in introducing a fully automatic transmission for its cars and trucks. So, the company licensed an automatic transmission design that was being built by BorgWarner. The BorgWarner contract agreement included that it would build half of Ford's transmissions; the other half would be built by Ford.

With this agreement in place, Ford broke ground on an assembly plant to build the remaining transmissions. The Fairfax transmission plant opened in 1950 and began manufacturing the Ford-O-Matic. This transmission was used in F-Series trucks from 1953 to 1964. This was a hydraulically controlled rear-wheel-drive (RWD) 3-speed transmission. It used a cast-iron case to house the hydraulic clutches, bands, and control valves with either aluminum or cast-iron bellhousing around the torque converter.

The original Ford-O-Matic accomplished two things. First, it used an integrated torque converter and planetary gearset to automatically shift smoothly without an interruption in torque from the engine. Second, the shifting pattern was revised from Park-Neutral-Drive-Low-Reverse (PNDLR) to Park-Reverse-Neutral-Drive-Manual Low (PRNDL) configurations, which served to reduce "shift shock" when changing gears and reduce torque shock when trying to rock a stuck car back and forth. The Ford-O-Matic was manufactured from 1951 until it was replaced by the C4 transmission in 1964.

In 1953, the Ford-O-Matic automatic transmission was used in Cadillacs for about three months after the Livonia, Michigan, Hydra-Matic automatic transmission plant burned down. It was also briefly used in some International and Dodge trucks as well as Checker Cabs.

Power King Engine

The Ford flathead engine era was coming to an end. The 1953 Ford pickup was the last that used the famous flathead V8. In fact, the 1953 trucks carried over all of the engines from the previous generation, including a 215-ci 6-cylinder with OHV, which was used in all of the light-duty trucks, and the 239-ci flathead L-Head V8 engine.

The big news came in 1954 with the introduction of a completely new 239-ci Y-block V8 OHV engine that produced 130 hp. This replaced the flathead V8 officially. This new OHV engine had the same displacement but produced about 15 percent more horsepower than the Flathead V8. Ford engineers had created about 400 experimental engines using an estimated 600,000 man-hours to develop the new 239 OHV engine to be sure of the engine's durability.

The new OHV 239 engine was referred to as the Power King. The 239 Y-block was named for its distinctive skirting, which made the form of the engine look like a *Y*. This engine developed 130 hp at 4,200 rpm with 214 ft-lbs of torque between 1,800 and 2,200 rpm. The compression ratio was 7.2:1. It used molded/cast steel rocker arms, intake valve stem seals, high-turbulence combustion chambers, aluminum alloy pistons with steel struts to control expansion, full-length water jackets, and a deep-skirt crankcase block for greater structural rigidity. The engine had the following features:

- Copper lead bearings
- Precision molded/cast alloy iron crankshaft for better vibration dampening
- Full-pressure lubrication system with an external oil pump and full-flow oil filter
- High-lift camshaft
- Chrome-plated top rings
- Integral valve guides for faster heat transfer
- Adjustable lifters

Ford made changes to the 1954 inline-6 engine, nicknamed the "Cost Clipper." It increased horsepower to 115 hp from 101 by increasing the displacement from 215 ci to 223 using a larger

cylinder bore (3.625 inches versus 3.56 inches) plus a new camshaft and other refinements. The new horsepower was 115 at 3,900 rpm with torque at 193 ft-lbs at 1,000 to 2,200 rpm.

1953

As noted, the naming changed for the 1953 F-Series. There were other significant changes in the truck's new dimensions and proportions. The grille took a different shape with horizontal bars spanning between the headlights. The front axle was moved rearward, creating more overhang in the front from 35.8 inches to 38 inches. The hood was longer and positioned between the two front fenders (called nested) instead of being positioned over the top of the front fenders. A curved windshield and wider cab were featured for greater driver and passenger comfort.

The headlight surrounds (bezels) were chrome again for 1953, but the hubcaps were still painted like the 1952 models. The tailgate used block capital letters for F-O-R-D rather than the script that was on previous models. The new Ford-O-Matic transmission was also an option, and a

As the second generation of the F-Series began, it had a new appearance, including a new grille with horizontal bars between the headlights, which is evident on this 1953 F-100. (Photo Courtesy Ford Motor Company)

3-speed manual transmission shifter was located on the steering column.

Some of the other options on the 1953 F-Series were a right-side taillight, electric windshield wipers, tinted glass, a heavy-duty fan, and a locking gas cap. The base price of the 1953 F-100 was $1,330. Ford sold 116,437 F-Series pickups in 1953 and 9,951 panel trucks were produced for this model year.

THE COMPETITION

While the F-Series Ford pickup truck was a class leader in truck sales, there were many other pickup trucks on the market.

Chevrolet (1920+)

As previously discussed, Chevrolet produced pickup trucks that were in direct competition with the Ford trucks, and still are to this day.

Dodge (1929+)

Dodge started building pickup trucks in 1929, and these trucks compete with the Ford pickups to this day.

GMC (1912+)

Today's GMC trucks are similar to Chevrolet pickup trucks, but this was not always the case. In the past, the GMC trucks featured longer wheelbases and/or different and unique engines that were not available in Chevrolet pickups. For example, the GMC featured a V6 engine from 1959 through 1974 that was never offered in a Chevrolet truck. GMC also used a 287-ci Pontiac V8 for 1955 and a 316-ci version in 1956, which were referred to as the GMC 288 and 316 engines, respectively.

Hudson (1937–1947)

The first true Hudson truck was built on the Essex car chassis. The Hudson Super Six pickup was a car-like pickup with the front of the Hudson car and a pickup bed behind the cab. It was built on the car body-on-frame (BOF) platform. This was similar to what Ford did many years later to create the Ranchero.

An interesting note was that Hudson hired a female designer to help with the design of Hudsons. Elizabeth Ann Thatcher was hired in the late 1930s as a designer, and she remained in that role until 1941 when she married Joe Oros. Joe Oros was a designer at Cadillac at that time but later moved to Ford.

Gale Halderman, a designer at Ford for 40 years, remembers: "I knew Elizabeth from her job at Hudson. I worked with her husband, Joe Oros, for many years and while designing the Mustang. I helped Joe design the 1957 Ford Galaxie. Because of the great sales, Joe was promoted to chief designer of Ford Studio. He immediately promoted me to a design manager. I had only been with Ford several weeks."

Jeep (1947–1992)

The Jeep brand had a pickup truck in various designs for 1947 until 1992. The Jeep pickup was updated and brought back into production for 2020 with the Gladiator.

Nash (1947–1954)

Nash, an independent vehicle manufacturer, produced the 133-inch-wheelbase Nash Model 3148 and the 157-inch Nash Model 3248.

Plymouth (1937–1941)

Plymouth produced a pickup truck starting in 1937 with four bodystyles built on a truck chassis shared with Dodge. Plymouth called them the PT series (for Plymouth Truck), and included the Express (pickup) and a cab-and-chassis (with full-length running boards and rear fenders). Production ended in 1941 at the start of the World War II.

Studebaker (1955–1960)

Studebaker produced trucks from 1955 until 1960 in 1/2-ton, 3/4-ton, 1-ton, 1½-ton, and 2-ton versions. The smaller trucks were equipped with either an inline 6-cylinder or a V8 engine, whereas the larger trucks were only available equipped with a V8.

The second year of the second generation was 1954, which saw the grille change with a slanted-forward appearance and three air openings underneath the grille. (Photo Courtesy Ford Motor Company)

1954

In addition to the aforementioned new OHV V8 engine, the 1954 F-Series saw the Ford-O-Matic transmission added for the F-250 and F-350. The horsepower increased on the inline 6-cylinder engine, making it a popular choice for this truck. Horsepower increased to 115 hp (from 101).

The front "fat fenders" used on a 1954 F-100 were classic and added to the look of the truck. Also notice the straight steel front bumper and the black-painted steel running board under the door. This truck features whitewall tires, which were rarely found on a work truck. (Photo Courtesy Richard Truesdell)

The interior of a 1954 F-100 shows the use of a column-mounted shifter for the 3-speed manual transmission. Also, the brake and clutch pedals as well as the accelerator pedal linkage travel through the floor of the cab. The plain instrument panel features all of the gauges and speedometer in one assembly. (Photo Courtesy Richard Truesdell)

Below: The 1954 F-100 had the fuel filler cap located behind the driver's door, the exhaust tailpipe exited behind the rear bumper on the driver's side, and the push-button door handle and the styled front and rear fender shared a similar wheel opening shape. The license plate was located under the left-side taillight, which was used to light the license plate from the same housing to save cost and weight. (Photo Courtesy Richard Truesdell)

Cosmetically, very little was changed for the 1954 truck. There was a new grille, which was slanted forward slightly and had three air openings underneath its center. All V8-equipped trucks used the "V8" emblem in the center of the grille, while the deluxe cab had three chevrons on each side of the emblem. There were more features added to the interior including armrests, a dome light, and a cigarette lighter. The 1954 F-100 standard base price was $1,318.

The side-mounted spare tire on this 1954 F-100 features a period-correct size (6.00-16), but white sidewall tires were rare on a pickup truck. The wheels were 16 inches in diameter, larger than most passenger cars at the time that had 14- or 15-inch-diameter wheels. The larger-diameter wheels on a pickup truck required, of course, larger tires. These larger-diameter wheels and tires had a higher weight-carrying capacity compared to similar size passenger cars. (Photo Courtesy Richard Truesdell)

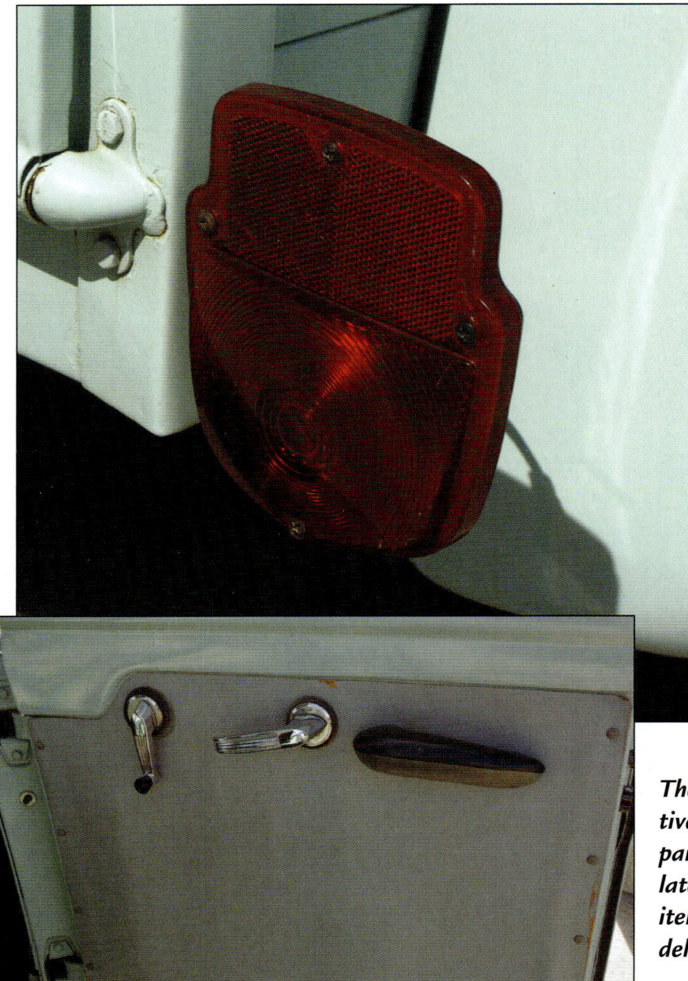

Taillights of a 1954 F-100 were installed on both the left side and the right side of the truck. The shape was similar to the Ford logo, as seen on the front hood and running board. The light assembly was simply attached to the rear side of the bed and not incorporated into the rear fender. It was also equipped with screws that allowed easy access to the bulb, making maintenance and service easier than many current model pickup trucks. (Photo Courtesy Richard Truesdell)

The door panel of a 1954 F-100 featured an armrest, which was a relatively new feature for pickup trucks. Notice the easy-to-clean inner door panel. Very little if any sound deadening was used on trucks until much later when trucks started to feature the same driver and passenger comfort items that were used in passenger cars. (Photo Courtesy Richard Truesdell)

The 6-cylinder OHV engine of a 1954 F-100 is mostly stock except for replacement spark plug wires that were routinely replaced during service anyway. The large, black, round object at the top of the engine is an oil bath–type air filter. Instead of a pleated paper air filter that is commonly used today, early engines used a design that forced the incoming air down into the air filter housing and then upward before traveling downward again into the top of the carburetor. The air filter has engine oil in the lower section of the filter housing. Air can be made to change direction quickly, but the dirt in the air has greater mass and cannot make as rapid a change in direction as the air. This causes the dirt to be trapped in the pool of oil. Routine maintenance included changing the oil in the oil-bath air filter. (Photo Courtesy Richard Truesdell)

This 1955 Ford F-100, with all the styling updates, is considered a classic by many collectors. The whitewall tires were generally not seen on pickups of this time. They do seem to make this truck stand out more.

A large rear window is one of the main improvements on the 1955 F-100. This, along with a one-piece large front windshield, was where Ford managed to show up rival Chevrolet. The combination offered an expansive, wide-open view.

1955

The Ford pickup truck remained basically unchanged for 1955. The exceptions were that a larger engine was available at 256 ci that produced 140 hp and new rear leaf springs (52 inches long by 2 inches wide) increased the maximum GVW for the F-100 to 5,000 pounds. Ford stayed with the same bodystyle as the 1954 F-Series. The larger curved windshield that was introduced in earlier models was still being used and being labeled as a safety improvement.

Chevrolet also introduced a new modern pickup truck for 1955. The new 1955½ Chevrolet trucks featured a wraparound windshield and flush-mounted fenders and doors. A special version called the Cameo featured a highly styled slab-sided fiberglass bed (cargo body).

The 1955 F-Series did have minor cosmetic changes. The most notable change was the new *V*-shaped grille. It consisted of two bars with a drop V in the upper bar; this symbol indicated which engine the truck had (a star for a 6-cylinder and a V8 emblem for the 8-cylinder). These emblems appeared to be floating atop the *V*-shaped portion of the grille. The side emblem was embellished using a chromed circle that had F-100, F-250, or F-350 inside it. There was a custom-cab paint coat option that had a two-tone paint scheme that combined Snowshoe White with any other color. The base price of a 1955 F-100 was $1,460.

One of the most notable changes for the 1955 truck model year was the new V-shaped grille, which consisted of two bars with a drop V in the upper bar. It had an indicator of the truck's engine with a star for a 6-cylinder and a V8 emblem for the 8-cylinder. These emblems appeared to be floating atop the V-shaped portion of the grille.

1956

In an effort to counter the new Chevrolet pickup with its major body change of the previous year, Ford made two big changes for the 1956 F-Series. First was the addition of a larger wraparound windshield. Second, a new 12-volt electrical system was added.

Wraparound Windshield

The F-100's new windshield was used with vertical door pillars. This had a positive effect on the F-Series popularity, and these big-window pickups are still admired and sought by collectors. Some models featured an optional large wraparound rear window that was 824 square inches of glass, which was almost the size of the front windshield (almost 1,000 square inches of glass).

With a larger windshield, Ford had to reengineer how the windshield wipers operated. The new wipers would sweep through their own arc of travel across the windshield. The new openness of the 1956 design provided more visibility than any other pickup truck on the market in 1956.

12-Volt System

The 12-volt electrical system, which included the ignition system, had been used in Europe and on diesel trucks for some time. It was first used in

The exterior of 1956 models changed the A-Pillar to accommodate a larger wrap-around windshield. The A-Pillars were now vertical, allowing for extra glass space. (Photo Courtesy Frazier Motor Company)

The 1956 models are the most popular and collectible among the second-generation trucks in part because of the new front window treatment, the new larger V8 engine, a 12-volt electrical system, and the addition of optional power steering. (Photo Courtesy Frazier Motor Company)

The dash instrumentation was changed in 1956 to this half-moon instrument cluster. While gauges were used for fuel level and temperature, the oil and battery indicators were idiot lights. (Photo Courtesy Frazier Motor Company)

To accommodate the new, larger wrap-around front windshield, Ford changed how the wipers operated. Each wiper swept through its own arc on the windshield. (Photo Courtesy Frazier Motor Company)

the United States in 1953, when General Motors used a 12-volt electrical system in its Oldsmobile, Buick, and Cadillac cars. The Chrysler Crown Imperial also had the 12-volt system.

Other Features

In 1956, the cab style was also changed to further accent the roof's new styling and incorporate a visor above the front windshield. The headlamps also had a slight visor over them. There were virtually no other changes in the truck body from the 1955 F-Series.

The front grille was very similar to the 1955 for the V8-equipped trucks but without the floating V8 emblem. The 6-cylinder-equipped trucks no longer had the star or any other designation on the front to indicate it was a 6-cylinder truck. The side emblem had also been changed to have the F-100, F-250, or F-350 and a red circle over a chrome spear with Ford lettering in red.

The body, fenders, and bed remained unchanged from the 1955 truck with new colors being added. The custom cab provided a two-tone paint scheme that consisted of Colonial White on top with any other available color on the body. The F-100 was built on a 118-inch wheelbase and offered an 8-foot bed for more cargo space.

The standard 1956 interior had a new high-dial half-moon instrument cluster along with red and gray plaid upholstery as the standard interior. All standard and custom cab interiors offered safety features, such as the lifeguard steering wheel and new double-grip door latches that prevented accidental door opening in the event of an accident. For the first time, power steering was available on the F-100, which had previously only been available on the F-250. Ford was pushing its truck safety features while seat belts were still an option.

V8 Engine Size

The V8 engine size increased to 272 ci and the power increased to 172 hp, whereas the inline 6-cylinder engine remained the same at 223 ci but was now producing 137 hp. Ford replaced the 3-speed heavy-duty manual transmission with the medium-duty BorgWarner model T 89B. The standard 3-speed manual, 3-speed overdrive manual, and 3-speed manual were the same and still offered. The V8-equipped F-100 with manual transmission had a larger 10.5-inch clutch that provided increased surface area. The Ford-O-Matic automatic transmission was still an option on the truck and was still being advertised by Ford as the best transmission for towing when connected to a V8 engine. The price for the standard F-100 with the 6.5-foot bed was $1,577, while the new 8-foot bed truck cost $1,611.

Conclusion

The 1950s proved to be an amazing decade for the Ford Motor Company. Competition with Chevrolet in both cars and trucks was heated. It seemed sales figures were always neck and neck with each other, and it was a battle of who could one-up the other or be the first one out with the latest and greatest vehicle technology. Trucks were definitely part of Ford's marketing plan.

Many trucks moved off the farms and into houses with two-car garages in the middle of newly constructed subdivisions. The second-generation Ford F-Series really showed the pivot that took place at the Blue Oval in how Ford viewed trucks and in how the American consumer wanted the pickup truck to be.

POWER STEERING

Ford began offering hydraulic power steering on its V8-equipped cars in 1953 and on the F-250 in 1955. In 1956, Ford offered hydraulic power steering as an option on the F-100.

This early power steering system used a hydraulic cylinder with a piston (Power Steering Ram) to provide controlled energy to the steering linkage, so the driver put forth less effort to turn the steered wheels.

The 1955–1956 hydraulic power steering systems used an engine-driven power steering pump to provide hydraulic pressure. The hydraulic cylinder had its piston rod anchored to the frame at one end with the cylinder body attached to the relay (intermediate) steering rod at the other end. At the very end of the relay rod was a control valve assembly that had a tie-rod end connected to one end and the other end fastened to the steering gear pitman arm. When the driver turned the steering wheel, the pitman arm moved and also moved the control valve in either a right- or left-turn position. It would send power steering fluid pressure to either the right- or left-turn side of the hydraulic cylinder. This would provide hydraulic assist to the steering linkage at the relay rod.

This system had a direct mechanical connection between the steering wheel and the linkage that steers the wheels so if the power-steering system failed, you could still steer the truck manually.

Ford Light-Duty Truck Paint Colors (1953–1956)

Color	Available Year and VIN Code			
	1953	1954	1955	1956
Raven Black	A	A	A	A
Dark Blue Metallic	–	–	–	B
Sheridan Blue	B	B	–	–
Banner Blue	–	–	B	–
Glacier Blue	C	D	–	–
Light Blue	–	–	–	D
Aquatone Blue	–	–	C	–
Grey	–	–	–	H
Woodsmoke Gray	D	–	–	–
Waterfall Blue	–	–	D	–
Snowshoe White	–	–	E	–
Seafoam Green	G	–	–	–
Sea Sprite Green	–	–	G	–
Sea Haze Green	–	H	–	–
Light Green	–	–	–	G
Torch Red (Vermillion)	N	R	R	R
Meadow Green	R	U	U	U
White (Two Tone)	–	–	–	E
Yellow	–	–	–	M
Goldenrod Yellow	–	V	V	–
Primer	P	P	P	P
Specialized Colors	SS	SS	SS	SS

Note: Information included in this chart is designed to be inclusive. Dependent upon reference, year, and carryover, information may vary.

Note: 1953–1956 color codes on the VIN plate are listed as "Color."

Ford Light-Duty Truck Engines (1953–1956)

Year	Engine	Horse-power (hp)	Torque (ft-lbs)	VIN Code
1953	215-ci inline 6-cylinder OHV	101	185 at 1,300–1,700 rpm	D
	239-ci L-head V8	110	194 at 1,900–2,100 rpm	R
1954	223-ci inline 6-cylinder OHV	115	193 at 1,000–2,200 rpm	D
	239-ci V8 OHV	130	214 at 1,800–2,200 rpm	V
1955	223-ci inline 6-cylinder OHV	115	195 at 1,200–2,400 rpm	D
	239-ci V8 OHV	130	215 at 1,800–2,200 rpm	V
	256-ci V8 OHV	140	228 at 1,900–2,400 rpm	Z
1956	223-ci inline 6-cylinder OHV	137	202 at 1,600–2,600 rpm	D
	272-ci V8 OHV	172	260 at 2,100–2,600 rpm	V

Note: Information included in this chart is designed to be inclusive. Dependent upon reference, year, and carryover, information may vary.

Note: Engine VIN example: The underlined letter "D" F10D5F100001 indicates the placement in the engine VIN and the engine in the example is a 223-ci inline 6-cylinder.

Ford Light-Duty Truck Transmissions (1953–1956)

Year(s)	Model	Automatic/Manual	Number of Gears	Transmission
1953–1955	F-100	Manual	3	Standard
1953–1955	F-100	Manual	3	Heavy Duty
1953–1955	F-100	Manual	3	3-Speed with Overdrive
1953–1955	F-100	Manual	4	Optional
1953–1955	F-100	Automatic	3	Ford-O-Matic
1956	F-100	Manual	3	BorgWarner T89B Medium Duty
1956	F-100	Manual	3	Standard
1956	F-100	Manual	3	Heavy Duty
1956	F-100	Manual	3	3-Speed with Overdrive
1956	F-100	Manual	4	Optional
1956	F-100	Automatic	3	Ford-O-Matic
1953–1956	F-250	Manual	3	Standard

Note: Information included in this chart is designed to be inclusive. Dependent upon reference, year, and carryover, information may vary.

Ford Light-Duty Sales and Prices (1953–1956)

Year	Model	Wheelbase (inches)	Length (inches)	Bed Length (feet)	Height (inches)	Width (inches)	Gross Vehicle Weight (pounds)	Price	Number Manufactured
1953–1956	Ford F-100 1/2-ton pickup	110/118*	189.1/203.2*	6.5/8*	75.5	75.7	4,000–5,000	$1,292–$1,616	505,184**
1953–1956	Ford F-250 3/4-ton Express pickup	118	203.2	8	Varies	75.7	6,900–7,400	$1,450–$1,760	93,042***

Note: Information included in this chart is designed to be inclusive. Dependent upon reference, year, and carryover, information may vary.

* In 1956, Ford offered the F-100 1/2-ton Express that was based on the F-250 frame.

** Is a total of all F-100 1/2-ton pickup body, bed, engine, and cab types.

*** Is a total of all F-250 3/4-ton Express pickup body, bed, engine, and cab types.

FORD F-SERIES THIRD GENERATION (1957–1960)

"The third generation represented the 40th anniversary of the first truck for Ford. So much had changed at Ford and with the truck during four decades of production."

As one of the greatest decades in American history began to wind down, some great vehicles were on the roads. The 1957 Chevy and 1957 Ford are arguably two of the greatest cars to have been produced in America. The 1957 Ford actually outsold the 1957 Chevrolet, yet the 1957 Chevy is one of the most iconic cars of all time. Both are considered highly collectible.

The year 1957 was good for Ford trucks too. Ford launched the third generation of its F-Series pickup truck. It represented a further evolution of the pickup with an attractive and bold styling that featured a flat-style side bed known as the Styleside truck. This design became the foundation of light truck bed design for many years at Ford.

In May 1957, Ford discontinued building trucks at the Highland Park Ford Plant in Highland Park, Michigan. All light- and medium-duty trucks were transferred to 10 other plants throughout the United States. The production of the F-350 and larger heavy-duty trucks were transferred to the Kentucky Truck Assembly Plant in Louisville, Kentucky. With the new assembly plants, Ford was able to offer the Styleside truck with 6.5- or 8-foot beds and the Flareside truck also with 6.5- or 8-foot beds.

This beautiful two-tone 1960 F-100 is an example of the design from the last year before the switch over to unibody construction. Notice the front bumper and rear step bumper. Rear bumpers were optional, and customers could choose which dealer-installed bumper they would want, if any at all. (Photo Courtesy Steve Kennedy)

The 1959 Custom Cab Ford F-100 shows the attractive styling of the trucks in this era. The two-toned paint scheme was part of the Custom Cab trim. (Photo Courtesy Shannon Gregory)

styling lasted well into the 21st century and had a significant role in Ford truck history. The F-Series integrated the hood into the bodywork with a clamshell design, and this feature would be part of the F-Series for the next 20 years.

During this generation, two types of pickup boxes (beds) were offered. The traditional separate bed with fenders was known as the Flareside. Many still call this style of pickup a "step side" because there is a step behind the cab where a person could stand to get access to the content in the bed. The inside of the bed was straight from the front and back, making loading and unloading sand and gravel easy.

The second type of box was called the Styleside. It featured the same continuous lines from the front to the rear and integrated the pickup bed, cab, and front fenders together. With this design, the inner fenders were inside the bed of the truck and did not provide an access step to the side of the bed.

The third generation represented the 40th anniversary of the first truck for Ford. So much had changed at Ford and with the truck during four decades of production. Henry Ford II was fully entrenched and comfortable in his role as president of Ford. He hired a hotshot executive from the Pennsylvania area to be Ford's national marketing manager. His name was Lee Iacocca, and he went on to make automotive history at Ford and later at Chrysler. Iacocca oversaw such significant projects as the Ford Mustang and the Ford Escort, as well as escalating the Lincoln brand to a prestigious level. By the end of the third-generation F-Series, Iacocca was named vice president and general manager at Ford in 1960.

Styleside Versus Flareside

Following its competitors at Dodge and General Motors, Ford created its updated design by widening the front bodywork to integrate the cab and front fenders together. This

In 1957, the Styleside pickup set the trend for what truck beds would be like for the generations of trucks that followed for all manufacturers. Prior to this, truck beds were only as wide as the rear wheels. The Flareside had fancy-looking fenders that give the appearance of extra width, but it was not until the Styleside that the Ford truck bed gained in width. The Styleside's bed was stretched out to 73 inches and narrowed to 49 inches in the middle to make room for the wheelhouse. That 49 inches is the magic measurement because this means that 4x8 sheets of plywood or drywall could be carried flat on the floor of the bed.

This beautiful 1957 truck has no rear bumper, which is how trucks of this era were delivered from the dealer. The driver- and passenger-side mirrors were likely dealer installed. The chrome bezels and grille indicate a higher trim than the more basic trims of the era. (Photo Courtesy Chad Horwedel)

Overall, the 1957 F-100 Styleside had about 8 percent more cubic feet of cargo room than the 1956 F-100 Flareside. On short-wheelbase 1/2-ton trucks, the Styleside gained even more room with a 24-percent increase. The truck bed's box was made of welded all-steel construction throughout the floor, side, corners, and tailgate. It was good for consumers to have two options; however, the Styleside was the popular choice by a 5:1 margin. Most buyers liked the new, stylish, elongated-looking pickup over the Flareside.

Third-Generation Powerplants and Performance

The third-generation F-Series saw advancement and development in styling but not so much in the engine and performance arena. Ford carried over the engines and transmissions from the second-generation F-Series.

The standard engine on the 1957 F-Series was the 223-ci inline six (I6) that developed 139 hp and the optional engine was the 272-ci (4.5L) V8 that developed 171 hp. The 272 came with a new air filter that stopped 90 percent of the dirt that the ordinary oil bath cleaners missed. This was the first use by Ford of a cellular element filter, which replaced the old oil-bath style.

The standard transmission for 1957–1960 was the 3-speed manual. Optional transmissions included a 3-speed manual with overdrive, a Ford-O-Matic automatic transmission, a 3-speed manual medium-duty transmission (BorgWarner T89B), and a 4-speed manual transmission. In 1958, Ford introduced the 292-ci V8 that developed 186 hp to keep competitive with the growing popularity of the V8 engines from Dodge and Chevrolet. The 292-ci engine was used in Ford trucks, namely the F-100, through 1964.

One of the big changes that occurred during the third generation took place in 1959, when Ford introduced its first four-wheel-drive (4WD) truck that was manufactured completely in-house. Prior to this, Ford had used Napco, Marmon Herrington, and American-Coleman to convert to 4WD. In

The two-tone exterior and interior indicate that this 1959 F-100 was a higher trim. The owner restored this truck to a nearly stock interior. The wraparound rear glass gave it a lot of style and differentiated it from other rivals. (Photo Courtesy Shannon Gregory)

A slightly modified (lowered) 1957 F-100 features a unique chrome grille (with V8 emblem), chrome headlight bezels, and a front bumper that were seldom seen on trucks of this era. Also notice the right-side outside rearview mirror, which was added by the dealer or the owner. It does not have a rear bumper, which was common for this era. (Photo Courtesy Greg Gjerdingen)

1959, the Willys-Overland company, which built the 4WD Jeep, had 65 percent of the 4WD market followed by International, which had an estimated 15 percent, and GM had the rest of that market. Ford steadily climbed its way up to gaining a huge share of the 4WD light truck market.

The factory F-100 4WD was offered on both the Flareside and Styleside pickup trucks and available with the 6-cylinder or V8 engine. While the 3-speed manual was standard, buyers could only get 4WD with the 4-speed manual transmission.

Another change to the 1959 model year occurred as a result of the 4WD addition. In order to handle the rugged terrain that 4WD trucks encountered, Ford strengthened the engine and transmission mounts and added more steel around the door openings. Ford also improved the torsional strength of the chassis by 18 percent. This was done by increasing the size of the rear crossmembers with heavier gauge steel and by adding gussets to the truck side rails and crossmember attachment areas.

A 1957 Ford F-100 is attached to a camper. The painted grille and painted white bumper plus the "dog dish" hubcaps show that it is a base trim level truck. (Photo Courtesy Richard Truesdell)

This 1957 F-100 features a solid-color grille and front end instead of using a separate color for the grille opening. There is no V8 emblem on the center of the grille, which indicates it is a 6-cylinder model. (Photo Courtesy Jim Johnson)

Later in 1959, Ford introduced the Spicer (Dana) Power-Lok locking differential (a limited-slip differential) for its two-wheel-drive (2WD) trucks. This differential was available for both the 6-cylinder and the V8 engines. You could get the Power-Lok differential in a choice of the 3.73:1 or the 3.9:1 final drive gear ratio.

By the 1960 model year, the optional heavy-duty springs for 1959 were now standard. By the end of the decade, Ford addressed issues the 292 V8 had with oil consumption by incorporating a new piston ring design that used three chrome-plated control rings. In 1960, a new ignition system was used with a breaker point design. It had been used on the heavy-duty truck engines, such as the 401- and 534-ci engines, and it was now standard on the 292 V8. Also, on the 292 V8, Ford changed the cast-iron cover on the oil pump to a steel cover and used a pressure relief valve that eliminated sticking from sludge.

1957

In 1957, the Styleside pickup set the trend for what truck beds would be like for the generations of trucks that followed. The Styleside 1957 F-100 no longer had the big round fenders of the previous generation. This new design allowed more room under the hood and more space in the cab.

Ford adapted the wire grille and large center bar from the past models and added this into the 1957 design. Ford also maintained the older positioning of the parking turn signal lights and located them directly beneath the headlights on the 1957 truck.

The new trucks featured:

- An all-new cab with integral running boards.
- Chrome-plated front bumper offered as a regular production option (RPO) on the pickup truck for the first time.
- The front fenders were flush with the hood and the doors.
- The hood wrapped over the side and was flush with the front fenders.
- The top of the hood featured ribs that not only added strength to the hood but also gave it an interesting style not seen on pickup trucks before.
- The sides were also styled with creased lines over the front wheel opening.

Both styles sold for the same price, even though the newer Styleside was often thought to be a premium design. This design was started by Chevrolet with the fiberglass bed called the Cameo.

As a result of the exterior changes, there were also significant changes to the interior of the 1957 F-100. The F-100's interior featured a long bench seat that had plastic seat upholstery with a woven appearance. Ford used a new lifeguard steering wheel, which was a safety feature for the driver because it would collapse in a front collision. Seat belts were available as a dealer-installed option.

Ford continued to offer its upgraded Custom Cab interior for 1957 at an additional cost of $68.30, and the automaker would also put an emblem on the door of the Custom Cab interior. The Custom Cab interior featured upgrades such as an acoustic headliner, instrument panel trim, and insulation behind the dash to help reduce road noise. The Custom Cab option also included adjustable dual sun visors, a dome light with a manual switch, and armrests on both doors.

In both the standard and Custom Cab models, Ford offered the Hi-Dri ventilation system to keep the drivers and passengers comfortable on long trips. It was located at the base of the windshield and was operated by dual controls. This allowed the driver and the passenger to receive fresh air individually or at the same time.

Truck chassis strength was increased in 1957 by using 18-gauge steel floor pans that were much heavier than previous models. This improvement also helped to decrease road noise in the cab. The use of suspended brake and clutch pedals eliminated dust, heat, and cold from entering the clearance holes in the floor pan. All of these changes show the subtle and deliberate attention to the interior comfort of trucks. The civilization of the truck was continuing with rider comfort and safety being taken into consideration.

The 1957 truck windshield was more than 2 inches wider than on the 1956, and the standard rear window was 41 square inches smaller. The Flareside still used a wood bed floor with the steel skid strips, and the taillights were still connected to the bed with brackets. The tailgate on both models still had the Ford logo lettering stamped in the steel and used white striping around the body-colored letters.

This year, Ford was able to hide truck running boards within the rocker panels of the truck, making them visible only when the door was open. This gave the truck a slimmer and more streamlined appearance and also made it easier to accentuate the truck with the two-tone paint scheme.

During the third generation, the 1957 model was the only member of this class with single headlights. F-100 trucks built from 1958 to 1960 were the only model years that Ford used four headlights.

In 1957, the starting price of a Styleside or Flareside was $1,789 with the 110-inch wheelbase and 6.5-foot bed. The 118-inch wheelbase model with the 8-foot bed sold for $1,828.

1958

With the success of the 1957 F-Series, Ford decided to keep things just the way they were and made only very minor changes to the appearance of the 1958 Ford F-100. Ford changed the front appearance by adding quad headlights and upgrading the grille.

The quad headlights provided the biggest difference between the 1957 and 1958 truck. Ford also put quad headlights on its full line of trucks and cars. Ford advertising called the quad headlights *Safety Vision*, which focused on how this added illumination provided greater vision at night and at dusk. The new grille emphasized the new headlights with a large crossbar that ran across the front and had an eggcrate center section. Ford advertising touted that it cost less to own and less to run, and it lasted longer than the competition. There was no change to the truck's interior in 1958.

The Custom Cab was a $68.37 option and came with color-keyed vinyl upholstery, a headliner, instrument panel trim, additional insulation, adjustable sun visors, a dome light, and armrests on both doors. Electric-powered windshield wipers were added for 1958. Previously, the wipers were powered by vacuum off of the top of the mechanical fuel pump and engine vacuum.

In 1958, the Chevrolet Cameo was dropped from the GM product line in favor of wider-bed trucks similar to the third-generation F-Series. Ford had the competition reacting, and even Dodge and International followed suit with similarly styled trucks in 1959.

The Ranchero was a modified Ford Galaxie station wagon. It shared most of the platform on the front and became more of a truck on the back end. Pictured here is a slightly modified 1959 Ranchero. (Photo Courtesy Richard Truesdell)

The Ford Ranchero rode and drove like a passenger car, yet was designed to be used as a light-duty pickup. (Photo Courtesy Richard Truesdell)

This beautiful 1958 two-tone M-100 has aftermarket wheels and tires but is otherwise stock. This truck was offered exclusively in Canada. (Photo Courtesy Randy Brown)

The 1958 Mercury M-100 truck was a rebadged Ford F-100 and, as such, was similar in almost every way. (Photo Courtesy Randy Brown)

FORD RANCHERO

Ford was the first to introduce a station wagon–based pickup truck that looked like the coupe with a rear pickup truck bed instead of a station wagon body. You can argue that the Ranchero was a distant cousin to today's crossovers, which have both truck- and car-like features. The same is true of the Ranchero, which Ford produced from 1957 to 1979. There were seven generations of Rancheros produced by Ford. It sold more than 500,000 total units of the Ranchero over this life span.

When it was introduced in 1957, there was nothing else like it on the road. Some of the features of the new Ranchero included:

- Unique roof and upper rear panels
- Double-wall pickup bed box liner, tailgate liner, and load floor
- Spare tire stored behind the passenger with a tool compartment behind the driver's seat.
- 118-inch wheelbase, the same as the Ford station wagon in 1957–1959.
- The Ranchero had a gross vehicle weight (GVW) of 4,600 pounds. (GVW was the weight of the vehicle plus the maximum cargo weight it was designed to carry)

The Ranchero was built on the same assembly line as the passenger cars and included many of the same powertrains and options that were available on the sedan or station wagon versions of the full-size Fords of that era. In 1959, General Motors launched its own version of the Ranchero with the legendary El Camino.

This 1959 F-100 is the Custom Cab trim. That trim level is indicated on the driver-side door just above the door handle. (Photo Courtesy Creative Commons)

The M-100 was the Canadian version of the F-100. The styling was quite similar, as indicated by this gorgeous two-tone M-100. (Photo Courtesy Randy Brown)

The instrumentation inside F-100 trucks of this era were very basic. Inside this 1959 F-100, the instrumentation shows gauges for fuel and engine temperature as well as warning lights for the generator and oil. Notice at the bottom are left and right knob vents. When these are pulled, they control airflow into the cab. Also visible is the choke, which was needed to start the engine. (Photo Courtesy Ted Nelson)

1959

As noted, the most dramatic change for the 1959 F-Series was in the addition of the Ford-built 4WD system. Visually, the 1959 truck did not appear that much different from the 1958 with the exception of the new grille.

The wide center bar of the grille was progressively smaller from what appeared on the 1957 F-100. The new 1959 grille had four center bars around a slightly thicker one at the top. The grille still wrapped around the four quad headlights and it had rectangular parking lights that were still positioned below the headlights. The new truck had a large intake in front of the hood, which featured

A slightly modified 1960 F-100 with a chrome grille and bumper. Its white roof is a variation of the two-tone color scheme often found on higher trim F-100s of this era. (Photo Courtesy Joel Guevara)

This slightly modified 1960 has a chrome grille but a painted front bumper. There are no outside mirrors present, which was a regular occurrence for trucks of this era. The hubcaps shown are known as dog-dish hub-caps. (Photo Courtesy Steve Kennedy)

The 1960 grille of the F-100 is similar to the 1959 version. These were the only two trucks of this genera-tion that had vent openings with the Ford logo centered on the hood.

The distinctive front-end styling is showcased on this modified 1960 F-100. (Photo Courtesy Jon Carr)

mesh with Ford lettering across the front of it. The rest of the 1959 body was the same as the 1958 F-Series.

A review in the September 1959 issue of *Motor Life* magazine helped drive sales of the 1959 F-Series when the magazine noted that the truck was stable on the open road and had impressive acceleration. In this article, it mentioned that the 292 V8 propelled the F-100 from 0 to 60 mph in 12.23 seconds. This is incredibly slow by today's standards, but this was impressive power and performance for trucks at that time. The base price for the 1959 110-inch wheelbase 4WD truck was $2,512.46.

1960

In 1960, Ford continued to change the front grille without changing much of the body of the 1960 truck. The grille now had a top crossbar that was larger than the inset bars below it. The grille still wrapped around the headlights with the parking lights inset into the grille. The air intake on the hood was also altered slightly. Instead of the mesh grille, Ford added two separate intake openings divided by a new gear and lightning Ford crest. The side emblems also changed. The emblems featured a rocket with the Ford emblem.

The rest of the 1960 F-Series exterior was pretty much the same as 1959 with some small refinements made to the engine and the interior. The 1960 F-Series had new weatherstripping, which reduced the wind and road noise. There was a new comfortable front seat, which used cotton padding to improve the ride. Ford used a 1.25-inch-thick foam pad to increase comfort. The nylon upholstery used vinyl-ribbed bolsters and a patterned headliner, which helped to provide a more car-like feel to the F-Series.

The Custom Cab models had matching two-tone door panels. The white steering wheel with a chrome horn ring was a carryover from 1959, and the new seats had striped nylon Saran upholstery with vinyl.

Falcon Ranchero

Starting with the 1960 model year, Ford changed the Ranchero that was based on the full-size passenger car chassis to the unit-body Falcon station wagon body. The Ranchero featured the same powertrain as the first Falcon passenger car with a 144-ci (2.4L) inline 6-cylinder that was rated at 90 hp. The size was much smaller, changing from a wheelbase of 118 inches of the 1959 model to 109.9 inches for the 1960 Falcon-based Ranchero. While a lot smaller than the previous generation, it did have an 800-pound load capacity.

A 1959 F-100 features the Ford emblem centered between two vent openings. The horizontal bars attach the headlights to each other.

Conclusion

One of the most exciting decades in American history was over. Ford Motor Company had its share of successes and failures, yet the vision for the F-Series was clear. The American consumer interest was increasing and Ford, through marketing, demographic study, and at times imitating its competition, was hitting its groove on truck design. The third-generation F-Series saw incredible styling and a revolutionary new presentation of the truck bed. Power and comfort were put back into the spotlight, and this theme continued into the formative 1960s, just in time for more volatility and a changing American mindset.

The blue dot installed in the center of the taillight was a popular modification of trucks in the 1950s. From a distance, the taillights appear purple.

Pickup trucks during this generation carried this F-100 emblem on the side. (Photo Courtesy Creative Commons)

Ford Light-Duty Truck Engines (1957–1960)

Year	Engine	Horsepower (hp)	Torque (ft-lbs)	VIN Code
1957	223-ci inline 6-cylinder OHV	139	207 at 1,800–2,700 rpm	D or J
	272-ci V8 OHV	171	260 at 2,100–2,600 rpm	K, L, or V
1958	223-ci inline 6-cylinder OHV	139	207 at 1,800–2,700 rpm	J
	272-ci V8 OHV	181	262 at 2,200–2,700 rpm	K or L
	292-ci V8 OHV	186	269 at 2,200–2,700 rpm	C
1959	223-ci inline 6-cylinder OHV	139	207 at 1,800–2,700 rpm	J
	292-ci V8 OHV	186	269 at 2,200–2,700 rpm	C or D
1960	223-ci inline 6-cylinder OHV	139	203 at 2,000–2,600 rpm	J
	292-ci V8 OHV	172	270 at 2,000–2,600 rpm	C or D

Note: Information included in this chart is designed to be inclusive. Dependent upon reference, year, and carryover, information may vary.

Note: Engine VIN example: The underlined letter "J" F10J8G100001 indicates the placement in the engine VIN and the engine in the example is a 223-ci inline 6-cylinde

Ford Light-Duty Truck Paint Colors (1957–1960)

Colors	Available Year and VIN Code			
	1957	1958	1959	1960
Raven Black	A	A	A	A
Dark Blue	B	–	–	–
Midnight Blue	–	B	–	–
Caribbean Turquoise	–	–	–	B
Wedgewood Blue	–	C	C	–
Indian Turquoise	–	D	D	–
Colonial White	E	E	E	–
Starmist Blue	F	–	–	–
Silvertone Green	–	F	–	–
Sky Mist Blue	–	–	–	F
April Green	–	G	G	–
Gunmetal Gray	–	H	–	–
Willow Green	J	–	–	–
Monte Carlo Red	–	–	J	J
Turquoise	–	–	–	K
Azure Blue	–	L	–	–
Holly Green (Dark)	–	–	L	L
Gulfstream Blue	–	M	–	–
Corinthian White	–	–	M	M
Seaspray Green	–	N	–	–
Primer	P	–	–	–
Torch Red	R	R	R	–
Special Paint	S	–	–	–
Mint Green	–	–	S	–
Woodsmoke Gray	T	–	–	–
Silvertone Blue	–	T	–	–
Meadow Green	U	U	U	–
Academy Blue	–	V	V	V
Adriatic Green	–	–	W	W
Goldenrod Yellow	–	X	X	X
Inca Gold	Y	–	–	–

Note: Information included in this chart is designed to be inclusive. Dependent upon reference, year, and carryover, information may vary.

Note: 1957–1960 color codes on the VIN plate are listed as "Color."

Ford Light-Duty Truck Transmissions (1957–1960)

Year	Model	Automatic/ Manual	Number of Gears	Transmission
1957–1960	F-100	Manual	3	Standard
1957–1960	F-100	Manual	3	Medium Duty
1957–1960	F-100	Manual	3	3-Speed with Overdrive
1957–1960	F-100	Manual	4	Optional
1957–1960	F-100	Automatic	3	Ford-O-Matic
1957–1958	F-250	Manual	3	Standard
1957–1958	F-250	Manual	3	Medium Duty
1957–1958	F-250	Manual	3	3-Speed with Overdrive
1957–1958	F-250	Manual	4	Optional
1957–1958	F-250	Automatic	3	Ford-O-Matic
1959–1960	F-250	Manual	3	Standard
1959–1960	F-250	Manual	3	Medium Duty
1959–1960	F-250	Manual	3	3-Speed with Overdrive
1959–1960	F-250	Manual	4	Optional
1959–1960	F-250	Automatic	3	Heavy-Duty Cruise-O-Matic

Note: Information included in this chart is designed to be inclusive. Dependent upon reference, year, and carryover, information may vary.

Ford Light-Duty Trucks Sizes and Prices (1957–1960)

Year	Model	Wheelbase (inches)	Length (inches)	Bed Length (feet)	Height (inches)	Width (inches)	Gross Vehicle Weight (pounds)	Price	Number Manufactured
1957–1960	Ford F-100 1/2-ton Styleside and Flareside	110/118	189.1/203.2	6.5/8	75.5	75.7	4,000–5,000	$1,631–$2,134	449,843*
1957–1960	Ford F-250 3/4-ton Styleside and Flareside	118	203.2	8	Varies	75.7	4,900–7,400	$1,786–$2,245	57,469**

Note: Information included in this chart is designed to be inclusive. Dependent upon reference, year, and carryover, information may vary.

Note: From 1957 to 1960, Ford offered a F-110 1/2 ton with a bed length of 6.5 feet, a wheelbase of 110 inches, and a GVW of 4,000 pounds.

Note: In 1958, Ford offered a F-140 1/2 ton with a bed length of 8 feet, a wheelbase of 118 inches, and a GVW of 4,000 pounds.

Note: From 1957 to 1959, Ford offered a F-260 3/4 ton with a GVW of 4,900 pounds.

* Is a total of all F-100 1/2-ton Styleside and Flareside body, bed, engine, and cab types.

** Is a total of all F-250 3/4-ton Styleside and Flareside body, bed, engine, and cab types.

FORD F-SERIES FOURTH GENERATION (1961–1966)

"The garish exterior styling of the third-generation F-Series gave way to a more streamlined and timeless styling for the fourth-generation F-Series (1961–1966)."

Coming out of the seemingly happy-go-lucky times of the 1950s, America was now in a new decade. This decade would be filled with cultural clashes, international clashes, and even the assassination of an American president.

A recession that started in 1957 was starting to recover in the early 1960s. As a result of the economic downturn, vehicle manufacturers started producing smaller economy cars, such as the Ford Falcon released in the 1960 model year.

Internally at the Blue Oval, the design mentality changed too. While the 1950s-era trucks had flashy exteriors, they also had sparse interiors. The garish exterior styling of the third-generation F-Series gave way to a more streamlined and timeless styling for the fourth-generation F-Series (1961–1966). The fourth-generation F-Series introduced several firsts to the truck line including:

- The first unibody pickup was created to reduce manufacturing costs.
- Twin I-Beam independent front suspension was developed.
- The first crew cab was introduced.

Inside the design studio, trucks were looked at in the same way as cars, with a focus on interior comfort. Prior to this, items such as rubber floor mats were one of few options available to truck buyers. The interiors were still very basic. Starting with

The rear view of 1961 F-100 shows the handles used to lock and unlock the tailgate. This was an improvement over earlier trucks that used a hook connected to a chain to keep the tailgate fastened to the bed of the truck. The letters FORD are stamped into the tailgate and are simply body color, as is the rear bumper (Photo Courtesy Richard Truesdell)

Tow ratings were not precise during the 1960s. Generally, the rule of thumb was if you can move it, you can tow it. Even this 1965 F-100 long-bed Custom Cab had enough towing capability and brake control to move this 1967 camper in Arches National Park in Utah. During this era, the dangers related to towing excessive amounts at highway speeds were not even considered. (Photo Courtesy Ted Nelson)

the fourth generation, the F-Series had designers' attention and, as a result, the aesthetics of the interior were dramatically improved. All this was good, since the truck was being bought by families in the suburbs, not just rural America. The truck was gaining in popularity in the middle class and the pickup truck was even being considered by many as daily drivers. This was a real pivot in the market segment, and Ford responded with the fourth-generation F-Series.

The 223-ci 6-cylinder engine in a 1961 F-100 shows that the ignition coil located between the second and third spark plug from the front looks like it is installed upside down. In fact, this is the correct way to install the coil. This type of coil has transformer oil inside the cylindrical metal housing to help cool the primary and secondary coil windings. Placing the coil in this fashion keeps the insulating oil near where the secondary coil is located to help prevent the high-voltage output arcing from the primary windings to the steel housing. Also, helping to prevent undesirable arcing, the plastic used is mustard colored and does not contain any carbon, which can make it conductive to high voltages. This coil design is called a "mustard top" coil. (Photo Courtesy Richard Truesdell)

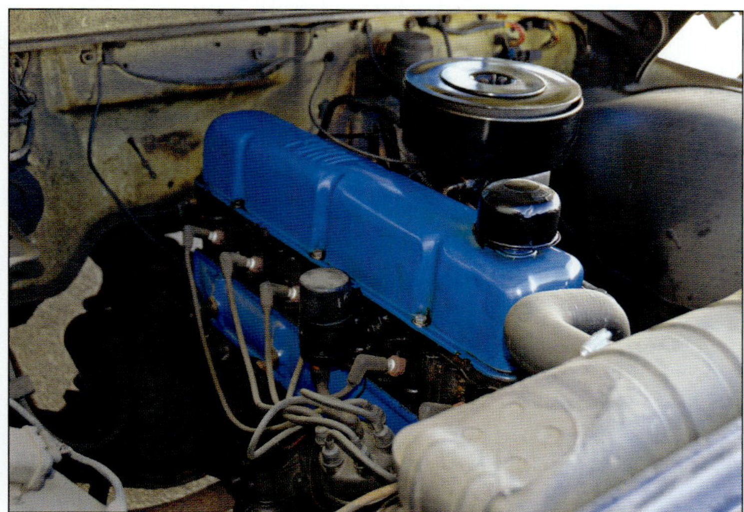

This is another angle of the inline 6-cylinder engine used in the 1961 F-100. The valve cover (top) and the side cover (lower) that cover the valvetrain are painted blue with the rest of the engine painted black. (Photo Courtesy Richard Truesdell)

The interior of a 1961 F-100 is shown. Notice that the 3-speed manual transmission is column mounted and the brake and clutch pedals are suspended from the dash panel. The stock-appearing steering wheel is covered with an aftermarket vinyl covering likely used to add grip and to help insulate hands from a cold or hot steering wheel. On the passenger's side, notice that there is no armrest and that the inner door panel is metal. It is a far cry from today's truck interior. (Photo Courtesy Richard Truesdell)

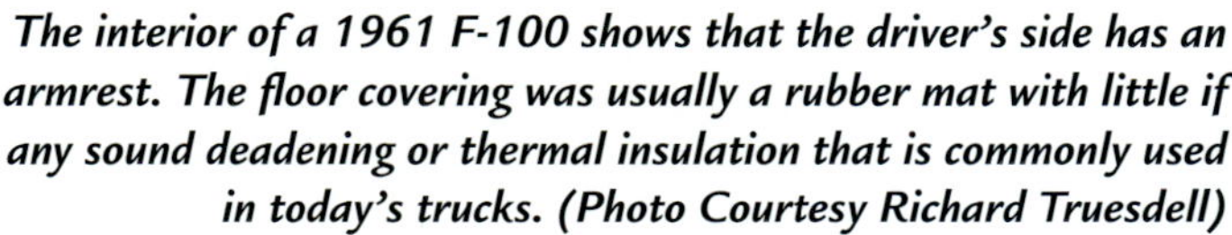

The interior of a 1961 F-100 shows that the driver's side has an armrest. The floor covering was usually a rubber mat with little if any sound deadening or thermal insulation that is commonly used in today's trucks. (Photo Courtesy Richard Truesdell)

Pictured here is a tailgate handle of a 1961 F-100. Placing the opening handle inside the tailgate allowed for a wider tailgate opening. (Photo Courtesy Richard Truesdell)

This 1962 F-100 Flareside was stock except for aftermarket wheels. Notice that the grille and bumper are painted white in this example. This truck also has a rear side outside rearview mirror, something that did not come from the factory but was often added at the dealer or by the owner after purchase. (Photo Courtesy Robert André)

Pictured here is the left rear taillight of the 1961 F-100. Notice the use of a reflector on the left rear only, which was there to provide a reflection from headlights of any vehicle approaching from the rear. (Photo Courtesy Richard Truesdell)

The speedometer of this 1961 F-100 is surrounded by other instruments, including engine coolant temperature, oil pressure, and charging system ammeter. The instrument panel was constructed from stamped steel without any changes to make it look better; instead, it was simply functional and cost effective for Ford. (Photo Courtesy Richard Truesdell)

Unibody Construction

For 1961, Ford expanded on the previous generation's Styleside F-100 with new 6.5- and 8-foot-long truck beds. They featured an integrated cab and bed known as unibody, or unit body. These were constructed with the cab and pickup bed in one continuous piece with no gap between them, similar to a unibody car.

The integrated body made the truck look more like passenger car styling and also resulted in a 1.5-inch lowering of the step-in height to the cab. The back of the cab served as the front of the pickup bed. The single-wall bed sides were spot welded directly to the door sills. The one-piece cab and box body were still mounted to a traditional frame-style chassis. It was still body-on-frame and not technically a unibody frame.

There was one major disadvantage and a fundamental problem of the unitized cab and bed. When a heavy load was placed toward the rear of the bed, the stress on the body often caused the doors to pop open. That's not a good thing to have happen when driving at highway speed. If a heavy load was placed toward the front of the bed, the stress caused the door-sills to deform, causing the doors to be jammed shut.

The unitized cab with bed design was only used on the F-100. A separate cab and bed were used for the F-250 and higher series of Ford trucks. Ford discovered that the unitized body was not strong enough to handle the rigors of the 4WD vehicle in addition to the other problems of the unitized body. So, the unibody trucks were dropped midway through the 1963–1964 model year. The result was that some 1963 trucks and the 1963–1964 4WD trucks used the bed from the 1957–1960 F-Series.

Econoline

In 1960, Ford introduced the Econoline van, which replaced the F-Series panel truck. The Econoline van was designed by the passenger car division at Ford and not the truck division. It was designed to compete against the VW bus. The Econoline (unofficially referred to as the E-100) had a 90-inch wheelbase and was 168 inches long, 76 inches wide, and 70 inches high. It had a 3,300-pound GVW.

The Econoline van was available in three different configurations: delivery van, station bus, and pickup. The delivery van had panel truck doors at the rear and on the right side. This van featured a huge interior space of 204 cubic feet, which was large considering the relatively small outside dimensions.

The station bus was another version of the Econoline truck and featured room for eight passengers with two bench seats in the rear (three people each) plus driver and passenger bucket seats in the front. Windows were used instead of sheet metal on the sides, so visibility was good.

The Econoline pickup was another version of the delivery van, except that instead of a closed rear section, it had an open bed that was 85 inches long, 63 inches wide, and 23 inches deep. The E-100 was only offered as a pickup truck during the van's first generation and was discontinued in 1967.

The Econoline was immediately popular. It was bare-boned but useful. It was mostly available as a transport vehicle and in company fleets. The Econoline represented Ford's response to the equally popular Volkswagen bus and van.

By 1963, both General Motors and Dodge offered rivals. The Econoline was a success for Ford. Ford of Canada marketed a Mercury Econoline from 1961–1965. This was because Lincoln-Mercury dealerships were more well-represented in some parts of rural Canada.

The Ford Econoline was a truck-based van with unusual looks. It first appeared as a 1960 model year vehicle. Throughout its life, the Econoline took on a more van-like, traditional appearance as opposed to this early-generation Econoline. (Photo Courtesy Randy Stern)

The Ford Econoline was an unusual vehicle that was available in three configurations: delivery van, bus, and pickup truck. The Econoline was Ford's response to the Volkswagen Bus, which was extremely popular during this era. (Photo Courtesy Randy Stern)

This 1964 Ford Econoline was a special order by the US Army. It was used as a support vehicle at Fort Rucker in Alabama. The Econoline's engine was located between the driver and the passenger with access through the removal of the engine cover. (Photo Courtesy Joe Unger)

1961

Kicking off this new generation, there were big changes in store for the 1961 Ford truck. The unibody cab was the biggest deal for this model year, but F-100 also got a new look. Some of that is attributed to the unibody design, which gave the truck straighter and cleaner lines. It also increased the cargo capacity.

Many automotive historians consider the fourth-generation F-Series to have the best fit and finish of any other truck in Ford's history. Although the unibody had major flaws, from a design aspect, it gave it a pure look. The new fourth generation included:

- Up front, four headlights were replaced by two headlights.
- The grille took on a new look with a wide opening that stretched across the front and was surrounded by molding.
- The front was still very square with four vent openings underneath the pointed edge that ran along the front width of the hood.
- The Ford truck badge was centered on the front of the hood and the sides used the rocket-style F-100 logo.
- The tailgate of both the Flareside and Styleside F-100 was standardized, eliminating the chain style in favor of the hinge support system. This minor change was in response to the loud clatter the chain style made on the previous generation.
- With more designer focus, Ford continued to improve the cab comfort of the F-100 by fitting the truck with a large front windshield for extra visibility.
- A new electric center windshield wiper system was now standard (it was previously available as an option).
- Inside the cab, additional foam was put into the bench seat along with extra sound deadening insulation to provide a more-comfortable and quieter ride.
- Styleside trucks had woven brown upholstery with bolsters and the lifeguard steering wheel as a safety feature.
- Additional interior amenities included a dome light, a passenger-side sun visor, a glove box, and a headliner.

The Custom Cab options continued to feature the two-tone instrument panel that matched the two-tone exterior. The chassis for the 1961 F-Series remained unchanged. The F-100 with the 8-foot bed had a GVWR of 5,000 pounds, but the 4WD models, which were only available as a Flareside, had a GVWR of 3,500.

From a mechanical standpoint, little was changed on the 1961 F-100. There was a 223-ci 6-cylinder engine. The 262-ci V8 was the preferred option, which had a rating of 172 hp. The 3-speed manual was still the standard transmission, while a 4-speed manual and the Ford-O-Matic automatic transmission were popular options.

In 1961, Ford updated its car-based Ranchero truck. It was based on the Ford Falcon, and the Ranchero had a new convex grille as viewed from the side. The engine size was increased from 144 to 170 ci by using a longer stroke with the power increased from 90 to 101 hp.

The base price of the Styleside pickup was $1,981 for the 6.5-foot bed and $2,017 for the 8-foot bed. The Flareside price was $1,966 for the 6.5-foot bed and $2,001 for the 8-foot bed. Production was down in 1961 with only 62,410 Stylesides and 3,361 Flaresides being produced.

Falcon Ranchero

For the 1961 model year, Ford offered the 170-ci (2.8L) 101-hp 6-cylinder inline engine in addition to the standard 144-ci (2.4L) 85-hp 6-cylinder in the Ranchero. The styling and other features were the same as offered in the 1961 Falcon sedan and station wagon.

According to Gale Halderman, a Ford designer for 40 years, sound and thermal insulation were the most expensive items in the interior of any vehicle. Gale said that if costs had to be reduced, there was a certain order followed.

First, sound and thermal insulation was reduced. There were several reasons for this. It required a lot of labor to install at the factory. The insulation added to the weight of the vehicle. The cost of the insulation itself was a big factor. While the insulation was not removed entirely, the thickness and the quality of the material were reduced to save money. According to Gale, few people could tell the difference unless they drove an identical vehicle with the standard and then the lesser amount of sound deadening material back-to-back. The chances of this happening were not likely, so vehicle manufacturers could achieve this cost saving with relative ease.

Second, the quality of the interior fabric used on the seat(s), door panels, and headliner (inside roof fabric) was reduced to save costs. While all fabric was tested to ensure long life and wear as well as fade resistance, using a lighter weight fabric or a step down in quality often resulted in huge savings.

Finally, carpet thickness was reduced to reduce vehicle weight and cost. Trucks often did not include carpet, and when it was offered as an option, few realized that there are many different thicknesses and grades of carpet. As a result, using carpet in a pickup truck was thought to be a huge step up in the interior look and feel regardless of the thickness or grade.

1962

With the truck market changing rapidly, Ford stood pat for the 1962 F-Series. Due to customer concerns over the integrated cab/bed of the 1961 F-100, Ford rushed the production of a separate bed using the 1957–1960 F-100 design.

Cosmetically, only a few changes occurred. The 1962 model included a crosshair in the center of the grille. The Ford logo was moved to just above the four hood vents, where it would stay for almost 20 years. The rest of the truck's body remained the same as 1961, including the hood side emblem.

Mechanically, the only change that occurred for the 1962 F-Series was with the transmission. The Cruise-O-Matic automatic transmission replaced the Ford-O-Matic as the go-to automatic transmission. The interior remained unchanged, with the exception of the Custom Cab trim.

The Custom Cab option included two-tone door panels and instrument cluster and chrome trim around the instrument cluster. It had a white steering wheel with chrome trim and dual sun visors. Additional insulation in the cowl (firewall) helped block heat and noise from the engine compartment. The Custom Cab exterior also had more chrome trim around the windshield and grille than the standard model.

The 1962 Falcon Ranchero featured a new slotted grille with flat-top headlight surround. Its new hood and front bumper design had integrated parking lights. The taillights and white-lettered wheel covers were also new for 1962.

The 1962 Econoline pickup featured a higher gross vehicle weight than before, now listed at 3,600 pounds, up from 3,300 pounds due to heavy-duty rear leaf springs.

The base price of the 114-inch wheelbase Styleside was $2,006, while the Flareside was $1,979. The 122-inch wheelbase model cost $2,015 for the Flareside and $2,042 for the Styleside.

1963

Still reacting to the unibody disaster of 1961, the remaining line of the F-100 was changed back to a separate bed and cab. This change first appeared in the spring of 1962 on 4WD trucks and was expanded to the 2WD trucks in the 1963 model year. In the spring of 1963, the unitized body trucks were still available, but they were eventually phased out altogether from this model year.

There were minor cosmetic changes made to the grille, which now featured a floating rectangle shaped opening with turn signals. All models were available with the 6.5- and 8-foot beds, but only the Flareside model used a wood bed with steel skid strips. The push to add car-like comfort continued.

For the 1963 model year, changes were made to improve driver and passenger comfort. The foot pedals were moved closer to the floor to create more legroom. Synthetic foam cushioning was added to the bench seat to make it more comfortable. Door pockets with zippered openings were added as an option.

Ford upgraded the F-Series suspension system to be more like the larger trucks by adapting a new single I-Beam front axle combined with leaf springs and a stiffer frame. The I-Beam suspension was used on the F-Series until the introduction of the Twin I-Beam independent suspension in 1965.

The 223-ci 6-cylinder engine carried over as did the 292-ci V8. The transmission remained unchanged from the previous model year. Pricing remained steady for the F-Series. Prices ranged from $2,000 for the 114-inch-wheelbase Flareside to $2,066 for the non-unibody 122-inch-wheelbase Styleside. Starting in 1963, the truck segment became even more competitive with additional trucks from General Motors, Chrysler, Jeep, and International.

6,000-MILE OIL CHANGES

When Ford announced that it was recommending the oil change interval be extended to 6,000 miles or 6 months instead of the previously specified interval of 3,000 miles or 3 months, everyone was surprised, and many were shocked. The move was done for several reasons including:

1. To help reduce the maintenance cost for owners of new Ford cars and trucks in an effort to improve sales.
2. Engineers thought that engines were more efficient, which reduced the need to change oil as often as previously specified.
3. To help reduce the time needed for service by the average vehicle owner.

In 1963, several factors led to an increased number of miles being put on vehicles. The gasoline prices were relatively low, and the new interstate highway system was nearly complete. People could travel farther to visit family and friends and to go on vacations. The population was also increasing due to the baby boom of World War II, and more people were driving, so the family car was used for longer periods throughout each day.

Reducing the number of oil changes required from four times a year to twice a year resulted in substantial savings to the average car owner, not only in money, but also time needed to take the vehicle in for service. All of this was before vehicles were equipped with an oil life monitor (OLM) that can actually let the driver know when the driving conditions have been met and when an oil change is needed.

The new oil change interval was discussed and debated by service technicians and vehicle owners for years. Other major vehicle manufacturers also started to recommend longer oil change intervals in an effort to keep up, as this was a huge selling point to those considering purchasing a new vehicle.

Today's vehicles, depending on how and under what conditions the vehicle is being driven, can be driven for a year and up to 12,000 miles before an oil change is needed or recommended. But back in 1963, a 6,000-mile oil change interval was almost unheard of and considered by many to be potentially harmful to the life of the engine.

Ford Ranchero

For 1963, the Ford Ranchero received a new horizontal bar grille, amber parking light lenses (which used non-amber clear bulbs instead of previously used amber bulbs behind a clear parking light lens), and restyled taillights.

Ford Econoline

The Ford Econoline van and pickup continued with just minor changes. A new option for 1963 was an additional door on the driver's side, making it available with a total of eight doors (two on the right, two at the rear, two on the left side, and two cab doors).

The grille of the 1964 F-100 is highly stylized. The eight rectangles sit between the circular headlights. As such, these trucks are easy to identify. (Photo Courtesy Misty Sleeth)

For this generation, 1964 is considered the nicest interior. More padding was added to the seats of the F-100, padded sun visors were added, and it now had a three-spoked steering wheel. (Photo Courtesy Misty Sleeth)

There were a lot of significant changes to the bed of the 1964 F-100. But also, the tailgate featured, for the first time, a single-hand release system. (Photo Courtesy Misty Sleeth)

1964

By 1964, the unibody style was completely phased out of production. There were minor body changes to this model year including:

- Ford made the roof 1 inch higher, which provided more headroom for the passengers.
- Ford added more sound-deadening insulation (26 pounds of noise and thermal insulation), making this the quietest F-Series truck to date. There were even padded sun visors as an option.
- There was a new three-spoked, color-coded steering wheel, which was an attractive cosmetic change.
- Outside, only a minor change occurred to the grille. There were now eight open squares across the front divided into four vertical rows.
- The headlights still featured chrome surrounds, and turn signals were located inside the headlights.
- Chrome trim was used around the grille on some models; the Ford letters were placed above the grille and were spaced apart more on the 1964 truck.

The Styleside F-100 now had a new separate cargo bed. The big news that was pioneered by Ford was the first double-side cargo bed. Before, the cargo bed consisted of a single sheet of steel on the sides. If a heavy load shifted and struck the inside of the bed, it created a ding or dent on the inside that was also seen on the outside of the cargo bed. By using a double-wall construction, a dent on the inside would not be seen on the outside. The new cargo bed was styled to blend with the character lines of the cab. The inside of the cargo bed measured 99 inches long, 70 inches wide, and 19 inches deep. It was the first industry use of a single-hand tailgate release.

Ford lettering was stamped larger on the outer sheet metal and the vertical brake lights were larger on the 1964. In addition, Styleside trucks had a toolbox option. The toolbox was located on the inside of the bed just behind the passenger wheel well.

The 1964 engines and transmissions remained unchanged from 1963. The price of the 114-inch-wheelbase 6-cylinder model was $1,964 for Flareside and $1,979 for Styleside. The long-bed 8-cylinder model was priced at $2,000 for Flareside and $2,016 for Styleside.

Ford Econoline

Changes were minor and included an upgraded cab interior and headliner, a locking glove box door, left-hand cargo doors (optional), and an optional heavy-duty package. The powertrain remained unchanged for 1964.

Ford Ranchero

The Ranchero continued to follow the bodystyle of the Falcon, which had a major styling update for 1964. Gone were the rounded corners in favor of an angular design. A Sedan Delivery version was first offered in 1964.

1965

Things were great at the Blue Oval. The company was basking in the glow of the Mustang's success. For 1965, Ford pickup truck sales were up 22 percent. The automaker sold a record 489,510 trucks, including the Econoline vans and Falcon Rancheros. This represented a year of big changes for

Ford trucks. There was a new trim line known as the Ranger; a new special edition known as the Camper Special; and a new, revolutionary suspension system.

Cosmetically, there were quite a few changes to the 1965 F-100. A new grille featured a revised set of rectangle openings set across two horizontal bars and placed between the two headlights and bezels. The turn signal lights were moved up above the chrome grille surround, and the Ford lettering stretched out between the lights. An option for 1965 was to mount a grille guard to the top of the bumper with two braces attached to the frame. The grille guard was a low-profile design that did not interfere with the turn signals or headlights.

The interior for 1965 remained mostly the same as the 1964 model. The Custom Cab had bright chrome script lettering across the outside of the door that was larger and more visible than in 1964.

In 1965, Ford introduced the Ranger package that featured bucket seats, carpeting, and an optional center console. These changes were used in the marketing of the Ranger option.

Paying close attention to the developing recreational vehicle lifestyle that was occurring in the country, Ford created a special edition known as the "camper special." This featured a longer wheelbase of 128 inches (an increase of 6 inches). The long chassis was available in the F-100 and F-250 4x2. This included dual outside Western-style mirrors, a camper special emblem on the fenders, an extended tailpipe, and a 70-amp-hour battery. The camper special packages also had the option of either the new 300-ci inline 6-cylinder engine or the 352-ci V8. Both were equipped with either Cruise-O-Matic automatic transmission or the 4-speed manual. The instrument panel on the camper special featured oil pressure and ammeter gauges.

In 1965, Ford joined the rest of the automotive industry in adopting the use of an alternator, also called an AC generator, instead of the DC generator of its previous product line. Motorcraft, a division of Ford Motor Company, made most of the alternators used on domestic Ford vehicles.

The standard engine in 1965 was a new 240-ci inline 6-cylinder that developed 150 hp at 4,000 rpm with 234 ft-lbs of torque at 2,200 rpm. The optional 6-cylinder engine primarily found on heavy-duty F-100s was the larger 300-ci inline 6-cylinder that developed 170 hp at 3,600 rpm with 283 ft-lbs of torque at 2,400 rpm. (The 300-ci engine had a longer stroke.) The V8 option in 1965 was the new (to the truck line) 352-ci engine that developed 208 hp at 4,400 rpm with 315 ft-lbs of torque at 2,400 rpm. The 223-ci I6 and 292 V8 had been dropped.

Ford Econoline

The Econoline van featured minor changes, including moving the rear license plate bracket from the rear bumper to the rear cargo door. As a result of this change, the bumpers were the same front and rear, thereby reducing costs.

Ford Ranchero

The 1965 Ford Ranchero was basically a carryover from the 1964 model year but replaced the optional 260-ci V8, which was discontinued, with a 289-ci (4.7L) V8 for 1965. Also, for 1965, an alternator replaced the DC generator that was used on Fords in prior model years.

For the 1965 F-Series, prices ranged from $2,000 to $2,125 for 1965 F-100s, based on style and truck size.

This 352-ci V8 in a 1965 F-100 shows what many owners do to improve the safety and appearance of their trucks from this era. This large V8 features chrome-plated valve covers to add some style, as well as a low-restriction chrome-plated air filter. In the background, notice that the stock single-cylinder master cylinder has been updated to a much safer dual master cylinder design and newer vacuum booster power brake system.

The rear of a 1965 F-100 pickup truck shows the painted Ford lettering on the tailgate and the central tailgate opening handle that is used to unlatch both sides of the tailgate using one hand. This truck also features a two-tone paint scheme (white over blue) plus a chrome rear bumper and aftermarket dual exhaust tailpipes.

The full wheel covers used on this 1965 F-100 instead of hubcaps that only covered the lug nuts was a great way to enhance the look of a truck. The use of white sidewall tires was rarely seen on work trucks, but many owners used them on daily driver trucks. Toward the end of the 1960s, Ford trucks were being used by families instead of just as work trucks.

The front end of the 1965 F-100 shows a painted front grille and bumper with a blue body color and a white top. This rust-free example is mostly stock except for aftermarket wheels, which were commonly used to dress up trucks. (Photo Courtesy Travis Davis)

The chrome door edge guards were added by the owner to add interest to the normally plain side view. The toolbox in the bed usually means that this truck was used for business. (Photo Courtesy Travis Davis)

HOW THE TWIN I-BEAM SUSPENSION CHANGED THE F-SERIES

Introduced in 1965, the Twin I-Beam front suspension featured strong forged-steel twin beams that cross and provide independent front suspension operation with the strength of a solid front axle. Using two steel I-Beams allowed each front wheel to move up and down independently, which provided a smoother ride than the previously used straight axle, called the mono-beam by Ford.

Early versions of the Twin I-Beam systems used kingpins, while later models used ball joints to support the steering knuckle and spindle. Coil springs are usually used on Twin I-Beam suspensions. The Twin-I-Beam suspension was used for rear-wheel-drive trucks (4x2) for the first 15 years and then finally adapted to 4WD trucks and called the Twin Traction Beam system, in 1980. Previously the 4x4 trucks used a leaf spring solid front axle (non-independent) design. The Twin I-Beam and Twin Traction Beam suspension systems were used on Ford trucks until 2002.

The Twin I-Beams were basically like long lower control arms. To control longitudinal (front-to-back) support, a radius rod was attached to each beam and anchored to the frame of the truck using rubber bushings. These bushings allowed the

This Ford advertisement showcases the new revolutionary Twin I-Beam suspension. The front wheels operate independently on their own axle. (Photo Courtesy Ford Motor Company)

A 1965 Custom Cab long bed is shown towing a 1967 camper in front of the historic Hackberry Store along Route 66. (Photo Courtesy Ted Nelson)

front axle to move up and down while still insulating road noise and vibration from the frame and body. When the radius rod bushing on a Ford truck or van deteriorated, the most common complaint from the driver was noise.

Besides causing tire wear, worn or defective radius rod bushings can cause a clicking sound heard during braking or a clunking noise heard when the truck hits bumps in the road. When the bushing deteriorates, the axles move forward and backward with less control. Noise is the first sign that something is wrong.

The Twin I-Beam suspension represented a true turning point for Ford. Earlier in the decade, Chevrolet had already modified its suspension system to improve ride quality. With this introduction, the Ford truck went through a significant metamorphosis. In 1965, with the introduction of this new, more-comfortable suspension, Ford focused on passenger and driver comfort and putting the rough-riding, crude reputation of early trucks behind it. The Twin I-Beam suspension would stay with Ford and its truck line for the majority of the 20th century.

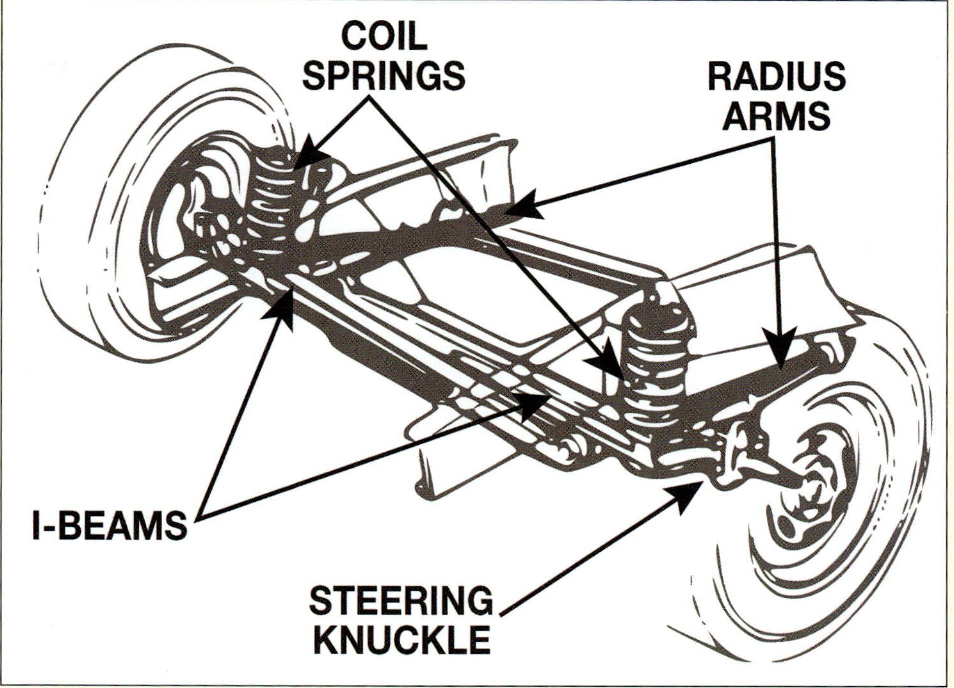

This 1965 F-100 has the Twin I-Beam emblem and two-tone paint with blue used on the lower body and white on the upper body panels. This truck had a Custom Cab trim level because of the use of the chrome side trim and full wheel covers.

1966

By 1966, Ford had become the number-two truck manufacturer in terms of total unit sales, just behind its rival, General Motors. Ford's truck sales totaled 536,427 units in 1966. Much of the sales success was due in part to the introduction of the Ford Bronco.

The Bronco was introduced in August 1965. The body was unique and built by the Budd Company. The base model was topless, had no doors, and featured 4WD. Other Bronco models featured a roof just over the cab or a longer roof covering the rear area on the Wagon version. The Bronco featured a solid front axle with coil springs and a leaf spring rear suspension. The Bronco was intended to compete against Jeep, which dominated this segment, and the International Scout as well.

For the F-100 and the F-250, there were only a few minor changes. There was a new grille that had two large openings above a series of stamped rectangular openings. This was the last year of this new-look grille, which was synonymous with the fourth-generation F-Series.

The 1966 Ford Bronco featured no doors or roof and had 4WD as standard to compete against the Jeep. Other models included a door and a roof over just the front seat or over the seat and the rear section as well. Notice the center of the front wheels where the front hubs could be locked to the drivetrains for off-road use only. If the 4WD system was used on dry pavement, severe and damaging vibrations would be created. (Photo Courtesy Richard Truesdell)

The rear of the 1966 Ford Bronco shows the handle used to open the rear tailgate, similar to the system used on the F-100. The rear license plate was located on the tailgate instead of under the rear bumper to help provide more road clearance for when the Bronco was used off-road. (Photo Courtesy Richard Truesdell)

The spartan interior of the 1966 Bronco is similar to that of a Jeep. Notice the lockable glove box and the suspended brake and clutch pedals. This Bronco was equipped with white bucket seats that look to be the same units used in the Ford Mustang. Also, notice the padded sun visors as one of the safety features that Ford started to include in the 1960s. (Photo Courtesy Richard Truesdell)

In 1966, the 4WD truck could be ordered in both the 115- and 129-inch wheelbase for the first time; previously, it was only available in the 129-inch size. Another big change for 1966 involved the introduction of the F-250 crew cab, which was a six-passenger vehicle. It had a full bench seat in the rear along with four doors. Due to the fact that this was a larger truck, the standard F-250 8-foot bed was shortened to 6.5 feet. The crew cab was available in either the Styleside or Flareside. This truck was built on a 147-inch wheelbase and maintained the 7,500-pound GVWR. All engines and transmissions for the 1966 F-Series were carryovers.

Ford Econoline

Ford updated the Econoline van with more length, calling it the Econoline Super Van. It featured a lengthened body that allowed for increased cargo capacity, as well as added safety features such as seat belts and a padded dash.

Ford Ranchero

The 1966 version of the Ranchero was a one-year model with both Falcon and Fairlane using the same platform. The 1966 model was labeled as the Ford Ranchero and did not include the Falcon name. Features of the 1966 Ranchero included:

- Falcon front sheet metal was on a modified station wagon platform.
- Late 1966 model year Rancheros used the same front sheet metal as the Fairlane.
- Seat belts were standard equipment for the 1966 model year.
- Engines available included:
  - 170-ci (2.8L) inline 6-cylinder
  - 200-ci (3.3L) inline 6-cylinder
  - 289-ci (4.7L) V8
- Transmissions included the 3-speed automatic and the column-shifted 3-speed manual.

The base price of the 6-cylinder F-100 was $2,069 for Flareside and $2,085 for Styleside short beds. The base price for the long bed model was $2,015 for the Flareside and $2,121 for the Styleside.

Conclusion

If the 1950s represented a return to greatness for Ford, then the 1960s represented Ford vaulting into dominance. Following up on the success of its car line and the launch of the Mustang, Ford did not forget about advancing the pickup truck. More good things were to come for the F-Series, and Ford's pickup truck success was still climbing with no peak in sight.

Ford Light-Duty Truck Engines (1961–1966)				
Year	Engine	Horsepower (hp)	Torque (ft-lbs)	VIN Code
1961	223-ci inline 6-cylinder OHV	135	203 at 2,000–2,600 rpm	J
	292-ci V8 OHV	172	270 at 2,000–2,700 rpm	C
1962	223-ci inline 6-cylinder OHV	135	200 at 1,800–2,400 rpm	J
	292-ci V8 OHV	160	270 at 1,800–2,000 rpm	C
1963	223-ci inline 6-cylinder OHV	135	203 at 2,000–2,600 rpm	J
	262-ci inline 6-cylinder OHV	152	237 at 1,800 rpm	B
	292-ci V8 OHV	160	270 at 2,000–2,700 rpm	C
1964	223-ci inline 6-cylinder OHV	135	200 at 1,800–2,400 rpm	J
	262-ci inline 6-cylinder OHV	152	237 at 1,800 rpm	B
	292-ci V8 OHV	160	270 at 2,000–2,700 rpm	C
1965	240-ci inline 6-cylinder OHV	150	234 at 2,200 rpm	A or J
	300-ciinline 6-cylinder OHV	170	283 at 1,400–2,400 rpm	B
	352-ci V8 OHV	208	315 at 2,400 rpm	D
1966	240-ci inline 6-cylinder OHV	150	234 at 2,200 rpm	A
	300-ci inline 6-cylinder OHV	170	283 at 1,400–2,400 rpm	B
	352-ci V8 OHV	208	315 at 2,400 rpm	D or Y

Note: Information included in this chart is designed to be inclusive. Dependent upon reference, year, and carryover, information may vary.

Note: Engine VIN example: The underlined letter "C" F10CK350001 indicates the placement in the engine VIN and the engine in the example is a 292-ci V8.

Ford Light-Duty Truck Transmissions (1961–1966)				
Year	Model	Automatic/ Manual	Number of Gears	Transmission
1961–1966	F-100	Manual	3	Standard
1961–1966	F-100	Manual	4	Optional
1961–1966	F-100	Automatic	3	Ford-O-Matic
1961	F-250	Manual	3	Standard
1961	F-250	Manual	4	Optional
1961	F-250	Automatic	3	Cruise-O-Matic
1962–1964	F-250	Manual	3	Standard
1962–1964	F-250	Manual	4	Optional
1962–1964	F-250	Automatic	3	Cruise-O-Matic
1962–1964	F-250	Manual	3	Medium Duty
1965–1966	F-250	Manual	3	Standard
1965–1966	F-250	Manual	4	Optional
1965–1966	F-250	Automatic	3	Cruise-O-Matic
1965–1966	F-250	Manual	3	Heavy Duty
1965–1966	F-250	Manual	3	3-Speed with Overdrive

Note: Information included in this chart is designed to be inclusive. Dependent upon reference, year, and carryover, information may vary.

Color	Available Year and VIN Code					
	1961	1962	1963	1964	1965	1966
Raven Black (Black)	A	A	A	A	A	A
Caribbean Turquoise	B	B	B	B	B	B
Milk White	–	C	–	–	–	–
Arctic Milk White	–	–	C	–	–	–
Pure White	–	–	–	C	C	C
Light Blue	D	–	–	–	–	–
Starlight Blue	D	–	–	–	–	–
Peacock Blue	–	–	–	–	–	D
Viking Blue	–	E	E	E	–	–
Baffin Blue	–	F	–	–	–	–
Arcadian Blue	–	–	–	–	F	F
Chrome Yellow	–	G	–	G	G	G
School Bus Yellow	–	–	G	–	–	–
Sahara Beige	–	–	–	–	–	H
Rangoon Red	–	J	J	J	J	J
Monte Carlo Red	J	–	–	–	–	–
Driftwood Gray	–	–	K	–	–	–
Bengal Tan	–	–	–	K	–	–
Tan	–	–	–	–	K	–
Holly Green (Dark)	L	L	L	L	L	L
Corinthian White	M	M	M	–	–	–
Wimbledon White (White)	–	–	–	M	M	M
Frost Turquoise	–	–	–	–	–	N
Tropical Turquoise (Peacock)	–	–	–	–	O	–
Prairie Bronze (Palomino)	–	–	–	–	P	–
Antique Bronze	–	–	–	–	–	P
Mint Green (Light)	S	–	S	S	S	–
Poppy Red	–	–	–	–	–	S
Sandshell Beige	–	T	T	–	–	–
Navaho Beige	–	–	–	T	T	–
Academy Blue	V	V	V	V	–	–
Yellow	–	–	–	–	V	–
Marlin Blue (Medium)	–	–	–	–	W	W
Goldenrod Yellow	X	X	–	–	–	–
Glacier Blue	–	–	Y	–	–	–
Silver Blue	–	–	–	–	Y	Y
Skylight Blue	–	–	–	Y	3	3
Phoenician Yellow	–	–	–	–	7	–
Springtime Yellow	–	–	–	–	8	8
Primer	–	–	–	–	–	9

Note: Information included in this chart is designed to be inclusive. Dependent upon reference, year, and carryover, information may vary.

Note: 1961–1966 color codes on the VIN plate are listed as "Color."

Year	Model	Wheelbase (inches)	Length (inches)	Bed Length (feet)	Height (inches)	Width (inches)	Gross Vehicle Weight (pounds)	Price	Number Manufactured
1961–1966	Ford F-100 1/2-ton Styleside and Flareside	114–129	189.1	6.5/8	75.5	75.7	5,000–5,600	$1,966–$2,121	1,000,327*
1961–1966	Ford F-250 3/4-ton Styleside and Flareside	122–129	189.1	8	Varies	75.7	7,400–7,500	$2,120–$2,244	228,065**

Note: Information included in this chart is designed to be inclusive. Dependent upon reference, year, and carryover, information may vary.

Note: From 1961 to 1963, Ford offered a F-101 1/2 ton with a GVW of 4,000 pounds, and from 1964 to 1966, the F-101 1/2 ton had a GVW of 4,200 pounds.

Note: From 1961 to 1963, Ford offered a F-260 3/4 ton with a GVW of 4,900 pounds, and from 1964 to 1966, the F-260 3/4 ton had a GVW of 4,800 pounds.

* Is a total of all F-100 1/2-ton Styleside and Flareside body, bed, engine, and cab types.

** Is a total of all F-250 3/4-ton Styleside and Flareside body, bed, engine, and cab types.

FORD F-SERIES FIFTH GENERATION (1967–1972)

The fifth generation of the F-Series truck was overshadowed by the real star of Ford at the time: the Mustang. The Mustang launched three years prior and had already sold more than a million units. It was the muscle car era. America was in love with these cars that were squatty, sporty, and fast—pretty much the opposite of what trucks were. However, the truck was not forgotten; it still had its place among all the Mustang buzz.

Ford still invested heavily in the next generation of F-Series. From 1967 to 1972, Ford produced the fifth-generation Ford F-Series pickup trucks and commercial trucks. Some enthusiasts call this generation the Bumpsides. These trucks had sharper styling lines, a larger cab and greenhouse (the area of the body that includes the glass), and expanded and more-powerful engine options.

Capitalizing on the successful platform of the fourth generation, Ford managed to improve upon the success of that truck by making minor engineering tweaks. With the success of cars such as the Mustang, the Fairlane, and the Cobra, Ford knew how to engineer power. The horsepower increase for the F-Series was significant and necessary, although the real performance era of trucks was still more than two

> "These trucks had sharper styling lines, a larger cab and green-house (the area of the body that includes the glass), and expanded and more-powerful engine options."

Starting with the 1967 model year, Ford turned its design attention to the interior of the truck. Instead of a crude, basic dashboard, higher-quality materials were added to the dashboard and the instrumentation was reorganized. This was the first drastic interior redesign in the truck's history to that point.

decades away. Government-mandated emissions standards hit the automotive industry hard for both cars and trucks. While this generation of trucks started off getting more engine options and more horsepower, it would end with far less power.

Styling Applied to Pickup Trucks

For the fifth generation, attention was given to the styling of the pickup truck. Designers focused on paint color, interior style, and overall comfort. Before this fifth generation of trucks was over, the F-Series became the best-selling truck in America.

Gale Halderman, designer of the original Ford Mustang, was promoted to Director of Truck & Tractor Design in November 1968. He said that this generation was really the first time that interior styling was a factor for trucks. "Before then, there really wasn't much to a truck," he said. "Rubber floor mats were all you got prior to that."

For 1967, the longer front bench seat was covered in color vinyl upholstery, which matched the dashboard and other interior elements. Ford continued to add more cushioning to make the seat more comfortable too. Halderman said there was a design element used on the dashboard to help hide the instrument panel and make it look less commercial. Ford referred to this as the "swept away instrument panel."

This 390-ci V8 is in a 1970 F-250 that was fully restored to factory appearance. This truck is equipped with factory air-conditioning and power brakes. (Photo Courtesy Richard Truesdell)

This 1970 F-250 has been restored to factory-new condition. Notice the tool storage compartment on the passenger's side of the bed. Other options or accessories on this truck include vertical bumperettes on the front bumper and clearance lights on top of the cab. Also notice the full wheel covers with white sidewall tires and the two-tone paint and passenger-side outside rearview mirror. (Photo Courtesy Josh Fear)

This Ranger trim is equipped with air-conditioning, as seen below the dash. The vents are only incorporated in the evaporator housing and did not discharge through any vents in the dash. The blower motor is also visible under the glove box. (Photo Courtesy Richard Truesdell)

This 1970 Ford F-100 is equipped with some options, including a radio (per the antenna on the cab in front of the windshield on the passenger's side) and a passenger-side rearview mirror. (Photo Courtesy Josh Fear)

The two-tone color scheme of green with white on the lower body and the roof makes this 1970 Ford F-100 stand out. This truck has clearance lights over the cab and a spare tire at the rear of the bed, which was not the stock location. Spare tires were usually under the bed at the rear of the truck. (Photo Courtesy Josh Fear)

The new dash also had a larger glove box with a push-button latch and adjustable air vents for both vehicle occupants. The steering wheel was now painted the same color as the interior. The headliner was a standard feature that came in beige, blue, green, or red. Driver and passenger seat belts were now standard equipment. This design also included a lap belt in the center.

On the Custom Cab models, Ford added a chrome horn ring to the color-matched steering wheel, door armrests, and locks on both driver's and passenger's doors.

During the latter part of the 1960s, Americans were driving more miles in pickup trucks. It was still somewhat uncommon for a truck to be a daily driver, but it was viewed as a necessity for the weekend warrior. Thanks to extra disposable income, Americans were buying boats and campers and enjoying many of the National Parks and historic sites.

With the Vietnam War raging and much stricter government emissions standards for automakers, Ford still managed to produce an attractive, viable pickup truck that appealed to the masses. In 1971, President Richard M. Nixon issued a price freeze and repealed the Federal Excise Taxes on cars and light trucks. These changes affected the auto industry and contributed to substantial sales gains due to lower taxes.

Let's Go Camping!

During the end of the fourth generation of the F-Series, Ford launched a special-edition Camper Special that accommodated special slide-in camper trailers. These trailers were becoming quite the rage, surpassing the standard and traditional motorhome recreational vehicle sales.

GETTING STRICT ON EMISSIONS

Air quality standards were first addressed by federal regulation in the Clean Air Act (CAA) of 1963. The CAA of 1970 created the US Environmental Protection Agency (EPA) on December 2, 1970. The state of California created its own clean air environmental agency called the California Air Resources Board (CARB), which was established in 1967, when then-governor Ronald Reagan signed the Mulford-Carrell Act that combined the Bureau of Air Sanitation and the Motor Vehicle Pollution Control Board.

In 1970, CARB mandated a reduction of oxides of nitrogen for vehicles that were to be sold in California. Meeting this requirement led to the lowering of the engine compression ratios so that lead-free gasoline could be used.

In 1972, Ford adopted SAE standard J1349 horsepower ratings, which were also required to be published using the net amount of power with the engine equipped with all of the accessories. In the past, the power ratings were based on the gross horsepower. That meant that the power of the engine was measured without a water pump or an alternator. Gross power was often 20 percent higher compared to the net horsepower rating. Using the net rating meant using a full exhaust system as well as all of the accessories that are normally powered by the engine. This extra load on the engine reduced the available power to move the vehicle.

Real engine performance also suffered in 1972 in order to be compliant with the latest federal emissions laws. These laws required retarding both ignition (spark advance) and valve timing in 6,000-pound or lower GVW vehicles.

For the fifth generation, Ford expanded further on this camping craze. In 1967, Ford developed a partnership with Travel Industries Company to manufacture camper shells for the Ford F-250. This shell was made from lightweight plastic, making it 40 percent lighter than the standard camper shells. In addition, the camper shell had more interior space and was sold through Ford dealers. It was at this same time that trucks were starting to be looked at by more American consumers as a personal-use vehicle.

Ford's Camper Special trim line started to gain in popularity, even among those who did not have recreational vehicles. The model

A 1967 F-250 Camper Special in almost new-like condition features black sidewall tires and dog-dish hubcaps. (Photo Courtesy Richard Truesdell)

The interior of an F-250 camper special had the steering column–mounted gear selector readout commonly referred to as the "PRNDL" (pronounced "prindle"). This name was used regardless of the letters or numbers in the vehicle. (Photo Courtesy Richard Truesdell)

A three-quarter view of the 1967 F-250 Camper Special that features a step rear bumper. A rear bumper was an option on most pickup trucks of this era and often was a dealer-installed option. (Photo Courtesy Richard Truesdell)

had a lot of versatility. It could easily haul lumber for daily use for contractors or the blue-collar worker, plus it would also accommodate the slide-in camper or tow-behind camper. The cost of the F-250 with the camper body shell was $1,995 for base models and up to $2,895 for trucks containing additional upgrades.

All of the Camper Specials had a 352-ci V8 and special springs and tires designed to match the chassis to the load. Ford offered the Camper Special as a bigger truck in 1967 with the F-350 Camper Special. This truck featured the following:

- A dual-rear-wheel chassis on a 159-inch wheelbase that was designed to carry a 14-foot-long camper with over-the-cab chassis-mounted camper units.
- A dual-rear-wheel chassis with a 135-inch wheelbase designed to carry a 12-foot camper unit.
- A single-rear-wheel chassis with 135-inch wheelbase that could support an 11-foot camper.
- A single-rear-wheel chassis with 159-inch wheelbase that could carry a 12-foot camper unit.

The Camper Special was designed and developed in reaction to rival Chevrolet, which also had a "camper special." The Chevrolet C30 Longhorn was similar in many ways to Ford's

Camper Special. America's thirst for camping and recreational vehicles, and to escape the cities and suburbs, continued until the late 1970s. Ford's Camper Special would end in 1979.

1967

The redesign of this generation started with the 1967 model year. The new pickup had a drastically different appearance. Gone were the rounded corners; the fifth-generation F-Series certainly has a more squared-off look.

There were several body changes as well. A new grille was wide, flat, and had four rows of stamped slots with the headlights at each end. A convex-shaped body relief ran from the front through the doors and through the cargo bed. The turn signal lights were moved underneath the headlights. The wide front bumper followed the contours of the grille and blended in with the fenders.

The interior redesign allowed for a bigger cab space. The cab was 3 inches wider than the previous model year, measured from the outside of the cab. There were an additional 4 inches of shoulder room, which is measured from door panel to door panel. This change meant that the door panels were made narrower. There are noticeable improvements to the overall

The interior of a 1967 F-250 equipped with a column-shift automatic transmission. This truck has some accessories that were added by the owner(s) and include a speaker in the kick panel and an aftermarket air-conditioning unit located under the dash. (Photo Courtesy Richard Truesdell)

quality and touchpoints within the interior of the 1967 F-Series.

Another significant change involved the chassis. The F-100's new chassis was built on a 115-inch wheelbase for the short-bed trucks and a 131-inch wheelbase for the long-bed trucks. The bed options were still 6.5 and 8 feet. F-250 models were built on the 129-inch-wheelbase chassis, while the crew cab was still on the 147-inch wheelbase.

The F-250 frame was upgraded in 1967 to incorporate 3.89-inch cross braces. These braces were used to stiffen the chassis and provide additional weight capacity. When compared to the F-100, the F-250 had 400 pounds greater carrying capacity, and its rear axle had nearly 2,000 pounds of greater payload. The F-250 used larger 12-inch brakes. The F-250 crew cab could also be ordered with or without the 6.5-foot bed.

Ford created a variety of other models in the F-100 line. There was the basic chassis with cab and a bare chassis for use by an up-fitter company to create ambulances and other commercial-type vehicles. These chassis models were sold to fleets for their conversions with the utility bodies. A new Ford crew cab four-door model was introduced in 1967 on a lengthened wheelbase of 149 inches, up from 131 for the standard F-100.

Engine development in the late 1960s was at all-time high, and most of the engine innovation was put into passenger cars, specifically the muscle cars. The F-100 carried the same powerplants from the 1966 model year. The 240-ci inline 6-cylinder was standard and remained unchanged. Ford also offered the 300-ci inline 6-cylinder. While the V8 option was still the 352-ci engine, 1967 was the last year for its use.

The 3-speed manual with overdrive was standard equipment. Other options included a 4-speed manual transmission and Cruise-O-Matic automatic transmissions.

The base price of the F-100 Styleside short bed was $2,237. The Flareside started at $2,198 for the short bed. The long-bed Styleside started at $2,273 with the long-bed Flareside starting at $2,237. Trim levels for the 1967 F-Series were Base, Custom Cab, and Ranger.

Econoline

Model year 1967 was the last year of the Econoline. Updates made to the 1967 version included a dual master cylinder. This change was mandated by federal law to be included in all vehicles for 1967. Other minor changes included two-speed wipers and backup lights.

Ranchero

The 1967 Ranchero used the same Falcon/Fairlane chassis and the Fairlane front sheet metal and trim. The interior trim was also

A commonly used measurement for pickup trucks is referred to as the "cab-to-axle" (CA) dimension. This is the distance, measured in inches, between the back of the cab to the centerline of the rear axle. For example, 56 inches was used on the 1967 F-100 to ensure that the truck has the right ratio and dimension to meet the gross vehicle weight (GVW) rating. Other important load-carrying factors include:

Gross axle weight rating (GAWR) — This is the maximum weight that can be placed on the front or rear axle. This rating is commonly listed on the "vehicle safety certification label" located on the driver-door pillar.

Tare weight — This is the weight of the chassis before the body is installed and includes the weight of all of the options plus fuel and coolant.

Wheelbase — The wheelbase is the distance between the center of the front and rear axles, usually measured in inches.

Cab-to-body — The cab-to-body (CB) measurement is the distance between the cab and the body. On a pickup truck, this dimension is not needed or used because the two are so close together.

Body length — The body length (BL) is the distance from the front of the body to the rear of the body.

Curb weight — The curb weight got its name from a vehicle sitting at the side of the road with a full tank of fuel, without a driver or passengers.

Payload capacity — The amount of weight a vehicle can safely carry is called the payload capacity. This is the gross vehicle weight rating (GVWR) minus the curb weight.

When any commercial vehicle is designed to carry a load, these dimensions are used to make sure that the vehicle can safely handle what owners want and need. For example, between 60 and 70 percent of the body should be forward of the center of the rear axle. The load on the axles (front and rear) should not exceed the GAWR of the axles.

---

from the Fairlane and was marketed as the "Fairlane Ranchero." The one-year-only model featured four headlights with two on each side stacked above each other. Updates made to the 1967 version included a dual master cylinder. The 1967 Ranchero was offered in Base, Ranchero 500, Ranchero 500/XL, and GT trims.

Bronco

The 1967 Ford Bronco was basically a carryover with a Sport option package available for the Bronco wagon. The sport package included chrome exterior trim as well as full wheel covers and red-painted "FORD" lettering on the grille. Updates made to the 1967 version included a dual master cylinder.

1968

The easiest identifying feature on a 1968 Ford F-100 is the side marker light. This was the result of a Federal Safety Standard Mandate that required all carmakers to add side marker reflectors or lights to their vehicles. Reflectors were required for the rear of all vehicles. Ford redesigned the hood emblems to incorporate reflectors. Their designers also added reflectors to the rear of the bed as part of the new safety standards.

Other exterior styling changes occurred, including a new grille with a top, middle, and bottom bar. Styleside beds and tailgates featured double-wall steel and an all-steel floor board. The Flareside truck still had a wood floor and a small running board between the bed and the cab.

From an interior standpoint, the truck continued to mirror cars with higher-quality materials. This was the first year for factory-installed air-conditioning (previously, air-conditioning was dealer installed). The use of interior chrome trim molding on the Custom Cab models was also available. Power steering was also an option this year, as well as power brakes. The heavier-duty Flex-O-Matic rear suspension was an option on the F-100. Previously, it had only been offered on the F-250 in 1967.

The 240-ci inline 6-cylinder engine was standard and remained unchanged. Ford also offered the 300-ci inline 6-cylinder and two new V8 engines: the 360 ci and the 390 ci.

The same 3-speed and 4-speed manual transmissions were available, as was the Cruise-O-Matic automatic transmission. The new V8 engines increased the Ford truck brand's reputation for being capable and powerful. Ford quickly became the go-to option for contractors. The pricing for 1968 increased to $2,357 for a base model short-bed Styleside, and $2,318 for the base model short-bed Flareside. All other prices remained unchanged.

Econoline

The Econoline van had an all-new body and suspension for 1968. However, due to a United Automobile Workers (UAW) strike, the van was delayed and released as a 1969 model. Those vans featured the following:

- Available in two wheelbase lengths: the standard 105.5 inches and the Super Van at 123.5 inches.

QUICK AND EASY MODEL YEAR IDENTIFICATION

Identifying the year of a truck is often hard. Here is a list of things to look for based on the model year:

1967 — A squared-off look with the headlights, a rectangular grille, and the parking lamps were under the headlights.

1968 — Federal standards required the use of side marker lights and reflectors.

1969 — The grille was the same as the 1968 grille except the black paint was changed to ivory for the standard grille. This was changed again to chrome at midyear.

1970 — The 1970 featured a new grille pattern, and the parking lights wrapped around the rear side markers.

1971 — For the 1971 model year, the grille design was changed to six rectangular sections on each side of a center vertical bar.

1972 — For the 1972 model year, the grille design was changed slightly to four rectangular sections on each side of the center vertical bar.

- The Twin I-Beam front suspension was now used.
- Curved side glass was used.
- Side marker lights were added to the 1968 models to meet federal regulations and backup lights were standard.

Ranchero

The 1968 Ranchero was now based on the Ford Torino chassis and styling, and it was larger than the 1967 version. The new-for-1968 design featured four headlights that were now side by side instead of stacked. Side marker lights were added to the 1968 models to meet federal regulations and backup lights were standard.

Bronco

Minor changes to the Bronco for 1968 included a new bumper and an optional swing-out rear-mounted spare tire. Side marker lights were added to the 1968 models to meet federal regulations and backup lights were standard. This was the last year for the open-body Bronco roadster.

1969

There were minimal changes to the 1969 F-100 regarding styling and interior design. The 1969 grille now had bigger openings and a horizontal crossbar. It was basically the same grille that was used in 1968 but without the black paint used to cover most of the vertical elements, thereby updating the grille. Ranger trucks had the center crossbar painted red and featured a red Ranger grille ornament in the center.

The F-100 pickup and E-100 (Econoline) were offered in three specialized packages aimed at very specific buyers:

The Heavy Duty could handle bigger loads and came standard with the Flex-O-Matic rear suspension. The Contractor's Special was available on the 8-foot bed trucks that came with heavy-duty front and rear springs, a rear step bumper, Western-style mirrors, and lockable contractor boxes on both sides of the bed. The Farm and Ranch included the Flex-O-Matic rear suspension, high side cargo boards that were added to the bedside to increase cargo height, a rear step bumper, and Western-style mirrors. Each special model carried its own insignia that was mounted to the front cowl.

The 4WD trucks carried the old monobeam suspension with coil springs and forward radius rods that were now fitted with free-running hubs. The 4WD trucks were not available with the Twin I-Beam suspension. Engines for 1969 were a carryover from 1968. However, in midyear 1969, Ford offered the new 302-ci V8 in the F-100. The same three transmissions carried over to this model year. The 1969 interior options included the Custom Cab, Ranger, and Explorer packages.

The 1969 Ford F-100 Ranger trim had a special red crossbar on the grille. The Ranger trim for the F-100 trucks of this era remains highly collectible. (Photo Courtesy Richard Truesdell)

The tailgate of the 1969 Ford F-100 had a bold look. The Ford logo was centered with large print instead of the script. (Photo Courtesy Richard Truesdell)

The interior of this 1970 Ford pickup includes a three-spoke steering wheel and a deluxe interior for the time.

Econoline

The 1969 Econoline was introduced in January 1968 as a 1969 model, skipping the 1968 model year designation.

Bronco

The Ford Bronco for 1969 was basically a carryover from the 1968 model year with just some minor trim changes and color choices being the only changes.

Ranchero

The Ranchero for 1969 featured a new grille and lower side body moldings. A GT version of the Ranchero featured a unique grille and body side C-stripe. The 1969 Ranchero offered some new bold colors being offered for the first time, including Poppy Red, Wimbledon White, and Calypso Coral.

1970

The biggest news for this model came on the manufacturing side, as Ford built a new heavy-duty truck plant in Louisville, Kentucky, that was devoted to trucks. This plant allowed Ford to focus on its light-duty truck line as well as the success it was having with the Econoline vans. By 1974, its production had increased 36 percent.

The 1970 F-100 featured a new grille and additional engine options to suit a wider range of potential customers. The focus in 1970 was to offer a plush interior so the truck would be allowed to fit a variety of lifestyles and uses. Hal Sperlich, who was named vice president of trucks from 1970 to 1972 for Ford and who also played a huge role in the Mustang, said he could see how the truck was evolving at this time. Even though his work would not impact the fifth-generation pickup, his phrase the "civilization of the truck" was well underway. With a new decade came even more attention to detail and a focus on gaining a much broader consumer base for the F-100.

The F-100 received updated trim levels for 1970. The base trim level was now called Custom. The next higher trim level was referred to as Sport Custom. The previously used highest trim level Ranger was now the third level of trim. The highest trim level was now called the Ranger XLT.

In 1970, the base trim for the F-100 was renamed the Custom trim. This gave it a more personable name and made it seem more luxurious than it actually was. (Photo Courtesy Colin Date/National Parts Depot)

Cactus Green was one of 48 paint combinations available for the 1970 F-100. (Photo Courtesy Colin Date/National Parts Depot)

Ford catered to the camping craze of the late 1960s and the 1970s by creating the Camper Special, which was available on the F-100 and F-250. Ford even manufactured a camper cab to go along with the Camper Special truck. (Photo Courtesy Colin Date/National Parts Depot)

Any of these bodystyle packages could be ordered as an option on the F-100 or F-250, which included the vinyl roof and a new sliding rear window. A total of 48 two-tone exterior paint combinations were available in 1970 on the Ford F-100. This was the most ever offered by Ford to date.

The 1970 F-Series offered a heavy-duty package, which was available on the 8-foot bed Styleside trucks. The package included heavy-duty front springs, a heavy-duty battery, a heavy-duty alternator and ammeter, oil pressure gauges, a rear step bumper, and Western swing-lock mirrors.

In 1970, Ford offered the base engine of the 240- and 300-ci inline 6-cylinder engines. The 302-ci V8 was an engine that produced 210 hp and 295 ft-lbs of torque. The other V8 engine options were carryovers, as were all three transmissions.

In 1970, Ford offered a rival V8 engine to the standard 360-ci V8 (pictured here). The 302-ci V8 was a new option that produced 210 hp and 295 ft-lbs of torque. By examining this engine bay, you can see that the era of creature comforts was upon us, as evidenced by the power steering pump, vacuum brake booster, and air-conditioning compressor. (Photo Courtesy National Parts Depot)

Econoline

The 1970 Econoline was a carryover from the 1969 model year vehicle.

Bronco

In 1970, the Bronco Sport became a unique model. It was no longer listed as an option package.

Ranchero

The 1970 Ranchero had a complete redesign, which was called a "Coke Bottle" design due to its curved lines. A new trim level, called the Ranchero Squire, was similar to the design of the Country Squire station wagon of that year and featured wood-grain side panels. A Ranchero line followed the passenger-car line for powertrain options, which included the new 351 Cleveland engine as well as the 429 Ram Air option.

1971

Ford had another big year in 1971. It was the first time since 1929 that Ford outsold rival Chevrolet in trucks. Ford sold 515,403 light-duty pickups, beating Chevrolet by 20,000 trucks.

Only a few minor cosmetic changes occurred for 1971. The grille became much larger and more pronounced. Halderman said when designing trucks, he always instructed his designers to go bigger than what they thought it should be with their sketches. "They needed to look tough," he said. Clearly all the designers at Ford were starting to get a good idea of what a Ford truck should look like, which was important from a design standpoint, according to Halderman.

This was the time in Ford's truck history where chrome started playing a bigger role. Grilles continued to get bigger with a pronounced look each model year.

A 1970 Ford Ranchero had paint that was used to highlight this unique car that was like a truck. Based on the Ford Torino, it used the passenger car components at the front with a pickup bed at the rear. (Photo Courtesy Richard Truesdell)

THE FORD CAROUSEL

During the early part of the 1970s, product planners and designers within the Ford Truck Studio were working on vans alongside trucks. Dick Nesbitt was one of the main designers in the Ford Truck Studio. He remembers a concept van that, in his opinion, was significantly better than the Ford Econoline and Club Wagon (station wagon) that was favored by Ford president Lee Iacocca.

This concept van, called the Carousel (or Carrousel), was considered a "garageable" van. Certainly this concept van was the precursor to what became the minivan. Ford eventually went to market late with a minivan in the 1980s with the Ford Aerostar.

Hal Sperlich was adamant that Ford needed to be first to market with a "garageable" van, but it fell on deaf ears with Henry Ford II. Eventually, the difference in opinion on many topics led to Sperlich's dismissal as well as Iacocca's. Iacocca and Sperlich emerged at Chrysler after their termination, and the first project they greenlighted was a minivan.

Prior to all this, Nesbitt was given the go-ahead to work on a concept for a van. What he came up with was called the Carousel. With hundreds of design sketches submitted for this project, it was Nesbitt's passenger's side that was chosen. He said, "A fully drivable metal fabricated prototype was constructed based off my design."

Nesbitt said both Sperlich and Iacocca loved the design concept and wanted to greenlight it. "It turned out Henry Ford II decided against the Carousel mostly because he thought it would take sales away from the Ford station wagons and trucks."

The Carousel concept was based on the "Nantucket" platform, which was the basis for the station wagon too.

Nesbitt said you could see a lot of his design from the Carousel in the Ford Aerostar, which was Ford's first minivan.

This sketch by designer Dick Nesbitt was a concept van called the Carousel (sometimes Carrousel). This sketch was approved by Lee Iacocca, who tried to push the concept of a minivan forward during his final years at the Ford Motor Company. If you look closely, this sketch looks like a Ford Flex full-size SUV. (Sketch Courtesy Dick Nesbitt)

Nesbitt's sketch was turned into a full-size prototype. It did not make it to production during this era, as both Lee Iacocca and Hal Sperlich were fired from Ford. This Carousel Concept was to be the precursor to the Ford Aerostar minivan, which wouldn't launch until the 1980s. Being front-wheel drive allowed this concept to have the interior room of a full-size van and yet have the smaller outside dimensions that allowed it to be kept in most garages. (Photo Courtesy Dick Nesbitt)

Some of the sizing and design cues of the Carousel eventually made their way through the Truck Studio and influenced the next generation of the F-Series.

"I personally consider the Carousel a key concept design of the 20th century. It was the most satisfying design project I was ever involved with at Ford," Sperlich said.

This photo shows what the Ford Carousel would've looked like. It had a stout grille and clearly shared looks with the Ford trucks of this era. Notice the use of outside rearview mirrors on both the driver's side and passenger's side. (Photo Courtesy Dick Nesbitt)

This sketch by Ford truck designer Bud Magaldi is from the early 1970s. It shows a representation of the minivan that Ford was working on. Trying to capitalize on the success of the Econoline, Hal Sperlich was convinced of the need of a minivan for Ford. Ultimately, Sperlich and Henry Ford II would not see eye to eye, Sperlich was fired, and Ford did not create a minivan until the 1980s. (Sketch Courtesy Bud Magaldi)

Another sketch from designer Bud Magaldi shows the minivan concept. In the design studio at that time, it had the code name Nantucket. If you look closely at this sketch, you'll see the name on the side of this van. This sketch did not get approved, as the minivan program was not given the greenlight by Henry Ford II. (Sketch Courtesy Bud Magaldi)

This sketch by Ford truck designer Bud Magaldi was for an early 1970s Ford Bronco. Magaldi had a 32-year-long career designing cars and trucks at Ford. This sketch of the Bronco did not get approved. (Sketch Courtesy Bud Magaldi)

In 1971, Ford built seven engine options in the F-Series trucks. This was the most they ever offered. Ford offered 86 percent of light-duty trucks with V8 engines, such as the 360-ci 2V pictured here. (Photo Courtesy National Parts Depot)

In 1971, Ford offered seven engine options in the F-Series. This was the most engines it would ever offer in any single year. According to Ford, 86 percent of light-duty trucks were equipped with V8 engines. A total of 43.7 percent of Ford light-duty trucks were equipped with automatic transmissions.

The same paint color options carried over from the previous model year, and most of the options remained the same too. The Ranger XLT now featured a wood-grain appliqué on the tailgate and featured a cargo light.

The F-250 had more options available, such as the day/night rearview mirror and a convenient lighting package that included a cargo light, an engine bay light, and courtesy lights.

Bronco, Econoline, and Ranchero

The Bronco, Econoline, and Ranchero were mostly carried over for the 1971 model year with few changes.

1972

At the tail end of its life cycle and with government emissions standards now dictating various aspects of the automotive industry, very little changed for the 1972 F-Series. Ford carried over the 1971 chassis and body with only minor changes. The 1972 grille looked very similar to the 1971 grille except with fewer divisions between the rectangular shapes in the center of it.

The F-100 chassis remained unchanged and was still based on the 115-inch-wheelbase short-bed trucks with the 130-inch wheelbase for the long-bed trucks. Both Styleside and Flareside beds were available in either 6.5- or 8-foot versions. The standard F-250 was built on the 131-inch-wheelbase chassis, while the crew cab was still built on the 159-inch wheelbase chassis. The camper specials on the F-250 were still outfitted with either the 360- or 390-ci V8 with a sliding rear window.

The base price for the 115-inch wheelbase 240 I6 F-100 was $2,703. The base price for the 131-inch wheelbase was $2,739, which was $189 less than the 1971 version. Styleside and Flareside F-250 models were both priced at $3,020. The crew cab was priced at $3,518.

Econoline

For the 1972 model year, a sliding rear door became optional. Also available in 1972 was a cutaway van chassis for use by up-fitters to create specialized vehicles and a cab-chassis version that had a box-van body. Other changes were minor with some changes to trim and color options.

Bronco

The 1972 Bronco was mostly a carryover from the 1971 with just some minor trim and color changes. The slow-selling Bronco half-cab was deleted from the lineup at the end of the 1972 model year.

Ranchero

The new-for-1972 Ranchero featured a larger design on a body-on-frame platform. Three models of the Ranchero were available as before: the 500, the Squire (still with the wood-grain paneling on the sides), and the GT. The power-train options remained mostly the same as what was offered for the 1971 model year with the addition of a 400-ci V8.

Conclusion

Ford came out on top of the 1960s in many regards. It was primed to carry on the success of the fifth generation into the next generation of F-Series pickup trucks, if it could somehow deal with tight government regulations. Of course, this would not be easy to do, and a national oil crisis was on the horizon too.

Ford Light-Duty Truck Engines (1967–1972)

Year	Engine	Horsepower (hp)	Torque (ft-lbs)	VIN Code
1967	240-ci inline 6-cylinder OHV	150	234 at 2,200 rpm	A
	300-ci inline 6-cylinder OHV	170	283 at 1,400–2,400 rpm	B
	352-ci V8 OHV	208	315 at 2,400 rpm	Y
1968	240-ci inline 6-cylinder OHV	150	234 at 2,200 rpm	A
	300-ci inline 6-cylinder OHV	165	294 at 2,000 rpm	B
	360-ci V8 OHV	215	327 at 2,600 rpm	Y
	390-ci V8 OHV	255	376 at 2,600 rpm	H
1969	240-ci inline 6-cylinder OHV	150	234 at 2,200 rpm	A
	300-ci inline 6-cylinder OHV	165	294 at 2,000 rpm	B
	302-ci Windsor V8 OHV	210	295 at 2,600 rpm	G
	360-ci V8 OHV	215	327 at 2,600 rpm	Y
	390-ci V8 OHV	255	376 at 2,600 rpm	H
1970	240-ci inline 6-cylinder OHV	150	234 at 2,200 rpm	A
	300-ci inline 6-cylinder OHV	165	294 at 2,000 rpm	B
	302-ci Windsor V8 OHV	205	300 at 2,600 rpm	G
	360-ci V8 OHV	215	327 at 2,600 rpm	Y
	390-ci V8 OHV	255	376 at 2,600 rpm	H
1971	240-ci inline 6-cylinder OHV	140	230 at 2,200 rpm	A
	300-ci inline 6-cylinder OHV	165	294 at 2,000 rpm	B
	302-ci Windsor V8 OHV	205	300 at 2,600 rpm	G
	360-ci V8 OHV	215	327 at 2,600 rpm	Y
	390-ci V8 OHV	255	376 at 2,600 rpm	H
1972	240-ci inline 6-cylinder OHV	150	234 at 2,200 rpm	A
	300-ci inline 6-cylinder OHV	101	223 at 1,600 rpm	B
	302-ci Windsor V8 OHV	130	222 at 2,000 rpm	G
	360-ci V8 OHV	145	264 at 2,200 rpm	Y
	390-ci V8 OHV	156	292 at 2,000 rpm	H

Note: Information included in this chart is designed to be inclusive. Dependent upon reference, year, and carryover, information may vary.

Note: Engine VIN example: The underlined letter "A" F10AV746001 indicates the placement in the engine VIN and the engine in the example is a 240-ci inline 6-cylinder.

Ford Light-Duty Trucks Paint Colors (1967–1972)

Color	1967	1968	1969	1970	1971	1972
Raven Black (Black)	A	A	A	A	A	A
Caribbean Turquoise	–	B	B	–	–	–
Frost Turquoise	B	–	–	–	–	–
Royal Maroon	–	B	B	B	–	2
Wind Blue (Light)	–	–	–	–	–	B
Pure White	C	C	C	C	C	C
Peacock Blue	D	D	–	–	–	–
Tucson Gold	–	–	D	D	–	–
Fiesta Tan	–	–	–	–	D	D
Beige Mist	E	–	–	–	–	–
Sky View Blue	–	E	E	E	E	–
Brook Blue (Medium)	–	–	–	–	–	E
Arcadian Blue	F	F	–	–	–	–
Mojave Tan	–	–	–	F	F	–
Mill Valle Green (Light)	–	–	–	–	–	F
Chrome Yellow	G	G	G	G	G	G
Cordova(n) (White)	–	–	H	H	–	–
Cactus Green	–	–	–	H	–	–
Yucatan Gold	–	I	–	R	–	–
Lime Gold	–	–	–	I	8	–
Rangoon Red	J	J	J	J	J	J
Grabber Blue	–	–	–	J	–	4
Empire (Green)	–	–	K	K	–	–
Carmel Bronze	–	–	–	K	–	–
Ivy Green (Medium)	–	–	–	–	–	K
Holly Green (Dark)	L	L	L	L	L	L
Wimbledon White (White)	M	M	M	M	M	M
Coach	–	–	N	–	–	–
Norway (Green)	–	–	N	N	–	–
Platinum	–	–	–	–	–	N
American Blue	–	O	–	–	–	–
Seafoam Green	–	–	–	–	O	–
Sea Pine Green (Medium)	–	–	–	–	–	O
Boxwood Green	–	P	P	P	K	K
Scandia Green (Medium)	–	–	–	–	P	P
Brittany Blue	Q	Q	Q	Q	–	–
Winter Blue	–	–	–	–	Q	–
Winter Green (Light Yellow)	–	–	–	–	–	Q
Diamond Green	–	R	R	–	–	–
Astra Blue	–	–	–	–	R	–
Sequoia Brown (Medium Ginger)	–	–	–	–	–	R
Poppy Red	S	–	–	–	–	–
Champagne Gold	–	–	–	S	–	–
Shenandoah Green	–	–	–	–	–	S
Candy Apple Red	–	T	T	T	T	T
Lunar Green	U	U	U	U	–	–
Empire Yellow	–	–	–	U	U	–
Medium Lime	–	–	–	–	–	U
Diamond Aqua	–	–	V	–	–	–

Ford Light-Duty Trucks Paint Colors (1967–1972) *CONTINUED*

Color	Available Year and VIN Code					
	1967	1968	1969	1970	1971	1972
Mallard Green (Dark)	–	–	–	–	V	V
Meadowlark Yellow	–	W	W	–	–	–
Tampico Yellow	–	–	–	W	–	8
Saddle Tan (Light Ginger)	–	–	–	–	W	W
Bay Roc Blue (Medium)	–	–	–	–	–	W
Marlin Blue (Medium)	–	–	X	–	–	–
Light Ginger	–	–	–	–	X	–
Light Goldenrod	–	–	–	–	–	X
Reef Aqua	–	–	Y	Y	Y	–
Chelsea Green	–	–	–	–	–	Y
Federal Red	–	Z	Z	–	–	–
Baja Beige (Medium)	–	–	–	Z	H	H
Grabber Green	–	–	–	–	Z	–
Hot Ginger (Light Copper)	–	–	–	–	–	Z
Coachman Beige	–	2 or N	2	–	–	–
New Lime	–	–	2	2	–	–
Calypso Coral	–	–	3	–	1	1
Prairie Yellow	–	–	–	–	2	K
Explorer Green	–	–	–	3	–	–
Swiss Aqua (Bright)	–	–	–	–	3	3
Twilight Green	–	4	4	–	–	–
Chrystal Green	–	–	–	4	–	–
Regis Red	–	–	–	–	4	–
Diamond Blue	–	–	–	5	N	N
Medium Brown	–	–	–	–	5	–
Yuma Yellow (Bright)	–	–	–	–	–	5
Pebble Beige	6	6	6	6	–	–
Acapulco Blue	–	–	–	6	–	–
Bahama Blue (Bright)	–	–	–	–	6	6
Harbor Blue (Medium)	7	7	7	7	7	7
Springtime Yellow	8	–	–	–	–	–
Morning Gold	–	–	–	8	–	–
Primer	9	–	–	9	9	9

Note: Information included in this chart is designed to be inclusive. Dependent upon reference, year, and carryover, information may vary.

Note: 1967–1972 color codes on the VIN plate are listed as "Color."

Ford Light-Duty Truck Transmissions (1967–1972)

Year	Model	Automatic/ Manual	Number of Gears	Transmission
1967	F-100	Manual	3	Standard
1967	F-100	Manual	4	Optional
1967	F-100	Automatic	3	Cruise-O-Matic
1968–1969	F-100	Manual	3	3-Speed with Overdrive
1968–1969	F-100	Manual	4	Optional
1968–1969	F-100	Automatic	3	Cruise-O-Matic
1970–1971	F-100	Manual	4	Standard
1970–1971	F-100	Automatic	3	SelectShift Cruise-O-Matic
1972	F-100	Manual	3	Standard
1972	F-100	Manual	4	Optional
1972	F-100	Automatic	3	SelectShift Cruise-O-Matic
1967–1969	F-250	Manual	3	3-Speed with Overdrive
1967–1969	F-250	Manual	4	Optional
1967–1969	F-250	Automatic	3	Cruise-O-Matic
1970–1971	F-250	Manual	3	3-Speed with Overdrive
1970–1971	F-250	Manual	4	Optional
1970–1971	F-250	Automatic	3	SelectShift Cruise-O-Matic
1972	F-250	Manual	3	Standard
1972	F-250	Manual	4	Optional
1972	F-250	Automatic	3	SelectShift Cruise-O-Matic

Note: Information included in this chart is designed to be inclusive. Dependent upon reference, year, and carryover, information may vary.

Ford Light-Duty Trucks Sizes and Prices (1967–1972)

Year	Model	Wheelbase (inches)	Length (inches)	Bed Length (feet)	Height (inches)	Width (inches)	Gross Vehicle Weight (pounds)	Price	Number Manufactured
1967–1972	Ford F-100 1/2-ton Styleside and Flareside	115/131	191/211	6.5/8	71	79	4,200–5,600	$2,198–$2,928	1,699,315*
1967–1972	Ford F-250 3/4-ton Styleside and Flareside	129/159	211/215	6.5/8	71	79	4,800–7,700	$2,409–$3,518	595,745**

Note: Information included in this chart is designed to be inclusive. Dependent upon reference, year, and carryover, information may vary.

Note: From 1967 to 1971, Ford offered a F-101 1/2 ton with a GVW of 4,200 to 4,500 pounds.

Note: Height on Ford F-100 1/2-ton 4WD is 74 inches and Ford F-250 3/4 ton is 77 inches.

* Is a total of all F-100 1/2-ton Styleside and Flareside body, bed, engine, and cab types, excluding production year 1970.

** Is a total of all F-250 3/4-ton Styleside and Flareside body, bed, engine, and cab types, excluding production year 1971.

FORD F-SERIES SIXTH GENERATION (1973–1979)

By the end of the sixth generation, Ford marketing came up with a slogan that stuck with the F-Series for many decades and carried the brand to the top of the segment: Built Ford Tough. The groundwork was laid by the early part of the sixth-generation F-Series to earn that tough reputation.

According to legendary Ford design executive Gale Halderman, the word *tough* was used a lot when sketching trucks.

"Trucks were always fun to design," Halderman said. "They had to look strong and sturdy with big front ends and tough-looking bodies." Even though Halderman was only a Truck Design Studio executive for a brief time, he remembered working on trucks fondly. The Truck Design Studio was well funded, and the designers were mostly left alone to stay on their mission. Halderman said the executives rarely stopped by or meddled in the direction of the division.

During the 1960s, Ford had laid the groundwork with a truck-specific factory in Louisville, Kentucky. The sixth generation represented an investment into design and the rebadging of Ford's pickup. The company had to be careful how to proceed with this reinvention and redesign. The F-Series needed to be tougher, but tougher meant the addition of more materials. Galvanized steel was introduced during this generation, which was necessary for the F-Series to survive and maintain its stature.

According to Hal Sperlich, who was vice president of Ford Trucks from 1970 to 1972, trucks before this time were a "rusty mess." Sperlich, who was never one

Turn signals were moved to the top of the grille above the headlights. It was the first year for this cosmetic change, and it is one of the easiest ways to detect a 1973 F-Series. (Photo Courtesy Trenton Taylor)

The engine of this 1977 F-250 has an aftermarket electronic unitized ignition system and aluminum radiator. For 1977, there were seven engine options for the F-Series, including five different V8 variants. (Photo Courtesy Richard Truesdell)

to shy away from the honest truth, said, "Our trucks prior to the sixth generation were rust buckets and hurt our long-term reputation." During Sperlich's 18 months directing the Truck Division, he feels he had a huge impact on the F-Series.

"We knew what needed to be done. We wanted to make the truck look more attractive and feel more family friendly," Sperlich said. "We achieved that as the interior had better looks, it was less raw, even the exterior looked better. Of course, adding galvanized steel helped make them last longer too."

It was during the 1970s that Sperlich said the truck truly became more civilized. "The F-Series was no longer just a contractor's tool but was a family vehicle."

This is when the F-Series started becoming part of family life in the suburbs, despite an oil crisis that had family household budgets in peril. It all started with the rugged, tough, and now bigger sixth-generation F-Series, which is often nicknamed the Dentside truck. It is ironic that the sixth-generation F-Series began the same model year as the OPEC embargo hit the United States.

Windsor and Cleveland Engines

The Ford Windsor V8 engine was a series built by Ford beginning in July 1961. The Windsor designation was for the family of engines sharing a common basic engine block design manufactured in Windsor, Ontario, Canada. Ford adopted the designation specifically to distinguish the 351-ci (5.8L) version from the Cleveland family of engines that had the same displacement but a different configuration. The Windsor was discontinued in 2001.

Production of the 221-ci Windsor V8 engine began in 1961 for installation in the 1962 Ford Fairlane and Mercury Meteor and later in the original Mustang in 260- and 289-ci displacements. The displacement most commonly purchased was the 302 ci (4.9L) later marketed as 5.0L with engines of

that displacement offered from 1968 until 2000. For the 1991 model year, Ford began phasing in its new 4.6/5.4L Modular V8 engine, which was to replace the small-block Windsor.

The 351C was a 335-series engine that was nicknamed the Cleveland engine after the engine plant in Brook Park, Ohio, in which most of these engines were manufactured. Brook Park is a suburb of Cleveland. The Cleveland-series engines were used in cars and light trucks (351M/400 only), at times concurrently with the Windsor small-block family, the 351 Windsor.

The Cleveland engines shared the same bore spacing and head bolt spacing as the Windsor. The 400-ci version of the Cleveland engine was based on the 351-ci block but with a 0.500-inch-longer stoke, making the displacement of 402 ci. However, it was advertised as displacing 400 ci.

All Cleveland series V8s had free breathing and large-port canted valve heads. Some versions had large main-bearing caps with four-bolt attachments. This was similar to the changes required to make a 302 Windsor into the 351 Windsor. As a result, this engine family has two block deck heights: a low deck at 9.206 inches (234 mm) and a tall deck at 10.297 inches (262 mm).

All Cleveland series V8s shared the same bore spacing and cylinder head bolt pattern as the Windsor V8s. Beyond these shared aspects, the Cleveland engines are very different internally from the similar-looking Windsor series. Some differences included:

- The Cleveland V8s used smaller 14-mm spark plugs and the radiator hose locations differed.
- All Cleveland valve covers were secured with eight bolts, whereas the Windsor used six bolts.
- Another difference between the Cleveland and Windsor engines was the timing cover. The timing chain of the Cleveland engine was recessed into the block, so the timing cover was flush with the front of the engine and nearly flat. The Windsor has a stamped timing chain because the timing chain sat proud of the block.
- The 351C-4V was marketed as a high-performance engine featuring large valves and ports and a closed combustion chamber.

This slightly modified 1973 F-100 has side exhaust, which isn't stock but is a common modification done by truck enthusiasts. The aftermarket 7-inch headlights have been updated to help improve road vision. (Photo Courtesy Trenton Taylor)

For 1973, the F-100 had a clean, tough look enhanced by the aftermarket 7-inch updated headlights and monochromic paint. This mild custom version features aftermarket wheels. (Photo Courtesy Trenton Taylor)

- The R-Code Cleveland used four-bolt main bearing caps.
- The 1970 engines were 11.0:1 compression and produced 300 hp at 5,400 rpm, while 1971 versions had a slightly lower compression ratio of 10.7:1, and produced 285 hp at 5,400 rpm. The M-code 351C required premium fuel.

The 351M was equipped with a 2-barrel carburetor and open-chamber small-port cylinder heads. The blocks were cast in either the Michigan Casting Center or the Cleveland Foundry. The "M" stood for the Michigan Casting Center. The 351M was the last pushrod V8 designed by Ford.

1973

The sixth generation started off with subtle changes. Galvanized steel was the big change, but the addition did not do a lot to change the overall appearance of the F-Series. Ford did not want to jump headfirst into drastic changes because the previous model years had sold so well.

Ford changed the appearance of the 1973 F-100 by adding a new grille that used inner squares with the headlight bezel removed. The two front headlights floated within the grille and seem to be moved slightly closer to the center. Unlike the 1971 and 1972 grilles, where the turn signals were below the headlights, the turn signals on the 1973 were moved on top of the headlights with an opening between them that had the Ford lettering across it.

One of the options for 1973 was a fiberglass bed cap that was contoured to fit level with the top of the cab and use the rear sliding window. Ford called this fiberglass cap the pickup box cover. The standard pickup box cover had tinted windows, two sliding windows on the sides, one window on the rear that lifted up, and a tailgate that opened with a locking latch. The deluxe model pickup box cover was the same, plus it had bright window trim, a roof-mounted vent, an interior dome light, and a color-matching body stripe.

Ford also added more molding and trim to make the 1973 Styleside look better. The body side molding that stretched across the side of the truck was now inset slightly in the sheet metal and used marker lights at each end. The cab of the truck was also slightly changed with the new hood that had a flatter front edge and stretched slightly to increase the room inside the cab.

The biggest change to the 1973 chassis was increasing to a 117-inch wheelbase for the 6.5-foot bed. The 1973 F-100

At the Louisville Assembly Plant, 1973 Ford trucks roll off the line. Ford used this plant to manufacture trucks starting in 1955. The F-Series trucks were manufactured at the plant from 1973 to 1981 and were followed by the Ford Ranger from 1983 to 1999. (Photo Courtesy Ford Motor Company)

frames were stronger and featured six crossmembers to handle heavier loads. Ford used a new one-piece floor wheelhouse stamping that made the body stronger. The 8-foot bed's wheelbase was increased to 131 inches and had the same crossmember structure as the 6.5-foot bed.

The 3/4-ton F-250 used the same chassis changes as the F-100. The standard F-250 chassis wheelbase was now 131 inches long and the crew cab was built on a 161-inch wheelbase.

The transmissions for 1973 included a 3-speed manual as standard, an optional 4-speed manual, and an optional Cruise-O-Matic 3-speed automatic transmission. Prices for the base model F-100 remained under $3,000.

Ranchero

The 1973 Ford Ranchero had federally mandated 5 mph bumpers as well as a new grille and integrated parking lights. This year also featured a new hood and front fenders.

Econoline

Few changes were made to the 1973 Econoline van. There were minor changes to some standard and optional equipment offered.

Bronco

The 1973 Bronco featured a new higher trim level option called the Ranger. It featured lower body side strips, cut-pile front and rear seat carpet, deluxe wheel covers, wood-grain door trim, cloth-insert bucket seats, and a fiberboard headliner.

1974

The biggest news of the 1974 model year was the creation of the Super Cab, which featured a cab extended by 22 inches. The Super Cab was offered with either a 6.5- or 8-foot bed on a 138.8- or 155-inch wheelbase. These were introduced by Ford to compete with the Dodge Club Cab that was introduced in 1973.

The Super Cab had more room behind the seat and could be ordered with either a rear full bench seat or two facing jumper seats that could fold out of the way. With either of these options, the truck had enough room for a family of four.

You can argue that this was the moment where Ford's F-Series started aiming itself at the modern American family. Even Gale Halderman pointed to this as monumental. "In the design studio, a second row of seats was a natural progression for the truck," he said.

Ford may have copied Dodge with the Super Cab, but it would set the standard for pickup trucks from this point forward. "The sixth generation helped set the industry benchmark," Hal Sperlich said.

The result paid off for Ford, as 1974 was the third-best sales year for Ford trucks in its history. This allowed the automaker to retain its number-one position over Chevrolet. The same three transmissions carried over for this model year.

In 1974, the F-100 offered sun visors and padded dashes as standard equipment along with keyless locking doors and courtesy light switches. Ford still had a number of specialized packages, including the Sport Custom Cab, Ranger, Camper Special, Ranger XLT, Heavy-Duty Special, and four different Explorer packages.

The base price for the Styleside and the Flareside 6.5-foot bed was $3,246. The 8-foot bed was $3,282. The base price for

This truck has towing mirrors added and the truck has been raised slightly for off-road use. (Photo Courtesy Steven Smith)

Ford truck designer Bud Magaldi sketched a concept for the 1975 F-150. In 1975, the truck received a new name, although the looks were very similar. (Sketch Courtesy Bud Magaldi)

the Super Cab 6.5-foot bed was $4,185. The 8-foot bed Super Cab was $4,221.

Bronco

The Bronco (referred to as U-100) was basically unchanged except for minor interior items, such as a lit gear selector and new colors.

Ranchero

The Ford Ranchero featured new front and rear bumpers and a new grille. New options available in 1974 included:

- Color-keyed seat belts (the same color as the seats instead of all of the seat belts being black)
- Low-back bucket seats
- Automatic temperature control
- Tilt steering column (with automatic transmission only)
- Cruise control (called speed control at the time)
- Power windows

1975

In 1975, the F-150 was born (by name only). It may have been a strategy in light of government regulations, but the F-150 was an instant success and overshadowed the F-100 immediately. The F-150 came standard with a fresh air heater and defroster, keyless locking doors, color-matching door panels, seat belts, two-speed windshield wiper/washers, dome and courtesy lights, a padded dash, a backlight instrument panel, a headliner, rubber floor mats, vinyl seats, a day/night rearview mirror, and bright door mirrors.

The 1975 F-150 Super Cab was offered on the 113-inch-wheelbase chassis and the longer 148-inch-wheelbase chassis with the 6.75-foot bed. The 155-inch-wheelbase chassis had the 8-foot bed. Ford also made the F-150 available in both Styleside and Flareside models.

The F-250 was also available in Styleside, Flareside, Super Cab, and crew cab models. Both the F-250 Super Cabs and crew cabs were built on the 155-inch-wheelbase chassis. The GVWR of the F-250 was higher in 1975. The standard F-250 had an 8,100-pound GVWR, while the F-260 had a 6,200-pound GVWR. The F-100 was also available in the 133-inch wheelbase.

The transmissions for 1975 included a 3-speed manual as standard with the 4-speed manual and Cruise-O-Matic automatic transmission as options.

The 1975 F-150 cost $4,002 for the 133-inch wheelbase. The F-100 retailed at $3,640 but required more expensive unleaded fuel. The Super Cab Styleside in the 155-inch wheelbase was the most expensive at $4,541.

Bud Magaldi was a designer in the Ford Truck Design Studio at this time. He had a 32-year career at Ford. The 1975 F-150 was one of the trucks he influenced. There was extra attention given to the interior.

This is a 1975 Ford F-100 Ranger XLT. Late in this model year, Ford changed the name from F-100 to F-150. (Photo Courtesy Ford Motor Company)

This truck reflects the name change from F-100 to F-150. This was done to avoid emissions-control restrictions. (Photo Courtesy Ford Motor Company)

During late 1975 and starting with the 1976 model year, Ford changed the name from F-100 to F-150. Ford continued to produce F-100 trucks until the early part of the 1980s. Pictured is a 1976 F-150. (Photo Courtesy Steven Smith)

"As we started adding extra features to the interior, it started to get more popular with the masses and viewed more than just as a work truck," Magaldi said. "During the 1960s and much of the 1970s, you wouldn't find a woman interested in driving a truck. During this transition, it gained more mass appeal, even with women. It became a vehicle you could take anywhere and any place—from the opera to the farm."

Econoline

Also new for 1975 were unit-body construction Econoline vans. The newly designed van featured the following changes compared to the 1974 Econoline vans:

- Increased front overhang (distance between the front of the van and the front wheels)
- Concave side grooves similar to those used on the F-100
- Longer bevel-nosed hood
- Many new options, such as AM/FM radio, cruise (speed) control, and air-conditioning
- A GVW of 6,050 pounds

Ranchero

The Ranchero for 1975 was basically a carryover from the 1974 version with minor trim and color option changes.

Bronco

The Bronco was basically unchanged except for minor trim and color option changes.

1976

With the F-150 being such a success, Ford did not do anything different for the 1976 F-150 model. There were some changes made to the less popular F-100 model. The biggest change was a new grille that resembled the 1972 F-100 but had the headlights more recessed with thicker crossbars. The turn signals were still above the headlights, and the Ford lettering stretched across an opening between the top of the grille in the bottom face of the hood.

Ford offered a series of special packages that included the Camper Special, Northland Special, Ranger Package, Ranger XLC, and the Custom Décor Group for the Super Cab models. It also introduced a new trim called XLT that included:

- Cut-pile carpet, making this truck more like a passenger car than a work truck
- "Super soft" vinyl used on the seat
- Deluxe full wheel covers with color-matching inserts

The 1976 F-Series used the new Tu-Tone paint schemes. You could choose between a regular Tu-Tone, which used a color accent on the roof and the upper back panel of the cab; Deluxe Tu-Tone; and the Combination Tu-Tone. The Deluxe Tu-Tone was only available on the Styleside and had the color panel within the truck side moldings. The Combination Tu-Tone was only available on the Styleside and featured both the roof and upper back panel along with the matching color within the truck side moldings.

The 4WD trucks were still unchanged, using the mono-beam front suspension axle with free-wheeling front axle hubs and the 2-speed transfer case and 4-speed manual transmission.

The 1976 F-150 cost $4,235 for the 133-inch wheelbase. The F-100 retailed at $3,873. The Super Cab Styleside in the 155-inch wheelbase was the most expensive at $4,541.

The 1976 4WD F-250 sat higher because of the heavy-duty suspension. This truck also features an 8-foot bed and a sliding rear window. (Photo Courtesy Matt Milkert)

The F-250s that were equipped with 4WD between the years 1967 and 1977 are often referred to as High Boys. The "divorced" transfer case is set farther back in the frame than on other trucks; therefore, designers had to lift the front by 3 to 4 inches, which meant they also had to lift the back. The trucks came off the factory line sitting higher than other Ford trucks, which earned them their nickname. (Photo Courtesy Matt Milkert)

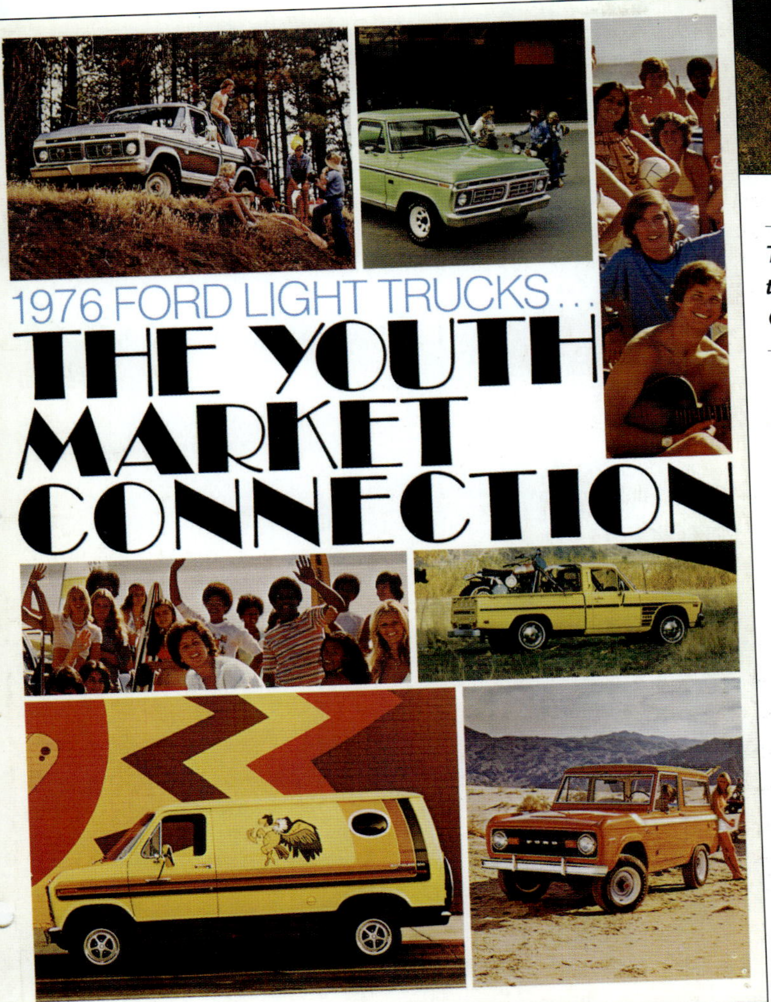

This advertisement shows how Ford marketed the F-Series trucks to a youthful audience. (Photo Courtesy Ford Motor Company)

Econoline, Ranchero, and Bronco

These were basically the same vehicles as they were in 1975 with just minor trim and color changes.

1977

After a record-setting sales year previously, the 1977 F-Series took a familiar spot on the sales chart as the top-selling vehicle in the United States. For this model year, there were some cosmetic changes that included smaller badging on the grille along with new insignias near the windshield. The bed received a rectangular fuel door to hide the gas cap. There was a new mirror design called the low-profile swing-lock. This mirror style is one of the easiest ways to tell a 1977 model.

The radiator support was made out of galvanized steel, but the front and rear wheel wells featured plastic splash

The side storage compartment of this 1977 F-250 had a lock and a key for underbed storage. This was a popular option for many work trucks. (Photo Courtesy Richard Truesdell)

This 1977 F-250 has been modified with some updates such as an aftermarket steering wheel and a center console with cup holders. (Photo Courtesy Richard Truesdell)

This well-worn 1977 F-150 has a chrome bumper and chrome down the side with dual trailer tow mirrors. (Photo Courtesy Matthew Johnson)

shields. The front fenders, the tailgate, the lower radiator reinforcement, and the rear cab corners were made from precoated metal. Truck undersides were coated with zinc primer.

The same three transmissions remained as carryovers from the other trucks of this generation. Ford offered two new engines for 1977: a 351 and a 400 ci, both V8s. These replaced the older 360 and 390 options.

Bill Moraniec, who worked in the Ford Truck Design Studio as a designer, said that to combat corrosion, which still occurred on the galvanized steel, designers used plastic fender liners for the 1977 trucks.

Moraniec said, "Weight reduction goals were achieved, as well as an added bonus of cost savings and design flexibility. Injection molding of plastics for interior and exterior ornamentation, grilles, bezels, molding, and so on replaced metal molding, stampings, and heavy diecast parts. Chrome plating plastic was perfected, thinner lightweight glass was used, and high-strength low-alloy steel (HSLA) was later introduced."

Ranchero

The new-for-1977 Ranchero was restyled like the Ford LTD II, which replaced the Torino that was the basis for the 1976 Ranchero. The same platform was used for the Ford LTD II, Ford Thunderbird, and the Mercury Cougar. The engine used included the 302-, 351-, and 400-ci V8s.

Econoline and Bronco

Basically, these were the same vehicles as in 1976 with minor trim and color changes.

1978

Ford advertising executives came up with an idea on how to brand the popular truck line in 1978. The company launched the Built Ford Tough campaign that year,

and, like the truck itself, it was a tremendous success. The Built Ford Tough ad campaign ran for more than two decades and is still often referred to in Ford's advertising today. Built Ford Tough is synonymous with the F-Series.

As for the 1978 F-Series, there were several significant cosmetic changes. The grille was replaced by a new, tougher-looking grille. It was larger than before and no longer combined the headlights and turn signals. The headlights were placed in housings besides the grille, and the park/turn signal lamps were now placed below the headlights. Additionally, a new chrome-plated Ford lettering set could now be seen on the hood immediately above the grille. Rectangular headlights replaced the round headlights, except on the Ranger and Custom trim levels. A contoured chrome bumper completed the new look.

According to Gale Halderman, using chrome was something they would often do in the design studio to add a new look. In the case of the Ford pickup, chrome added a tougher-looking appearance.

In 1978, a tilt steering wheel became available as an option. The 1978 F-Series had improved cab mounts, and door seals reduced the in-cab noise level. The F-150 Super Cab became available in 4WD. The bold-looking Free Wheeling special package was available along with a tubular black rear bumper bar, and chrome yellow-styled steel wheels were added to its previous appearance package (white wheels were optional).

Mechanically, a new 4-speed Overdrive manual transmission became available on 2WD pickup trucks with the 6-cylinder and the 5.0L (302-ci) and 5.8L (351-ci) V8 engines. The automatic transmission was still an option.

Ford launched a new top-tier trim called the Lariat. This became the luxury-level trim of the F-Series and featured

This sketch shows a Shorthorn F-Series that was based on the Ford Bronco. This sketch, by Ford designer Dick Nesbitt, was approved and produced as a Bronco in 1978. (Sketch Courtesy Dick Nesbitt)

One of the easiest ways to spot a 1977 model is by the side mirror. This new design was known as the low-profile swing-lock. (Photo Courtesy Bob Wilson)

two-tone exterior paint, special carpeting, a color-matched headliner, soft vinyl upholstery, and even a special black-plated tailgate. The Lariat trim stayed as the top-of-the-line trim for more than two decades, showing a glimpse of what trucks would look like in the future.

LITTLE LOUIE

This sketch shows a heavy truck concept known as the "Little Louie." It was created and designed by Andrew Jacobson out of the Ford Truck Design Studio. Jacobson said, "The Little Louie concept was influential within the Design Studio, as it added a lot of styling cues that a truck had not had at that time." (Sketch Courtesy Andrew Jacobson)

Prior to the sixth generation, the Truck Design Studio had been focused on its heavy truck design. Ford had invested heavily in improving the heavy truck product line. There was a level of fatigue within the designers in the truck studio. Ford would shuffle designers around from one studio to another, where one year they might work on trucks, and the next year they would work on cars or vice versa. According to design executive Gale Halderman, that was to keep the designers from getting stale and also spurred on the creative output.

Designer Andrew Jacobson sketched the Little Louie as a dually version of the F-250 so that it would have a convincing big-rig appearance. (Sketch Courtesy Andrew Jacobson)

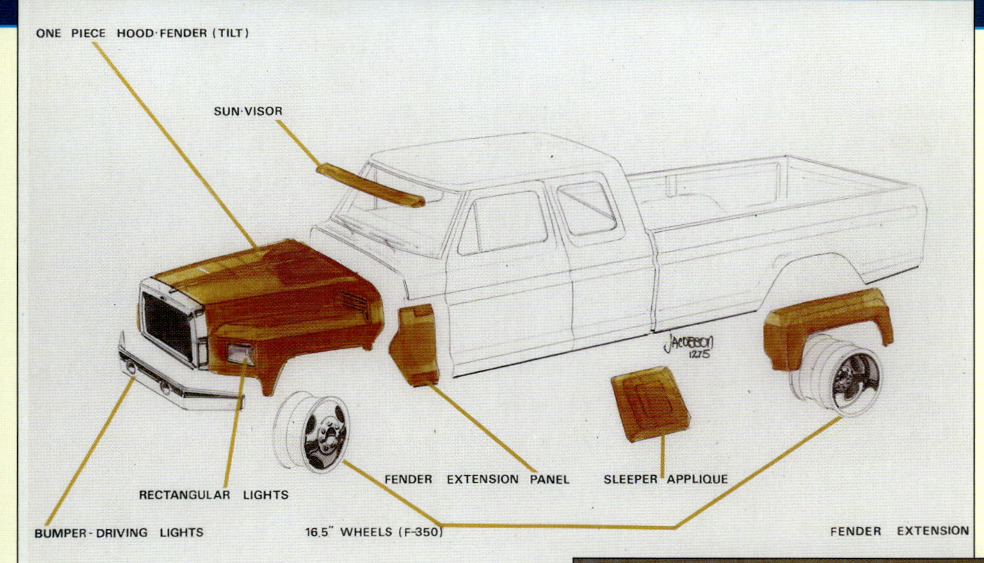

This sketch breaks down the different elements that made up the Little Louie concept truck. (Sketch Courtesy Andrew Jacobson)

Ford truck designer Andrew Jacobson is pictured here with the clay model version of the Little Louie. The truck concept he sketched got all the way to the approval process, where it was turned into a clay model. (Photo Courtesy Andrew Jacobson)

An offshoot from this mentality became a concept truck design called "Little Louie." Andrew Jacobson was a senior designer in the Ford Truck Design Studio and created the Little Louie.

"My concept was, why not take the design cues from the heavy-duty Ford Louisville Truck and adapt them to the F-250 and F-350," Jacobson said. "That way, those drivers who enjoyed the big rigs could have a smaller version of the Louisville truck." The Little Louie was born one Saturday morning from Jacobson's sketch pad.

"I came into work on an October Saturday morning on my own time and put the drawing together," Jacobson recalls. "I incorporated the tilt front end of a Louisville truck with the F-250. I did the illustration as a Super Cab version, as I could add an appliqué to show it with exposed external fuel tanks and a flatbed so that it would look more truck like." Jacobson sketched this truck as a dually version of the F-250 so that it would have a convincing big-rig appearance.

Jacobson said the rectangular lights (which existed in the Ford system) were also chosen to more closely echo the full-size Louisville Truck.

"The concept of a fiberglass tilt front end would allow easy manufacturing possibilities, as well as easy access for service to a production unit, and further reenforcing the Big Rig Design Concept," Jacobson said. "I was basically given the 'go ahead and do it, if you can find a way' by then–design vice president Gene Bordinat. The Little Louie was developed completely 'off the record' and in secret. The full-size model was completed in clay and painted orange."

The Little Louie concept was influential within the design studio. It added a lot of styling cues that a truck had not had at that time.

Jacobson said, "It brought to the forefront the concept of a 'tough truck.' The 'tough truck' concept went on to manifest itself in the grille work of the 1978 and 1979 F-Series pickups, and later the F-600 conventional medium-duty trucks that came out around the end of 1970," he said. Jacobson is proud of the Little Louie. "I do believe it has influenced the big, bold front ends that one sees on today's pickups, and was an interesting concept to show what a powerful pickup could look like."

Some of the styling highlights of the Little Louie include:

- A one-piece hood/fender
- Bumper driving lights
- Rectangular lights (which would be used in both the 1978 and 1979 sixth-generation F-Series)
- Fender extension panels
- A sleeper appliqué
- Twin exhaust stacks

Jacobson said the Little Louie is one of his favorite trucks he worked on over his 31-year career at Ford. Jacobson would eventually be named design director for trucks at Ford. "Even though the concept was done almost 40 years ago, it still makes a powerful, easily understood statement today."

Bronco

Ford redesigned the Ford Bronco and based it on the F-150. The Bronco was now almost similar to the F-150 but with the addition of a removable camper shell. This allowed Ford to compete with the Chevrolet Blazer by offering a larger and more luxurious Sport Utility Vehicle (SUV) while minimizing production costs since many parts were shared with the F-Series trucks.

Ranchero and Econoline

The 1978 Ford Ranchero and Econoline were the same vehicles as they were in 1977 with minor trim and color changes.

1979

The 1979 F-Series represents the last year of the sixth generation. The rectangular headlights were introduced for all trims, and the circular headlights were no longer available.

The grille insert that framed the headlights was either black or chrome to match the grille. The Free Wheeling package continued. Many collectors feel the look of the 1979 Free Wheeling F-150 typifies the pickup truck in the 1970s with its bold styling and aggressive features. Both the 1978 and 1979 F-Series are highly collectible.

A factory-installed CB radio, a popular hobby during this time, was added to the list of options for the F-Series.

The 1979 F-150 cost $4,235 for the 133-inch wheelbase. The F-100 retailed at $3,873. The Super Cab and Styleside in the 155-inch wheelbase were the most expensive at $4,541.

Bronco, Econoline, and Ranchero

The 1979 Ford Ranchero and Econoline were the same vehicles as in 1978 with minor trim and color changes.

Conclusion

The 1970s represent one of the best decades in Ford truck history. Ford took its spot atop the sales chart. The most amazing thing is that Ford managed to do all this with heavy government regulations in the middle of not one but two energy crises. With bolder styling, an improved interior, and the

This is a 1979 F-150 with the Ranger trim. It has been slightly modified with an aftermarket grille and bright metal rocker panels (which were not standard). It has 4WD, a 9-inch rear end, and a Dana 44 front axle with an NP203 transfer case. (Photo Courtesy Erick Simon)

A side-by-side comparison of two trucks from this era shows a 1979 F-350 Camper Special (left) and a 1977 F-100 (right). Even though Ford changed the name from F-100 to F-150, it continued to make the F-100 variant into the early 1980s. (Photo Courtesy Mark Krabbe)

Bud Magaldi's sketch shows the front of a truck concept. Magaldi said sketching trucks was fun and that adding features such as heavier grille bars could change the look of a truck, making it look tougher. (Photo Sketch Courtesy Bud Magaldi)

The sixth-generation F-Series is often referred to as Dentside Fords due to the styling cue found on the side panels. (Photo Courtesy Trenton Taylor)

introduction of the moniker "Built Ford Tough," these trucks lived up to that reputation.

"These trucks did everything," Magaldi said. "They could tow anything, and you could put anything in the back of it. And they lasted longer than cars. It really all started in the late 1970s, when we improved the quality of the interior appointments."

Galvanized steel, chrome accents, and square headlights helped add to that reputation and the mass appeal. But a new president was about to be elected, a second energy crisis was going on, and a Cold War was looming. Would the F-Series carry on with its success with yet another reinvention?

Ford Light Duty Truck Engines (1973–1979)				
Year	Engine	Horsepower (hp)	Torque (ft-lbs)	VIN Code
1973	240-ci inline 6-cylinder OHV	150	234 at 2,200 rpm	A
	300-ci inline 6-cylinder OHV	101	223 at 1,600 rpm	B
	302-ci V8	130	122 at 2,000 rpm	G
	360-ci V8	145	264 at 2,200 rpm	Y
	390-ci V8	160	290 at 2,000 rpm*	H
	460-ci V8	245	340 at 2,600 rpm*	J
1974	240-ci inline 6-cylinder OHV	150	234 at 2,200 rpm	A
	300-ci inline 6-cylinder OHV	101	223 at 1,600 rpm	B
	302-ci V8	130	122 at 2,000 rpm	G
	360-ci V8	145	264 at 2,200 rpm	Y
	390-ci V8	160	290 at 2,000 rpm*	H
	460-ci V8	245	340 at 2,600 rpm*	J
1975	240-ci inline 6-cylinder OHV	150	234 at 2,200 rpm	A
	300-ci (4.9L) inline 6-cylinder	120	223 at 1,600 rpm	B
	302-ci (5.0L) V8	130	122 at 2,000 rpm	G
	360-ci (5.9L) V8	143	264 at 2,200 rpm	Y
	390-ci (6.4L) V8	160	290 at 2,000 rpm*	M
	460-ci (7.5L) V8	245	340 at 2,600 rpm*	A or J
1976	240-ci inline 6-cylinder OHV	150	234 at 2,200 rpm	A
	300-ci (4.9L) inline 6-cylinder	120	223 at 1,600 rpm	B
	302-ci (5.0L) V8	130	122 at 2,000 rpm	G
	360-ci (5.9L) V8	143	264 at 2,200 rpm	Y
	390-ci (6.4L) V8	160	290 at 2,000 rpm*	M
	460-ci (7.5L) V8	245	340 at 2,600 rpm*	A or J
1977	240-ci inline 6-cylinder OHV	150	234 at 2,200 rpm	A
	300-ci (4.9L) inline 6-cylinder	120	222 at 1,600 rpm	B
	302-ci (5.0L) V8	130	122 at 2,000 rpm	G
	351-ci (5.8L) V8	160	262 at 2,200 rpm *	H
	360-ci (5.9L) V8	143	264 at 2,200 rpm	Y
	400-ci (6.6L) V8	169	276 at 2,000 rpm	S
	460-ci (7.5L) V8	220	340 at 2,600 rpm*	A or J
1978	300-ci (4.9L) inline 6-cylinder	101–120*	223 at 1,600 rpm	B
	302-ci (5.0L) V8	130	222 at 2,000 rpm	G
	351-ci (5.8L) V8	163	262 at 2,200 rpm *	H
	360-ci (5.9L) V8	143–145	264 at 2,200 rpm	Y
	400-ci (6.6L) V8	169	276 at 2,000 rpm	S
	460-ci (7.5L) V8	220	340 at 2,600 rpm*	A or J
1979	300-ci (4.9L) inline 6-cylinder	101–120*	223 at 1,600 rpm	B
	302-ci (5.0L) V8	130	222 at 2,000 rpm	G
	351-ci (5.8L) V8	156	262 at 2,200 rpm	H
	400-ci (6.6L) V8	169	276 at 2,000 rpm	S
	460-ci (7.5L) V8	220	340 at 2,600 rpm*	A or J

Note: Information included in this chart is designed to be inclusive. Dependent upon reference, year, and carryover, information may vary.

Note: The engine VIN from 1973 to 1979 is the fourth character.

Note: Approximately in 1975, engine displacement started using metric measurements.

* From 1978 to 1979, dependent upon year, carryover, and other factors, the 300-ci engine had four HP ratings: 101, 115, 117, and 120 hp. This data is an approximate value. Information regarding engine torque varies based on model and/or resource.

Ford Light-Duty Truck Transmissions (1973–1979)

Year	Model	Automatic/Manual	Number of Gears	Transmission
1973–1979	F-100	Manual	3	Standard
1973–1979	F-100	Manual	4	Optional
1973–1979	F-100	Automatic	3	SelectShift Cruise-O-Matic
1979	F-100	Manual	4	Overdrive
1973–1979	F-150	Manual	3	Standard
1973–1979	F-150	Manual	4	Optional
1973–1979	F-150	Automatic	3	SelectShift Cruise-O-Matic
1979	F-150	Manual	4	Overdrive
1973–1979	F-250	Manual	3	Standard
1973–1979	F-250	Manual	4	Optional
1973–1979	F-250	Automatic	3	SelectShift Cruise-O-Matic
1979	F-250	Manual	4	Overdrive

Note: Information included in this chart is designed to be inclusive. Dependent upon reference, year, and carryover, information may vary.

Ford Light-Duty Sizes and Prices (1973–1979)

Year	Model	Wheelbase (inches)	Length (inches)	Bed Length (feet)	Gross Vehicle Weight (pounds)	Price	Number Manufactured
1973–1979	Ford F-100 1/2-ton Styleside and Flareside	117/155	187–234	6.75/8	4,600–5,800	$2,889–$6,225	1,901,593*
1975–1979	Ford F-150 1/2-ton Styleside and Flareside	133/155	187–234	6.75/8	6,050–6,400	$4,002–$6,302	1,461,780**
1973–1979	Ford F-250 3/4-ton Styleside and Flareside	133/155	192–234	6.75/8	6,200–8,100	$3,183–$6,657	1,103,527***

Note: Information included in this chart is designed to be inclusive. Dependent upon reference, year, and carryover, information may vary.

* Is a total of all F-100 1/2-ton Styleside and Flareside body, bed, engine, and cab types.

** Is a total of all F-150 1/2-ton Styleside and Flareside body, bed, engine, and cab types.

*** Is a total of all F-250 3/4-ton Styleside and Flareside body, bed, engine, and cab types.

Color	Available Year and VIN Code						
	1973	1974	1975	1976	1977	1978	1979
Raven Black (Black)	A	A	A	A	A or 1C	A	A
Wind Blue	B	B	B	–	–	–	–
Pure White	C	C	–	–	–	–	–
Special White	–	–	–	C	9E	–	–
Blue Metallic	–	–	–	D	D	–	–
Bright Blue Metallic	–	–	–	–	–	D	–
Fiesta Tan	D	D	–	–	–	–	–
Medium Ginger Glow	–	–	D	4	–	–	–
Medium Vaquero Metallic	–	–	–	–	–	–	D
Brooke Blue	E	E	E	N	N	–	–
Nectarine Metallic	–	–	–	E	Y or 8T	Y	–
Cream	–	–	–	–	E	U	U
Mill Valley Green	F	F	F	–	–	–	–
Ginger Glow Metallic	–	–	–	F	–	–	–
Dark Brown Metallic	–	–	–	–	F or H	F or H	F or H
Chrome Yellow	G	G	G	G	G or 6S	G	–
Seapine Green	H	–	–	–	–	–	–
Baja Beige	H	H	I	–	–	–	–
Medium Copper	–	–	–	H or 2	2 or 8G	2	2
Rangoon Red	J	J	J	J	2V	–	–
Silver Metallic	–	–	–	J	1G	J or V	J or V
Boxwood Green	K	K	–	–	–	–	–
Autumn Tan	–	–	K	K	–	–	–
Castillo Red (Bright)	–	–	–	K	K	K	–
Light Medium Blue	–	–	–	–	–	–	K
Holly Green	L	L	–	L	7D	–	–
Chartreuse	–	–	–	L	L or 7R	–	–
Midnight Jade	–	–	–	–	–	L	–
Wimbledon White	M	M	M	M	M	M	M
Diamond Blue	N	–	–	–	–	–	–
Ivy Glow	–	N	–	–	–	–	–
Maroon	–	–	–	–	–	N	E
Dark Green (Mallard)	–	–	O or L	O	O or 49	–	–
Scandia Green	P	P	–	–	–	–	–
Vineyard Gold	–	–	P	–	–	–	–
Bali Blue (Light Blue)	–	–	–	P	8	8	–
Dark Nectarine Metallic	–	–	–	–	P or 8U	P	–
Winter Green	Q	–	–	–	–	–	–
Parrot Orange	–	–	Q	–	–	–	–
Tangerine	–	–	–	–	8F	Q	–
Sequoia Brown	R	R	R	R	–	–	–
Tidewater Aqua	R	–	–	–	–	–	–
Light Jade	–	–	–	–	R or 7A	R	R
Midnight Blue	S	S	S	S	S	S	S
Candy Apple Red	T	T	T	T	T	T	T
Limestone Green	U	U	–	–	–	–	–
Glen Green	–	–	U	U	–	–	–
Mallard Green/Dark Jade	V	O	V	B	B	B	B
Indio Beige	–	V	–	–	–	–	–
Medium Indio Blue	–	V	–	–	–	–	–
Baytree Green	–	–	–	V	–	–	–
Medium Copper Metallic	–	–	–	–	–	–	V
Saddle Tan	W	W	–	–	–	–	–
Ginger Glow	W	W or E	F	F	–	–	–
Medium Ivy Bronze Metallic	–	–	W	–	–	–	–

Color	Available Year and VIN Code						
	1973	1974	1975	1976	1977	1978	1979
Medium Green Glow Metallic	–	–	–	W	–	–	–
Durango Tan	X	–	–	–	–	–	–
Indio Tan	–	–	–	–	X	X	–
Bright Medium Blue	–	–	–	–	3T	–	–
Tan	–	–	–	X or 3	3 or 5V	7	–
Light Blue	–	–	–	–	3Y	–	–
Chamois	–	–	–	–	–	–	X
Burnt Orange	Y	Y	–	–	–	–	–
Baytree Green	–	–	Y	–	–	–	–
Mecca Gold	–	–	–	Y	–	–	–
Medium Golden Sand Metallic	–	–	–	–	–	–	Y
Hot Ginger/Copper Metallic	Z	Z	Z	Z	Z	–	–
Medium Tan Metallic	–	–	–	–	–	–	Z
Maroon Metallic	–	–	–	–	–	–	1
Medium Silver Metallic	–	–	–	–	1M	–	–
Pastel Lime	2	2	–	–	–	–	–
Royal Maroon	2	–	–	–	–	–	–
Cayan Red	–	–	–	2	–	–	–
Coral	–	–	–	–	2A	–	–
Lipstick Red	–	–	–	–	–	2U	–
Village Bright Green	–	3	–	–	–	–	–
Peppertree Red	–	–	–	3	–	–	–
Medium Blue Metallic	–	–	–	–	3D	–	–
Bright Dark Blue	–	–	–	–	–	S	–
Grabber Blue	4	–	–	–	–	–	–
Samoa Lime	4	4	–	–	–	–	–
Tan Metallic	–	–	–	4	4	–	–
Light Medium Pine	–	–	–	–	–	–	4
Bold Orange	–	5	–	–	–	–	–
Harness Tan	–	–	–	5	5	6	6
Copper Metallic	–	–	–	–	5Z	–	–
Dark Blue Metallic	–	–	–	–	–	–	5
Bahama Blue	6	–	I	I	I	I	I
Viking Red	–	6	6	–	–	–	–
Dark Brown	–	–	–	6	6	H	–
Bright Yellow	–	–	–	–	6E	–	–
Light Tan	–	–	–	–	6U	–	–
Harbor Blue	7	7	–	–	–	–	–
Gold Glow	–	7	7	–	–	–	–
Herron White	–	–	–	7	7	–	–
Light Chamois	–	–	–	–	–	7	–
Walnut Glow	–	–	–	–	–	–	7
Jade Metallic	–	–	–	–	7N	–	–
Medium Emerald	–	–	–	–	7U	–	–
Tampico Yellow	8	–	–	–	–	–	–
Sandpiper Yellow	–	8	–	–	–	–	–
Hatteras Green Metallic	–	–	8	8	–	–	–
Vista Orange	–	–	–	–	8G	–	–
Medium Blue Metallic	–	–	–	–	3D	–	8
Prime	–	–	–	–	–	–	9
White	–	–	–	–	9A	M	–
Dark Jade Metallic	–	–	–	–	46	–	–

Note: Information included in this chart is designed to be inclusive. Dependent upon reference, year, and carryover, information may vary.

Note: 1973–1979 paint color is listed on a VIN tag located on the driver-side doorjamb as "EXTERIOR PAINT."

FORD F-SERIES SEVENTH GENERATION (1980–1986)

Chapter SEVEN

"Perhaps the most significant change to the seventh-generation F-Series occurred in 1980 with the introduction of a new independent front suspension for 4WD trucks."

Ford continued the F-100 naming convention into the 1980s, which is evidenced here with the 1980 F-100 Ranger. (Photo Courtesy Ford Motor Company)

Ford had to walk a very fine line with the seventh generation of the F-Series. For the first time since 1965, light-duty trucks were based upon a completely new chassis and body. Changing the truck too much could cost Ford its place atop the sales charts in this emerging segment.

The seventh generation succeeded in being exactly what the consumer wanted at this time. It was narrower with a lower profile and a bit shorter. The bed size options remained, but as a result, the seventh-generation F-Series saw a reduction in weight, which increased the fuel economy.

This side-by-side comparison of a 1984 F-250 and a 2017 F-250 shows how the truck evolved during the last two-and-a-half decades. These are essentially the same size trucks but the 2017 appears much bigger. The 1984 F-250 was still quite crude in many ways, while the 2017 would be incredibly luxurious. (Photo Courtesy Trevor Parks)

TAILGATE UP VERSUS TAILGATE DOWN

Ford used the wind tunnel at Lockheed Aircraft Company in Atlanta, Georgia, for testing the coefficient of drag on its vehicles. According to Gale Halderman, the coefficient of drag results with either tailgate up or down were close.

Gale said that while the results were close to being equal, keeping the tailgate up in the normally closed position resulted in slightly reduced drag, and therefore would result in improved fuel economy at highway speeds. The reason the coefficient of drag was lower with the tailgate in the up position was that a cushion of air formed in the bed of the truck. This effect caused the passing air to ride over the pillow of air, reducing the overall drag at highway speeds.

Wind tunnel studies have proven that keeping the tailgate of a pickup truck up actually results in slightly better fuel economy than having it down. This beautiful red 1985 F-150 has dealer- or customer-installed grab bars on the top of the bed. (Photo Courtesy Jared Johnson)

The squared-off look was designed intentionally. During this time, trucks were tested for their coefficient of drag. Gale Halderman said that all clay modeled cars in the 1970s were put into the wind tunnel with talented clay sculptors literally shaving off areas that were creating unnecessary drag. Trucks, like cars, were being designed with the ultimate goal of improved fuel efficiency.

The bigger trucks (excluding the compact Rangers) of the seventh generation have been nicknamed as the Bullnose among enthusiasts. This nickname was given due to the similarity in looks of the grille and a bull's face and head. Bullnose trucks have forums and Facebook pages devoted to them, showing why the seventh generation continues to be a cherished collector truck.

The seventh-generation F-Series is highly collectible since, unlike many predecessors, the 1980–1986 F-Series had nice interiors and a comfortable ride. This was only the beginning of this trend, as the truck would continue its evolution toward luxury.

Twin-Traction Beam Suspension

Perhaps the most significant change to the seventh-generation F-Series occurred in 1980 with the introduction of a new independent front suspension for 4WD trucks. This was known as Ford's Twin-Traction Beam (TTB) suspension, which made Ford's trucks more off-road friendly without sacrificing the durability of a solid axle.

Preceding the launch of the seventh generation, Ford's engineers spent many months at the Ford Proving Ground

This lifted and modified 1984 F-250 has the addition of white steering dampers. These are used to help prevent the steering wheel from being jerked from the driver's hands when hitting rocks or bumps, especially when driving off-road. This bold front end shows why these seventh-generation trucks have been given the nickname Bullnose Fords. The similarity in looks reminds many of a bull's face and head. (Photo Courtesy Daniel Murphy)

facility in Arizona perfecting this suspension. Testing this new suspension for durability and comfort was of the utmost importance to Ford's engineers. The truck was incredibly popular already, and they could not have any setbacks or perceived quality issues.

While both the F-150 and the F-250 4WDs used the TTB front suspension, there were differences including:

- The F-150 used the light-duty Dana 44 front drive axle.
- The F-250 used the Dana 44HD front drive axle assembly with the Dana 50 being an optional front axle.

DIY Mindset

The average home price in 1980 was $47,200. This combined with free and loose loan regulations in the early part of the 1980s led to an increase in home ownership. With this growth came an increase in the weekend warriors and the DIY movement. Even Home Depot, which started as only a few hardware stores in Atlanta, Georgia, began establishing stores throughout the country.

The timing was right for the pickup truck to expand even farther into suburbia. Automotive historian John Heitmann chalks up the popularity of the pickup truck, and specifically the success of the Ford F-Series, to the growing families in suburban America.

"America was coming out of two oil shocks at this time," Heitmann said. "There was a burgeoning interest in home improvement and a growing DIY spirit. Society was changing and the economy was changing. Do-it-yourself America was thrusting ahead and the pickup truck was right there ready for them."

Heitmann said that younger families, which had one or two kids only, needed trucks for their weekend projects. "But they also wanted a comfortable interior space, not just something to haul around sheetrock," he said. So, in many ways, the development of the Home Depot crowd spurred on the growth and expansion of the seventh-generation F-Series. They really go hand in hand with what was happening in America and the housing market at the time.

Powertrain Improvements

The seventh-generation F-Series marked a major change in the powertrains used by the light-duty pickup line. In 1980, engineers referred to engine displacement size in liters instead of cubic inches. The standard engine was the tried-and-true 300-ci (4.9L) inline 6-cylinder engine equipped with a carburetor. A 232-ci (3.8L) V6 was used in 1982–1983 model years as an option but was dropped after 1983.

The small V8 engines included the 302 ci (5.0L). A smaller version displacing 255 ci (4.2L) was offered as a fuel economy option that was not very popular. The 255 ci was dropped after the 1983 model year. Electronic fuel injection (EFI) was introduced on the 302 (5.0 L) V8 as an option in 1984 and became standard on 302 engines in the 1985 model year.

The larger V8 gasoline engines included the 351- (5.8L) and 400-ci (6.6L) V8s. In 1984, Ford introduced the larger 460-ci (7.5L) V8, which replaced the 400-ci engine that model year. Ford also introduced a 420-ci (6.9L) diesel engine that was produced by International Harvester at its Indianapolis, Indiana, plant and then shipped to the Ford truck assembly plants. This indirect injected (IDI) diesel engine was used in the 1983–1987 model years. This engine was naturally aspirated and was never turbocharged.

Automatic Transmissions

The heavy-duty Ford C6 3-speed automatic transmission marketed as the Select-Shift Cruise-O-Matic was the standard automatic transmission for all years and came with most engine options. The Ford C6 was a heavy-duty automatic transmission built by Ford Motor Company between 1966 and 1996.

The C6, like the C4, used the legendary Simpson geartrain design. The Simpson gearset was named for its inventor, Howard Woodworth Simpson (1892–1963), who was an American automotive engineer. The Simpson gearset combines one sun gear with two carriers with planetary gears and two ring gears. A simple planetary gearset and a Simpson gearset can be combined to provide 4- and 5-speed transmissions.

Transfer Cases

Several different transfer cases were used; most were built by New Process Gear. NP205 and NP208F were the most common. Each transfer case used a stick-shift 4WD engagement

During the 1983 model year, Ford introduced a 7.5L V8 engine, as seen in this monochromatic tan 1983 F-150 pickup. (Photo Courtesy Daelin Stapley)

with four speeds: 4 Low, 4 High, Neutral, and 2 High. A Borg-Warner transfer case was also used.

Ford added its new automatic overdrive (AOD) 4-speed transmission as an option on light-duty models starting in 1981. The 4-speed manual was also added to go along with the 3-speed automatic. With the two new transmissions available, Ford was able to obtain an EPA rating of 21 miles per gallon (mpg) for its 2WD trucks and slightly less for 4WD.

1980

The debut of the seventh-generation redesign started with the 1980 F-Series. The seventh-generation grille was more prominently styled with horizontal bars and a vertical pattern. The square headlights were recessed inward. There were sharper lines on the front end and the corners. The chiseled appearance carried on from the front to the side profile with a more streamlined appearance.

The overall design of the seventh generation is of aerodynamics and modern looks. Ford was still spelled across the hood in chrome lettering just above the grille and spanned the width of the horizontal/vertical design of the grille. Later in this generation, the simple Ford lettering was replaced in favor of the now-famous Ford blue oval.

The 1980 F-Series debuted a new dashboard. It retained some of the same instrumentation as the previous generation but had a more modern feel. Overall, the response to the revamped interior was strong. Other highlights of the 1980 F-Series included:

- A repositioned hood release was now located inside the cab.
- A double-panel roof and additional sound deadening materials were added to decrease road noise and vibration.
- A resettable trip meter was introduced. This optional install was moved to the top of the speedometer as part of the optional Sport Instrumentation Group.
- The Sport Instrumentation Group also included the optional tachometer in the center of the cluster, as well as oil and ammeter gauges.

The F-100 continued to be offered, although it was far less popular than the F-150 and was soon discontinued. There were five trim options offered for the 1980 model year: Custom, Ranger, Ranger XLT, Ranger Lariat, and Explorer.

1981

The instant success of the 1980 model year gave way to very few changes for the 1981 model. The "egg carton" grille carried over for the 1981 model. Halogen headlights became standard. Real glass was still used for headlamps.

Four-wheel-drive models were given radial tires. The chrome Ford lettering remained on the hood and the tailgate, although this would be the last model year for that to appear on the hood. Styleside and Flareside beds were available, and the truck was available with a Super Cab as well.

For 1981, various special equipment orders were offered on all F-100s. A propane engine option used liquefied petroleum gas (LPG), commonly called propane. This option was popular with fleets because propane was less expensive, which reduced operating expenses. However, the energy of propane is about half that of gasoline, resulting in a much shorter range. This is why the propane option was best used for fleets that operated within a city so that the range of the trucks would not be a factor.

There were many interior and exterior options, including a cargo light, an inside hood release, variable speed windshield wipers, and stabilizer (anti-sway) bars.

Trim options for the 1981 included the base F-100 along with Custom, Ranger, Ranger XLT, and Lariat versions of the F-150. The popular Free Wheeling Appearance Package was again offered. It featured bumper guards, striping on the outside, and fog lamps. The 1981 F-Series was still available as a Styleside and a Flareside.

1982

The big news for the 1982 F-Series was the introduction of a 3.8L (232-ci) V6 engine. It came standard with a 3-speed manual transmission, but a 3-speed automatic and a 4-speed automatic overdrive were also available options. Ford stopped

The stock 1982 F-150 extended cab with the XLT Lariat trim was one of seven trims offered this model year. (Photo Courtesy Mike Cantu)

A 4WD 1982 F-250 with the 351-ci V8 engine and an automatic transmission was one of six engines offered this model year, four of which were V8s. (Photo Courtesy Lance Chambers)

using the name Ranger to describe an F-Series trim level, reserving it for a new line of small trucks built by Ford to replace the Mazda-built Courier. The Ranger debuted as its own nameplate in the 1983 model year.

The chrome Ford lettering was removed from the hood and replaced by a Ford oval plate that was centered in the grille. This new design stayed with the Ford trucks for the rest of the seventh generation, making the 1982 Ford F-Series the first time the blue oval made its appearance on a truck. Grille options in 1982 included a full chrome grille, a black grille, or the standard flat gray plastic grille. The headlight bezels also came in color options ranging from light gray, gray, dark gray, and black (the latter two were the most common).

For trucks equipped with the 5.8L V8, there was an electronic engine control (EEC), which had not been put in a Ford truck up until that point. Starting in 1982, many trim levels were available including Base, Fuel Saving (FS), XL, XLS, XLT Lariat, Explorer, and Eddie Bauer.

Seventh-generation XLS F-Series are considered a collector's truck, as these had blacked-out features in place of chrome, which gave them real distinction on the road.

1983

The model year 1983 saw the fewest changes among the entire seventh-generation F-Series. A large 7.5L (460-ci) V8 was introduced in the F-150 for 1983. There was also an available 6.9L diesel engine that offered an attractive combination of towing performance and fuel efficiency. Most of the changes for 1983 occurred in the bigger trucks with bigger engines. This change was likely due in part to fuel prices in America as the second oil crisis was waning and the economy was bustling.

The F-350 was given a crew cab with an 8-foot bed. Along the F-150 and F-100 line, there were some minor changes made to trim, paint colors, and option packages. The 1983 trim levels

FORD RANGER

Prior to 1982, there was a lesser-known compact truck that Ford sold called the Courier. It was based on the Mazda B1800. The Courier was produced from 1972 to 1982 and marked the beginning of a new class of compact trucks.

As part of the 1983 model class, Ford took the risk of watering down the F-Series sales by offering a smaller truck known as the Ranger. This compact pickup truck was produced from 1983 until 2011. During its first production run, the Ranger went through three generations, including a redesign in 1993 and again in 1998. Ford reintroduced the Ranger as part of the 2019 model year.

The Ranger had a cult-like following amongst truck enthusiasts, but sales never seemed to impact the sales of the F-Series. Rangers were widely popular in Latin America and South America. Due to the popularity, the Ranger was produced in Argentina to keep up with the demand in that global market.

The Ranger chassis eventually led to the development of the Ford Explorer, one of Ford's most successful nameplates of all time. The SUV craze of the late 1990s and into the 2000s was due in part to the success and thirst for smaller trucks like the Ranger. During the early 1980s, the Ford Bronco II also shared the platform with the Ranger, showing a continued interest in small, more rugged, off-road vehicles.

A beautiful red 1983 F-100 step side with a shorter truck bed and a painted front bumper and grille. This was the second-to-last model year that Ford would produce the F-100. (Photo Courtesy Ian Craig)

This 1983 F-100 interior shows the column-shifted 3-speed manual transmission and bench seat. Even with some of the visible wear and interior fading on this vehicle, there was not much to the interior. The color-keyed seat belts and black steering column were stock. (Photo Courtesy Ian Craig)

FORD AND EDDIE BAUER

Eddie Bauer was an outdoorsman who turned his passion into a brand. He started as a tennis outfitter with an outdoor retail store in Seattle, Washington. From there, his clothing line took off, and he was sought out to outfit mountaineers and adventurers. Soon, his name became synonymous with exploration and adventures.

As his brand escalated, he sold the business. Eddie Bauer LLC entered into a branding and licensing partnership with the Ford Motor Company in 1983. Ford launched the Eddie Bauer Ford Bronco in the 1983 model year and launched a line of vehicles under the Eddie Bauer brand with special badging and a special look. Vehicles that received this branding included Bronco, Explorer, Expedition, F-150, Excursion, Taurus X, and Aerostar. The Ford and Eddie Bauer partnership continued through 2010.

included XL, XLT Lariat, and XLS. The sporty XLS was discontinued after this year as was the F-100 trim and name.

1984

The 1984 model year marks the end of the F-100 name. Other significant changes also occurred during this model year. The body molding and interior trim were updated. The 1984 Ford F-150 was offered in XL, XLT, and XLT Lariat trims. Buyers had a choice of gas (V8 or inline 6-cylinder) or the 6.9L (420-ci) diesel (170-hp V8) engines, as well as a range of cab and bed configurations. The extended cab Super Cab was a popular Styleside choice. Flareside setups for the 1984 Ford F-150 included two-door and four-door cabs and long-bed and short-bed options.

The 5.8L (351-ci) V8 was upgraded to a High Output (H.O.) engine with a 4-barrel carburetor, a new camshaft, a larger air cleaner, and a low-restriction dual exhaust system. The result was a jump from 163 hp and 267 ft-lbs of torque to 210 hp and 304 ft-lbs of torque. Ford added EFI and the EEC-IV electronic engine control system to the 4.9L 6-cylinder, 5.0L V8, and the base 5.8L V8 engines. The 3.8L (232-ci) V6 engine was dropped from the F-Series lineup.

In 1984, Ford began using pre-coated steel and additional galvanized panels to help fight rust and corrosion. A new clutch safety switch kept the engine from cranking unless the

A 1984 Ford F-150 is shown here with the two-tone paint option of a blue body color and white sides and roof. (Photo Courtesy Gary Stull)

The interior of a 1984 F-150 that has 4WD with a manual transmission shows the far left pedal foot-operated parking brake. The transfer case is operated by the floor-mounted shift lever to the left of the transmission shifter. (Photo Courtesy Daylen Gilkerson)

clutch pedal was fully depressed. The F-Series key-in-ignition warning buzzer became standard equipment.

1985

In 1985, only minor cosmetic changes were made. Newly designed front disc brakes became standard. A new seam sealer and electro coat primer aided in corrosion protection. In 1985–1986 models, the upper accent moldings were moved below the front marker. For 1985, the rear tailgate molding on XLT models was updated and previewed the design of the 1987 model (and next generation). This molding has become increasingly rare and fetches a high price.

A cargo light was available as part of an optional equipment package. The combination stop/cargo lamp was not required until September 1, 1993, for the 1994 model year. The Lariat trim returned as the highest-level trim option for the F-Series. There was a dually version of the F-350 crew cab for the 1985 model year.

This 1985 F-250 has an 8-foot bed and an auxiliary fuel tank (seen by the two gas filler doors on the side). The truck is also lifted from the stock height and features aftermarket wheels and larger tires. (Photo Courtesy Mike Cochrane)

1986

Ford made just a few changes in the final year of the seventh-generation F-Series. Preferred Equipment Packages were made available to allow customers to choose what they wanted to add to their truck. Inside, some gauges that had been optional became standard equipment, including engine temperature, oil pressure, ammeter, and fuel level. New exterior colors added to this model year included Colonial White, Medium Silver Metallic, Dark Spruce Metallic, Dark Shadow Blue Metallic, and Dark Gray Metallic. Trims carried over unchanged from the previous model year. All F-150s were offered as Standard or Super Cab configuration with either Styleside or Flareside options.

Bronco

The Ford Bronco was updated for the 1980 model year while maintaining about the same size and powertrain options as the 1979 version. The Twin-Traction Beam front suspension used the light-duty Dana 44 front drive axle. The 1980–1986 Bronco used a leaf spring rear suspension with a Ford 9-inch drive axle assembly. The model changes for 1980–1986 consisted mostly of exterior trim and interior color options changes.

Econoline

The Ford Econoline continued mostly unchanged through 1986, using three different wheelbase models of 124- and 138-inch (standard van) and the Super Van with a 138-inch wheelbase. The Super Van had an extended rear overhang that added 20 inches to the overall length. Year-to-year changes mostly consisted of exterior trim and interior color options changes.

Conclusion

For 16 straight years, Ford had the best-selling truck in America. Changes made to the seventh-generation F-Series only solidified and diversified that further. Adding a smaller Ford Ranger did not hurt sales in the least and once again showed Ford was willing to take strategic chances when they were calculated and well planned.

When it comes to the seventh-generation F-Series, both engineering advances and design advances helped send it forward. The engineering advances and smaller size helped the most fuel-efficient Ford pickup truck barrel through the rest of the 1980s.

With the 5.0L V8 engine, this 1986 F-150 Lariat XLT had 190 hp and 285 ft-lbs of torque. (Photo Courtesy Joshua Reed)

Ford Light-Duty Truck Engines (1980–1986)

Year	Engine	Horsepower (hp)	Torque (ft-lbs)	VIN Code
1980	300-ci (4.9L) inline 6-cylinder	101–120*	223 at 1,600 rpm	E
	302-ci (5.0L) V8	130	222 at 2,000 rpm	F
	351-ci (5.8L) V8	156	262 at 2,200 rpm	G or W
	400-ci (6.6L) V8	153	309 rated	Z
1981	300-ci (4.9L) inline 6-cylinder	101–120*	223 at 1,600 rpm	E
	255-ci (4.2L) V8	115	206 at 2,200 rpm	D
	302-ci (5.0L) V8	130	222 at 2,000 rpm	F
	351-ci (5.8L) V8	156	262 at 2,200 rpm	G or W
	400-ci (6.6L) V8	153	309 rated	Z
1982	232-ci (3.8L) V6	109	184 at 1,600 rpm	3
	300-ci (4.9L) inline 6-cylinder	101–120*	223 at 1,600 rpm	E
	255-ci (4.2L) V8	115	206 at 2,200 rpm	D
	302-ci (5.0L) V8	130	222 at 2,000 rpm	F
	351-ci (5.8L) V8	150	280 at 1,800 rpm	G or W
	400-ci (6.6L) V8	153	309 rated	Z
1983	232-ci (3.8L) V6	109	184 at 1,600 rpm	3
	300-ci (4.9L) inline 6-cylinder	101–120*	223 at 1,600 rpm	Y
	302-ci (5.0L) V8	130	222 at 2,000 rpm	F
	351-ci (5.8L) V8	150	280 at 1,800 rpm	G
1984	300-ci (4.9L) inline 6-cylinder	115	223 at 1,600 rpm	Y
	302-ci (5.0L) V8	130	222 at 2,000 rpm	F
	351-ci (5.8L) V8	150	280 at 1,800 rpm	G
	351-ci (5.8L) V8	210	305 at 2,800 rpm	H
	420-ci (6.9L) V8 (diesel)	170	315 at 1,400 rpm	1
	460-ci (7.5L) V8	214	362 at 1,800 rpm	L
1985	300-ci (4.9L) inline 6-cylinder	101–120*	223 at 1,600 rpm	Y
	302-ci (5.0L) V8	150	250 at 2,600 rpm	N
	351-ci (5.8L) V8	150	280 at 1,800 rpm	G
	351-ci (5.8L) V8	210	305 at 2,800 rpm	H
	420-ci (6.9L) V8 (diesel)	170	315 at 1,400 rpm	1

Year	Engine	Horsepower (hp)	Torque (ft-lbs)	VIN Code
	460-ci (7.5L) V8	214	362 at 1,800 rpm	L
1986	300-ci (4.9L) inline 6-cylinderp	101–120*	223 at 1,600 rpm	Y
	302-ci (5.0L) V8	190	285 at 2,400 rpm	N
	351-ci (5.8L) V8	210	305 at 2,800 rpm	H
	420-ci (6.9L) V8 (diesel)	170	315 at 1,400 rpm	1
	460-ci (7.5L) V8	214	362 at 1,800 rpm	L

Note: Information included in this chart is designed to be inclusive. Dependent upon reference, year, and carryover, information may vary.

Note: The engine VIN in 1980 is the fourth character. From 1981 to 1986, the engine VIN is the eighth character.

* From 1980 to 1986, dependent upon year, carryover, and other factors, the 300-ci engine had four horsepower ratings: 101, 115, 117, and 120 hp.

Ford Light- and Medium-Duty Truck Paint Colors (1980–1986)

Color	1980	1981	1982	1983	1984	1985	1986
Black	1C	1C	1C	1C	1C or 99	1C	1C
Smoke Metallic	–	–	–	–	–	–	1D
Silver Metallic	1G	1G	1G	1G	1E	–	–
Light Smoke Metallic	–	–	–	–	–	–	1G
Medium Gray Metallic	1P	1P	1P	1P	–	–	–
Light Canyon Red Metallic	–	–	–	–	2E	2E	2E
Bright Bittersweet	–	–	–	–	2G	–	–
Candy Apple Red	2K	2K	2K	2K	2K	2K	–
Maroon	2L	2L	2L	–	–	–	–
Dark Red Metallic	–	–	–	2S	–	–	–
Midnight Wine	–	–	–	–	–	–	2W
Midnight Blue Metallic	3B	3B	–	–	–	–	–
Dark Blue Metallic	3D	–	3L	3L	3L	3L	–
Light Blue	–	–	–	–	3F	34	34
Medium Blue Metallic	–	3H	3P	3P	3P	–	–
Light Harbor Blue Metallic	–	–	–	3J	–	–	–
Bahama Blue	–	–	–	3T	3T	3T	–
Midnight Regatta Blue	–	–	–	–	–	–	3U

d Light- and Medium-Duty Truck Paint Colors (1980–1986) *CONTINUED*

or	1980	1981	1982	1983	1984	1985	1986
k Teal Metallic	–	–	–	4A	4A	4A	–
dium Dark Spruce tallic	–	4J	4J	4J	4J	–	4J
dium Spruce Metallic	–	4N	–	–	–	–	–
t Teal Metallic	–	–	–	4W	–	–	–
k Caramel Metallic	–	5G	5G	–	–	–	–
k Brown Metallic	–	–	5Q	–	–	–	–
ht Caramel	5T	–	–	–	–	–	–
d Metallic	6B	–	–	–	–	–	–
tel Sand	6D	–	–	–	–	–	–
ome Yellow	–	–	–	6S	6S	6S	–
	–	6U	6U	–	–	–	–
t Spruce Metallic	–	–	7B	–	–	–	–
dow Blue Metallic	–	–	–	–	–	–	–
y Green	–	–	–	7D	7D	7D	–
ht Regatta Blue Metallic	–	–	–	–	–	7H	–
k Pine Metallic	7M	–	–	–	–	–	–
k Chamois Metallic	8A	8A	–	–	–	–	–
dium Bright Bittersweet tallic	–	8D	–	–	–	–	–
per	–	–	–	8J	–	–	–
mois Metallic	8W	–	–	–	–	–	–
te	9A	9A	9A	9A	9A or 9F	9A	9M
cial White	–	–	–	9E	9E	9E	–
dium Copper Metallic	–	–	–	–	9H	–	–
ert Tan	–	–	–	9T	9P	–	–
t Desert Tan	–	–	–	9Q	9Q or 8Q	8Q	8Q
t Charcoal Metallic	–	–	–	–	9V	9V	–
Charcoal Metallic	–	–	–	9W	–	9W	–
dium Walnut Metallic	–	–	–	9Y	–	–	–
goon Red	–	–	–	22	22	22	–
ht Blue	–	–	–	32	–	–	–
t Regatta Blue Metallic	–	–	–	–	–	–	33
dgewood Blue	34	34	–	–	–	–	–
dium Dark Fire Red	–	–	–	–	51	51	51
dium Fawn Metallic	–	55	–	–	–	–	–
ow	–	–	–	61	61	–	–
t Spruce	–	–	74	–	–	–	–
t Medium Pine	76	–	–	–	–	–	–
Fawn Metallic	–	–	82	–	–	–	–
n	–	–	89	–	–	–	–

e: Information included in this chart is designed to be inclusive. Dependent upon ence, year, and carryover, information may vary.

e: 1980–1986 paint color is listed on a VIN tag located on the driver-side door- as "EXTERIOR PAINT."

Ford Light and Light/Medium Duty Truck Transmissions (1980–1986)

Year	Model	Automatic/ Manual	Number of Gears	Transmission
1980	F-100	Manual	3	Standard
1980	F-100	Manual	4	Overdrive
1980	F-100	Automatic	3	SelectShift Automatic
1981–1982	F-100	Manual	3	Standard
1981–1982	F-100	Manual	4	Optional
1981–1982	F-100	Manual	4	Overdrive
1981–1982	F-100	Automatic	4	Overdrive
1981–1982	F-100	Automatic	3	SelectShift Automatic
1983	F-100	Manual	3	Standard
1983	F-100	Manual	4	Overdrive
1983	F-100	Automatic	4	Overdrive
1983	F-100	Automatic	3	SelectShift Automatic
1980	F-150	Manual	3	Standard
1980	F-150	Manual	4	Optional
1980	F-150	Manual	4	Overdrive
1980	F-150	Automatic	3	SelectShift Automatic
1981–1983	F-150	Manual	3	Standard
1981–1983	F-150	Manual	4	Optional
1981–1983	F-150	Manual	4	Overdrive
1981–1983	F-150	Automatic	4	Overdrive
1981–1983	F-150	Automatic	3	SelectShift Automatic
1984–1986	F-150	Manual	3	Standard
1984–1986	F-150	Manual	4	Optional
1984–1986	F-150	Automatic	4	Overdrive
1984–1986	F-150	Automatic	3	Automatic
1980	F-250	Manual	3	Standard
1980	F-250	Manual	4	Optional
1980	F-250	Manual	4	Overdrive
1980	F-250	Automatic	3	SelectShift Automatic
1981–1983	F-250	Manual	3	Standard
1981–1983	F-250	Manual	4	Optional
1981–1983	F-250	Manual	4	Overdrive
1981–1983	F-250	Automatic	4	Overdrive
1981–1983	F-250	Automatic	3	SelectShift Automatic
1984–1986	F-250	Manual	3	Standard
1984–1986	F-250	Manual	4	Optional
1984–1986	F-250	Automatic	4	Overdrive
1984–1986	F-250	Automatic	3	Automatic

Note: Information included in this chart is designed to be inclusive. Dependent upon reference, year, and carryover, information may vary.

d Light and Light/Medium Sizes and Prices (1980–1986)

ar	Model	Wheelbase (inches)	Length (inches)	Bed Length (feet)	Height (inches)	Width (Inches)	Gross Vehicle Weight (pounds)	Price	Number Manufactured
80– 83	Ford F-100 1/2-ton Styleside and Flareside	117/133	188–208	6.75/8	69	77	4,700–5,150	$5,549–$7,068	487,712*
80– 86	Ford F-150 1/2-ton Styleside and Flareside	117/133/155	188–230	6.5/6.75/8	70	77	4,800–6,250	$5,697–$10,446	1,819,599**
80– 86	Ford F-250 3/4-ton Styleside	133/155	214–230	8	72	77	6,300–8,800	$6,515–$11,645	751,894***

te: Information included in this chart is designed to be inclusive. Dependent upon reference, year, and carryover, information may vary.

te: Production for the F-100 ended in 1983.

te that the F-150 4x4 had a height of 72.6 inches and a GVW up to 6,450 pounds. The F-250 4x4 had a height of 75 inches and a GVW up to 00 pounds.

a total of all F-100 1/2-ton Styleside and Flareside body, bed, engine, and cab types.

s a total of all F-150 1/2-ton Styleside and Flareside body, bed, engine, and cab types.

Is a total of all F-250 3/4-ton Styleside body, bed, engine, and cab types.

FORD F-SERIES EIGHTH GENERATION (1987–1991)

The prosperity of the 1980s continued in the United States, and the significant redesign of the eighth generation resonated with American consumers. By 1991, not only was the F-Series the best-selling truck in America (a title it had held for more than a decade) but it was also now the best-selling of all vehicle models in America.

It seemed appropriate that the F-150 would get a major refresh as it was celebrating its 50th anniversary in 1987. A new grille looked modern, and the composite headlights extending over the front quarter panels gave it a more rounded look. With an aerodynamic hood, this truck looked fresh to the American consumer.

The new grille earned this truck the nickname the bricknose due to the square appearance of the front end. It seemed that Ford was finding a groove in its timing of the F-Series redesigns. That, above all else, is a major factor for the truck's success. Ford had its finger on the American truck buyer's pulse.

The Flareside bed, which had clearly run its course, was discontinued during this generation. Although some purists liked the old-school look of the Flareside, there was a clear changing of the guard when it came to truck design. Ford was leading the way, and it showed in the eighth generation. This was also the beginning of the era of heavy customization to trucks. Owners would put lift kits on the truck to raise it higher off the ground. There were also those who wanted to lower them for a sportier, low-profile look.

Meanwhile, at the Ford Truck Design Studio, there was much energy and excitement about designing trucks according to Andrew Jacobson, who was truck design director for Ford starting in 1989. The excitement from the designers working on the best-selling vehicle in America showed inside the design studio.

"There was a special camaraderie in the Truck Studio," he said. "We were also blessed with a team of fantastic product planners, and some in marketing and engi-

This is a 1987 F-150 Super Cab. The eighth generation began in 1987 and represented the 50th anniversary of the Ford F-Series truck. (Photo Courtesy Ford Motor Company)

By 1991, the Ford F-150 was not only the best-selling truck in America but had also become the best-selling vehicle in America, surpassing cars. During the late 1980s and early 1990s, more Americans than ever were hitting the road in a pickup truck. (Photo Courtesy Lane Harris)

neering were very supportive of what we were doing. My thoughts on why the F-Series is Ford's best seller is that it is perceived as a good-looking, hard-working rig that can do anything, go anywhere, and last forever."

Jacobson said, during the late 1980s, through the entire 1990s, and even into the 2000s, the F-Series was the unsung hero and star of Ford, even though executives rarely stopped by the Truck Design Studio. Having that trust and freedom meant a lot and showed in how well executed the redesigns were each generation. The eighth generation was one of the best executed redesigns for Ford in the history of the F-Series.

HENRY FORD II (SEPTEMBER 4, 1917–SEPTEMBER 29, 1987)

Henry Ford II ran the Ford Motor Company from 1945 to 1980. He passed away in 1987, just as the eighth generation of the Ford F-Series launched. Many designers and executives who worked for or under him said he offered very little feedback on trucks and generally left the Truck Design Studio alone. (Photo Courtesy John Clor/Ford Performance Communications Archive)

Henry Ford II, who had taken over and essentially saved the Ford Motor Company in the 1940s and had run it until 1980, died of pneumonia at the age of 70 in 1987. Henry, sometimes known as HF2 or Deuce, was the eldest son of Edsel Ford and the eldest grandson of Henry Ford.

One of Henry Ford II's inspired moves was to hire 10 young up-and-comers known as the "Whiz Kids." Ford II envisioned these 10 men, right out of the Army Air Forces statistical team, as giving the company the ability to innovate and stay current. Two of them, Arjay Miller and Robert McNamara, went on to serve as presidents of Ford Motor Company themselves.

Henry Ford II took several steps forward and some back during his time at the helm of Ford Motor Company. He allowed the offering of public stock in 1956, which raised $650 million for the company. On the other hand, the Edsel cost the company almost half that. Henry Ford II hired Lee Iacocca, who was fundamental to the success of the Ford Mustang. He then fired Iacocca due to personal disputes in 1978.

Ford II formally retired from all positions at Ford Motor Company on October 1, 1982, upon reaching the company's mandatory retirement age of 65. However, he remained the ultimate source of authority at Ford until his death in 1987.

According to Gale Halderman, who worked nearly 40 years at Ford as a design executive, Henry Ford II never interfered much in the truck design. He said, "As long as it was on budget and made it to Job One, he rarely interfered on the truck side." Halderman said Ford II wasn't really a truck guy and in fact, most of the executives at Ford didn't drive trucks. Perhaps the lack of interference and attention allowed the "truck people" at Ford to shape the truck the way they saw fit.

F-150s and F-250s of this era were commonly called bricknose trucks due to the square-shaped front grille that resembled a brick. (Photo Courtesy Chris Wilson)

Most 1987 F-250s were imported into the United States. Assembly of these bigger trucks was done at two different assembly plants in South America. Ford developed a huge following in South America and Mexico as a result of the production plants Ford used in these areas. (Photo Courtesy Chris Wilson)

Powertrain

Fuel injection was added to the 4.9L inline-6 for 1987. In 1988, Ford became the first light-duty truck original equipment manufacturer (OEM) to sell a fully fuel-injected engine lineup. The 5.8L V8 and 7.5L V8 also gained fuel injection. Prior to the introduction of the eighth generation, the 5.0L V8 had fuel injection as an option for 1985 and was made standard in 1986.

In 1988, the diesel V8 from International (Navistar) was enlarged from 420 to 444 ci (6.9 to 7.3L) and allowed for an increase to 180 hp and 365 ft-lbs of torque. The 5.8L V8 and 7.5L V8 engines were equipped with electronic fuel injection in 1988.

Transmissions

In 1986, the 3-speed, column-mounted manual transmission had been discontinued, but the rest of the eighth generation was carried over from the 1986 trucks.

For 1987, the only transmissions available on Super Cab models were a 4- or 5-speed manual (regular cab models were also available with automatic transmission). The 4-speed manual transmissions were dropped after 1987 but could be ordered until 1989. In 1988, the 5-speed ZF S5-42 replaced the BorgWarner T19 in F-250 and F-350 models. For the F-150 and light-duty F-250, the heavier-duty BorgWarner T18 4-speed manual remained available, while the Mazda-built M5OD 5-speed manual was added to the model lineup for the

4.9L inline-6 and 5.0L V8-equipped models.

In 1989, the C6 3-speed automatic was replaced as the base automatic transmission with the 4-speed electronically controlled automatic overdrive unit (E4OD), though the C6 was still available as an option, mostly in F-250s and F-350s, until 1997.

Four-wheel-drive improvements included the addition of automatic locking hubs for the F-150 in 1989. Models with the 5.0L V8 also had an option of a "Touch Drive" electronic transfer case.

Chassis

Ford offered a 4WD swing-arm independent front suspension called Twin-Traction Beam (TTB) from 1980 through 1996. Based on its 2WD Twin I-Beam suspension from 1965, a Dana 44 differential was built into the driver-side (front) axle beam, transmitting torque to the passenger-side wheel with a double U-jointed axle shaft. The F-150 used radius arms and coil springs, whereas the 4WD F-250 and F-350 used leaf springs. The F-250 received TTB Dana 50 axles; the F-350 received a solid Dana 60 axle.

Some trucks, such as this 1988 F-250, were still basic and used primarily on farms, ranches, and by businesses. However, as trucks became more popular as daily transportation, luxury options began to appear more frequently in the order guides. (Photo Courtesy Danny Sanchez)

1987

In 1987, Ford's light-duty F-Series trucks and full-size Bronco companions were restyled with front ends that were more aerodynamic. They also got rear-wheel antilock brakes, as did the Bronco II. The new front-end design featured the following:

- Flush headlights (requiring only the bulb to be replaced if burned out, instead of the whole headlight)
- Wraparound parking lights
- A grille with 12 rectangular openings
- New front fenders, hood, and bumper added to the new, more streamlined look

The interior of the new generation trucks was also completely redesigned in 1987 and a Custom trim was reintroduced. A revised instrument panel had more legible gauges and a bigger glove box. Maintenance was made easier due to an easy-access fuse box and simplified belt replacement for the alternator, power steering pump, and air-conditioning compressor. The washer fluid reservoir had a wider opening, making it easier to access. Likewise, the brake fluid reservoir was now made of see-through plastic, making it much easier to visually check the levels. Many truck enthusiasts and mechanics point to these small maintenance changes as an important reason why the eighth generation was so popular.

Standard fuel injection on the base 4.9L 6-cylinder engine provided a 25-percent increase in horsepower. Heavy-duty models included F-250s and F-350s. Many were shipped as incomplete vehicles with no bed; these were intended to be used as tow trucks, box trucks, flatbed trucks, or dump trucks. However, owners could and did convert the models to pickup trucks.

The F-Super Duty also came with dual fuel tanks. The system used a single fuel gauge and a dash-mounted toggle switch to switch between the tanks. It came with a Power Take-Off (PTO) used to power attachments (such as winches or a dump bed) directly from the transmission. F-Super Duty models were rated at about 15,000-pound GVWR and came with either the standard 7.5L (460-ci) gas V8 or the optional 7.3L (444-ci) diesel V8. All wheels used on the Super Duty Ford trucks were 10-lug with dual wheels in the rear.

REAR WHEEL ANTILOCK BRAKES

Most of the early antilock brake systems (ABS) controlled the rear brakes only. This type of system was called single-channel ABS. Single-channel rear-wheel-only ABS is used on many rear-wheel-drive pickups and vans.

The Ford version was called Rear Antilock Brake System (RABS). GM and Chrysler versions were called Rear Wheel Antilock (RWAL)—pronounced "R wall."

For this system, there is a single speed sensor mounted in the differential or transmission. It is used for both rear wheels. Rear-wheel antilock systems are used where vehicle loading can affect rear-wheel traction. This is why it was used on pickup trucks and vans. Because the rear-wheel antilock systems have only a single channel, they are much less complex and less costly than their multichannel, four-wheel counterparts used in newer vehicles.

The F-250, F-250 Heavy Duty, and F-350 were built exclusively at the General Pacheco, Argentina, and São Bernardo do Campo, Brazil, assembly plants and sold as pickup truck models. Assemblies of F-250s, F-250 Heavy Dutys, and F-350s were shipped from South America to the United States as imports from 1987 to 1997.

1988

In 1988, a new line of Super Duty Ford F-350 trucks was introduced. These trucks filled a gap between the regular F-350s and the medium-duty F-600s. The standard engine was the 7.5L (460-ci) 385-series V8 engine with the 7.3L (444-ci) International diesel as an option. The 1988 F-Series dropped its available Flareside bed, but it would return a few years later.

For the F-150, Ford still featured a trim called Custom. It sounded fancy, but was actually the base trim and considered quite ordinary. The interior of the Custom had vinyl seats, rubber floor mats, and an AM radio. This bare-boned trim was a huge success as many truck owners still didn't "need" all kinds of fancy amenities.

The Custom trim represented, once again, Ford being in tune with its customer base, offering a simple and affordable trim that covered all they needed without any extra costly frills.

1989

The close of the decade fell in the third year of the eighth-generation redesign. Very little changed from 1988, as the 1989 F-Series truck's styling and options were a carryover. Ford's Bronco II and Ranger were restyled for the first time since their introduction. Both received aerodynamically smoother front ends. The Ford Ranger also added the standard rear-wheel antilock brakes that the Bronco II had received in 1987. New for the Aerostar minivan was a "midi" version with a longer body.

Interiors were also new, as were the standard antilock rear brakes. A new twin-spark plug cylinder head on the 2.3L four boosted horsepower by 10 to an even 100 hp. A 140-hp 2.9L V6 was also available in the Ranger.

One of the styling cues of the eighth generation was the split window on the rear side windows, as shown on this 1989 F-250. This design feature is one of the telltale signs of a bricknose Ford. (Photo Courtesy Lane Harris)

This 1989 F-150 is typical of the eighth-generation bricknose trucks with the square headlights and squared-off grille. This particular F-150 had a 300-ci (4.9L) inline 6-cylinder engine with manual transmission. (Photo Courtesy Isaias Zapata)

This 1989 F-150 had a width of 79 inches and a height of 72 inches. This truck has more rugged tires on it and shows how capable the F-150 was on and off the road as well as in inclement weather. This was part of the appeal of the F-150 during this era. (Photo Courtesy Amanda Knutson)

The Ford electronic engine control (EEC) is a series of engine control units (ECU) that were designed and built by the Ford Motor Company. They were introduced in the 1970s and went through several model changes.

EEC-I and -II used a common processor and memory. The EEC-II controlled the air-fuel ratio of the Ford model 7200 Variable Venturi (VV) Carburetor. This was the last carburetor designed and built by Ford in the United States. This carburetor was very expensive to manufacture because each carburetor had to be hand-calibrated in a pressure-controlled room.

The EEC-III system was used on certain 1981–1983 models. There were two different EEC-III modules: a Feedback Carburetor (FBC) and Central Fuel Injection (CFI). The distributors in EEC-III systems eliminated conventional mechanical and vacuum advance mechanisms. All timing was controlled by the engine control module. The increased spark of energy required greater separation of the distributor cap electrodes to prevent cross-fire.

The FBC module used the same Ford 7200 VV carburetor as the EEC-II. The CFI module fired two high-pressure (approximately 40 psi) fuel injectors, which were mounted in a throttle body and attached to a traditional intake manifold in the center valley of the 5.0L (302-ci) engine. CFI was available on all Ford vehicles with the 5.0L engine.

This 1991 Ford F-150 had an inline 6-cylinder engine with fuel injection. This engine was the only 6-cylinder engine optioned on the F-150 in 1991. Notice the long intake runners used to help the engine produce low-speed torque. This truck produced 145 hp and 265 ft-lbs of torque. (Photo Courtesy Joseph Mitchell)

Unlike previous EEC systems, the EEC-IV system used a small ignition module called the thick film integrated ignition (TFI or TFI-IV) module. It was grey in color and mounted on the distributor, whereas some later models have the TFI module mounted on a heatsink in the engine compartment.

1990

The 1990 F-Series trucks' styling and options were a carryover. The Sport Appearance Package was the only real addition to the 1990 F-Series. This package included special wheels and paint striping as well as a roll bar and off-road lighting. This showed off the F-150's versatility and showcased that it was a truck that could handle adventures. This suited the younger buyer of the pickup truck. With Jeeps so popular during this time, the F-150 stepped forward with the Sport Appearance Package to show its playful side.

The larger, more-powerful 4.0L Cologne V6 was added to the engine roster for both the Ranger and the Aerostar.

1991

At the end of the eighth generation there were a few notable changes for the 1991 F-Series. For F-150s, there was Electronic Touch Drive 4WD. This feature was only available on the 5.0L engine with the 4-speed automatic transmission. Still, this feature was popular and would be integrated on future models.

The eighth-generation F-Series lacked much chrome, which was intentional by the truck designers. Rather, elaborate paint schemes and even decals became popular. The 1991 F-150 had a two-tone paint feature known as the Bodyside. This version of the 1991, as the last of the eighth-generation F-Series, is still wildly popular among truck collectors.

Near the end of the 1990 model year, Ford released a new sport SUV called the Explorer. It was labeled a 1991 model and became the best-selling SUV in the United States. However, it spelled the end of the smaller two-door Bronco II. An optional 3.0L V6 replaced the 2.9L offered previously on 2WD Rangers and was still optional on 4x4s, gaining 5 hp to 145. Dress-up option packages included the STX option.

For 1991, a Nite trim package was introduced. It included blacked-out exterior trim, either a pink or blue/purple stripe, and a "Nite" decal on the sides of the cargo box.

The Nite package also included a dashboard badge, Nite floor mats, and a Nite-branded spare tire cover in the case of the Bronco. Other upgrades included 29-inch RWL tires, aluminum wheels, and a sport suspension. Any bed configuration could be selected, but it was single-cab-only for 1991. In addition, the option was available for 5.0L/302- or

FORD EXPLORER

In 1991, Ford stopped manufacturing the Bronco II and replaced it with an SUV called the Ford Explorer. This can be looked at historically as one of the most successful ideas in Ford's history. Right in the middle of the booming truck market with the F-Series being the best-selling vehicle in America, Ford launched a vehicle that arguably could eat into some of the F-Series market. It did not, as the 1992 F-Series continued to dominate.

What the Explorer represented was a gap in the automotive market for Ford. The Explorer sold more than 300,000 units in its first year, and by 1994, the third year in its existence, the Explorer was already the ninth best-selling vehicle in the United States (with the F-150 being at the top of that list that year). Competition in this emerging segment was limited. Jeep had the Grand Cherokee and Chevrolet had the S-10 Blazer (which would later just be called the Blazer). The Explorer has been through five generations of changes since its launch in 1991. A sixth generation of the Explorer launched in the 2020 model year.

Early in its production, the Explorer was offered with two-door and four-door options. By the third generation (2002), the Explorer Sport (two-door) was no longer offered. Many police forces chose a variant of the Explorer, known as the Interceptor Utility, as part of their fleet of vehicles.

The Explorer shared a chassis platform with the Ford Ranger and the Aerostar. Not using the F-150's chassis helped give the Explorer its own personality. It had car-like features the F-150 simply did not have. That made it appealing to those who would never be interested in buying a full-size pickup truck.

From 2001 to 2010, Ford offered the Explorer with a small truck bed as a counteroffer to the Ranger, which still had a work-truck feel. The Explorer Sport Trac, with its small truck bed and four doors, appealed to families. It is regarded as Ford's first midsize pickup truck (Ranger being a compact pickup truck). Since its inception and through the 2018 model year, Ford has sold more than 7.4 million Ford Explorers.

5.8L/351-powered trucks and Broncos (2WD or 4WD).

The other trim levels were Custom, XL, and XLT Lariat.

Conclusion

The 1980s were pivotal to the entire automotive industry, and certainly that was the case for Ford's popular F-Series. Gone were "three on the tree" shifters and carbureted engines. Trucks were looked at differently. They weren't just work trucks—they were family vehicles. The ease of repair of the eighth-generation F-Series resonated with DIY weekend warriors. Plus, the F-Series had better looks and significantly improved interiors that focused on comfort.

Hal Sperlich's notion of the "civilization of the truck" truly played out during the 1980s, an era filled with a Cold War, a popular actor turned president, and a housing boom that saw subdivisions spring up all over America. With the end of the 1980s and the beginning of the 1990s, Ford was well positioned for market dominance. The automaker didn't have to raise the bar, but it did. The competition was aware and merely playing catch-up. So, with such a success and now tagged as the best-selling vehicle (including cars) in America, how could Ford top that and continue the success into a new decade and new generation of pickup truck?

Ford Light-Duty Truck Engines (1987–1991)				
Year	Engine	Horsepower (hp)	Torque (ft-lbs)	VIN Code
1987	300-ci (4.9L) inline 6-cylinder	145	265 at 2,000 rpm	Y
	302-ci (5.0L) V8	185	270 at 2,400 rpm	N
	351-ci (5.8L) V8	210	305 at 2,800 rpm	H
	446-ci (7.3L) diesel V8	180	345 at 1,400 rpm	M
	460-ci (7.5L) V8	230	390 at 2,200 rpm	G
1988	300-ci (4.9L) inline 6-cylinder	145	265 at 2,000 rpm	Y
	302-ci (5.0L) V8	185	270 at 2,400 rpm	N
	351-ci (5.8L) V8	210	315 at 2,800 rpm	H
	446-ci (7.3L) diesel V8	180	345 at 1,400 rpm	M
	460-ci (7.5L) V8	230	390 at 2,200 rpm	G
1989	300-ci (4.9L) inline 6-cylinder	145	265 at 2,000 rpm	Y
	302-ci (5.0L) V8	185	270 at 2,400 rpm	N
	351-ci (5.8L) V8	210	315 at 2,800 rpm	H
	446-ci (7.3L) diesel V8	180	345 at 1,400 rpm	M
	460-ci (7.5L) V8	230	390 at 2,200 rpm	G
1990	300-ci (4.9L) inline 6-cylinder	145	265 at 2,000 rpm	Y
	302-ci (5.0L) V8	185	270 at 2,400 rpm	N
	351-ci (5.8L) V8	210	315 at 2,800 rpm	H
	446-ci (7.3L) diesel V8	180	345 at 1,400 rpm	M
	460-ci (7.5L) V8	230	390 at 2,200 rpm	G
1991	300-ci (4.9L) inline 6-cylinder	145	265 at 2,000 rpm	Y
	302-ci (5.0L) V8	185	270 at 2,400 rpm	N
	351-ci (5.8L) V8	210	315 at 2,800 rpm	H
	446-ci (7.3L) diesel V8	180	345 at 1,400 rpm	M
	460-ci (7.5L) V8	230	390 at 2,200 rpm	G

Note: Information included in this chart is designed to be inclusive. Dependent upon reference, year, and carryover, information may vary.

Note: From 1987 to 1991, the engine VIN is the eighth character listed.

Color	Available Year and VIN Code				
	1987	1988	1989	1990	1991
Chestnut Metallic	–	–	–	–	A9
Medium Mocha Metallic	–	–	–	–	DC
Mocha Frost Metallic	–	–	–	–	DD
Currant Red	–	–	–	–	EC
Electric Currant Red Metallic	–	–	–	–	EG
Medium Cabernet	–	–	–	–	EH
Wild Strawberry Metallic	–	–	–	–	EL
Vermillion	–	–	–	–	EP or E4
Light Crystal Blue Metallic	–	–	–	–	MK
Black	1C	1C	1C	1C or YC	MS or YC
Jewel Green Metallic	–	–	–	–	PB
Reef Blue Metallic	–	–	–	–	PC
Medium Platinum Metallic	–	–	–	–	RC
Black Ebony	–	–	–	–	UA
Green	–	–	–	–	W7
Medium Titanium Pearl Metallic	–	–	–	–	YG
Smoke Metallic	1D	1D	1D	1D or YW	YN, YV, or YW
Oxford White	–	–	–	–	YO or YZ
Silver Metallic	1E or 1Q	–	–	–	–
Light Smoke Metallic	1G	1G	1G	1G or YV	YV
Crystal Pearl Metallic	1L	–	–	–	–
Black	1R	–	–	–	–
Bronze Black Pearl Metallic	1S	–	–	–	–
Medium Charcoal Metallic	1Z	–	–	–	–
Medium Scarlet	–	2D	2D	2D or EN	EN
Light Canyon Red Metallic	2E	–	–	–	–
Medium Cabernet Red	–	2H	2H	2H or EH	–
Candy Apple Red	2K	–	–	–	–
Maroon	2L	–	–	–	–
Medium Canyon Red Metallic	2M	–	–	–	–
Bright Red	2V	–	–	–	–
Dark Blue Metallic	3L	–	–	–	–

Color	Available Year and VIN Code				
	1987	1988	1989	1990	1991
Bright Dark Blue Metallic	3N	–	–	–	–
Light Regatta Blue Metallic	3S	–	–	–	–
Bahama Blue	3T	–	–	–	–
Pawnee Tan	–	–	–	4D or AV	AV
Walnut Metallic	5D	–	–	–	–
Bright Orange	5F	–	–	–	–
Light Chestnut Metallic	5N	–	–	–	–
Wheat Metallic	6E	–	–	–	–
Bright Regatta Blue Metallic	–	7H	7H	7H or MG	MX
Bright Yellow	6N	–	–	–	–
Shadow Blue Metallic	7B	–	–	–	–
Holly Green	7D	–	–	–	–
Dark Shadow Blue Metallic	–	7N	–	7N or MJ	–
Dark Shadow Blue Metallic	7Q	–	–	–	–
White	9A or 9K or 9M	9M	9M	9M or YY	YY
Special White	9E	–	–	–	–
Desert Tan Metallic	9N	9N	9N	9N or AT	–
Walnut Metallic	9S	–	–	–	–
Light Chestnut	9T	9T	9T	–	–
Medium Walnut Metallic	9Y	–	–	–	–
Rangoon Red	22	–	–	–	–
Light Blue	34	–	–	–	–
Alpine Green Metallic	42	42	42	42 or SC	–
Medium Dark Fire Red	51	–	–	–	–
Bright Caramel Metallic	54	–	–	–	–
Light Sandalwood Pearl Metallic	63	–	–	–	–
School Bus Yellow	67	–	–	–	–
Dark Chestnut Metallic	–	95	95	95 or CE	–

Note: Information included in this chart is designed to be inclusive. Dependent upon reference, year, and carryover, information may vary.

Note: 1987–1991 paint color is listed on a VIN tag located on the driver-side doorjamb as "EXTERIOR PAINT."

Year	Model	Automatic/Manual	Number of Gears	Transmission
1987–1991	F-150	Manual	4	Standard (Overdrive) (1987)
1988–1991	F-150	Manual	5	Standard (Overdrive) (1988–1991)
1988–1991	F-150	Manual	5	Overdrive
1987–1991	F-150	Automatic	3	Optional
1987–1991	F-150	Automatic	4	Overdrive (AOD)
1987–1991	F-150	Automatic	4	Overdrive (E4OD)
1987–1991	F-250	Manual	4	Standard (Overdrive) (1987)
1988–1991	F-250	Manual	5	Standard (Overdrive) (1988–1991)
1988–1991	F-250	Manual	5	Overdrive
1987–1991	F-250	Automatic	3	Optional
1987–1991	F-250	Automatic	4	Overdrive (AOD)
1987–1991	F-250	Automatic	4	Overdrive (E4OD)

Note: Information included in this chart is designed to be inclusive. Dependent upon reference, year, and carryover, information may vary.

Year	Model	Wheelbase (inches)	Length (inches)	Bed Length (feet)	Height (inches)	Width (inches)	Gross Vehicle Weight (pounds)	Price	Number Manufactured
1987–1991	Ford F-150 1/2-ton Styleside and Flareside	117/133/138/155	194–232	6.5/6.75/8	70–72	79	4,800–6,250	$9,732–$1,6532	1,573,994*
1987–1991	Ford F-250 3/4-ton Styleside	133/155	210–232	6.75/8	73–79	79	4,800–8,800	$10,556–$18,970	620,239**

Note: Information included in this chart is designed to be inclusive. Dependent upon reference, year, and carryover, information may vary.

Note that the F-150 4x4 had a height of 74 inches and a GVW up to 6,250 pounds. The F-250 4x4 had a height of 79 inches and a GVW up to 8,860 pounds.

* Is a total of all F-150 1/2-ton Styleside and Flareside body, bed, engine, and cab types.

** Is a total of all F-250 3/4-ton Styleside body, bed, engine, and cab types.

"With more aerodynamic looks, smoothed edges, and significantly improved interior, the F-150 would, once and for all, put the crude work truck mentality out to pasture.**"**

FORD F-SERIES NINTH GENERATION (1992–1996)

America had just elected a new president thanks to a new generation of younger voters. College attendance was at an all-time high. Even though blue-collar jobs were still around, a white-collar, college-educated movement was well underway thanks to upstart high-tech businesses. The 1990s was the era of the internet with dot-com companies jumping into the Dow Jones and NASDAQ to varied levels of success. Microsoft Windows was on many household and office computers. Technology was embraced, even by the 30- and 40-somethings.

The combination of higher education and new technology helped usher in consumer confidence, which impacted the automotive industry and the truck industry. The ninth-generation F-Series would be known as the truck with mass appeal. Collectors and enthusiasts sometimes generically refer to this generation as an Old Body Style (OBS) Ford, as the redesign was the last generation to have the traditional boxy styling before designs that were more rounded became standard.

With more aerodynamic looks, smoothed edges, and significantly improved interior, the F-150 would, once and for all, put the crude work truck mentality out to pasture. The F-150 was now a family vehicle and even a daily commuter. Much of this was thanks to the advancements that occurred in the ninth generation.

On looks alone, the ninth generation was familiar. Some enthusiasts felt the changes made to the exterior were not drastic enough to differentiate it from the eighth generation. But the smoothed-out front end gave it a broader appeal.

In some ways, the styling blurred the lines between the F-150 and the newly launched Explorer. Some styling cues were indeed similar. This was to be expected since many of the same designers working on the SUVs were also working on pickup trucks, which was a common practice at the Blue Oval.

The ninth generation is considered an expansion of the eighth generation with a nod to the F-150 from the 1980s too. Ford even brought back the Flareside F-150 for

As Ford began the ninth generation of the F-Series truck, the F-150 received a new look with a focus on smoother edges and aerodynamics. (Photo Courtesy Ford Motor Company)

The ninth-generation Ford F-Series is a bit of a throwback in many ways. The styling cues, though a redesign, are subtle. Ford did bring back the Flareside F-150 for 1992. (Photo Courtesy Creative Commons)

DODGE RAM INFLUENCES THE TRUCK MARKET

Ford was always keeping an eye on the competition. General Motors had the GMC Sierra and the Chevrolet C/K. The smaller Chevrolet S-10 was not really a competitor to the bigger F-150. General Motors didn't launch the Silverado until 1999 to rival the F-150. However, Chrysler's Dodge Ram pickup was a legitimate rival.

The first-generation Dodge Ram was produced from 1981 until 1993. It was crude and lagged far behind the F-150 in sales and refinement. Former Ford executives Lee Iacocca and Hal Sperlich were at Chrysler at this time. Iacocca was Chrysler's president and Sperlich was president of North American operations. One of Sperlich's last big accomplishments at Chrysler was the creation of the second-generation Dodge Ram full-size pickup truck. Development for this truck began in 1986. Sperlich left Chrysler in 1988, but all the product planning had been completed during this time for the second-generation Dodge Ram.

"We remade this truck from the ground up," Sperlich said. "It was a completely new package. I was influenced from my time at the Ford Truck Studio when we had just introduced the Louisville Ford. The 1994 Dodge Ram was certainly influenced by the Louisville." Sperlich is incredibly proud of the end result of the 1994 Dodge Ram. It is one of his proudest accomplishments in his illustrious automotive career.

"When I was at the Ford Truck Studio, I liked the heavier trucks and their look. I admired the strength of the big deep bumpers and the drop fenders," Sperlich recalls. He influenced a similar look on the 1994 Dodge Ram. "That 1994 Ram was a good-looking, tough truck. I liked the powerful look of the hood and the tough chrome bumpers," Sperlich said. "That influence that we had on that truck is still there today. The Ram still has a look of strength and power."

The Dodge Ram won *Motor Trend*'s Truck of the Year for the 1994 model year. The instant success of the 1994 Dodge Ram helped elevate the entire truck segment and impacted the F-Series with stronger competition. It was the reason the ninth generation was so short lived and Ford got to market with a full redesign in 1997. In its first year, the 1994 Dodge Ram sold 240,000 units, compared to only 78,000 the year prior. Those sales nearly doubled in 1995 with more than 400,000 units sold, to nearly 500,000 units sold in 1996.

The 1994 Dodge Ram won Motor Trend's *Truck of the Year honors. Former Ford executive Hal Sperlich helped this truck achieve such success. As such, the 1994 Ram really raised the bar for the F-150 and had the Ford executives scrambling to improve upon the ninth generation. (Photo Courtesy Creative Commons)*

the 1992 model year. This was a styling tip of the cap to the more traditional truck buyers. For the first time ever, there was a high-performance version of the F-150 that certainly appealed to youthful truck buyers. The F-150 Lightning was created by Ford's Special Vehicle Team (SVT)—a group of high-performance enthusiasts at Ford that was charged with creating high-performance models. The souped-up F-150 Lightning continued the trend of factory high-performance trucks that was started by the Chevrolet 454 SS.

The ninth generation was the last F-Series to be produced as a complete range of trucks from a 1/2-ton pickup (F-150) to a medium-duty Class 6 truck. In the 1997–1998 model years, the larger models of the F-Series (F-250 and above) were split from the F-150 and became the Ford Super Duty trucks, related to the latter with a few powertrain components.

Models

The F-250, F-250 Heavy Duty (HD), F-350, and F-Super Duty were available in many different configurations from chassis cab base models up to XLT trimmed models with chrome and plush seating. The trucks came with a variety of engines. The 4.9L I6, 5.0L V8, and 5.8L V8 were the only options for the F-150 series trucks. The Heavy Duty trucks could be selected with a 5.8L V8, 460-ci V8, the 7.3L IDI (1992–1994), or the 7.3L Power Stroke (1994½–1997), which were the diesel options produced by Navistar International.

The F-250 HD was only available in 1996 and 1997, and it differed from the earlier F-250 in the trim. It also had a transmission cooler like the later Ford Super Duty trucks and also received a heavier rear axle, heavier springs, and shocks. As part of the 4WD off-road package, the HD was available with several skid plates underneath.

The F-350 trucks were only available with 8-foot beds, while the F-250 could be optioned in different ways (crew cab short bed and extended cab short bed). The F-250 HD came with these options for 1996 and 1997 only. The crew cab short-bed and extended cab short-bed trucks are very rare, as they were only produced for a little over a year.

Ninth-Generation Models			
F-Series	**Type**	**Model Year**	**GVWR (pounds)**
F-150	1/2 ton	All years	6,250 max
F-250	3/4 ton	1992–1995	8,300 max
F-250 Heavy Duty	Heavy Duty 3/4 ton	1995–1997	8,800 max
F-350	1 ton	All years	10,000 max
F-Super Duty (chassis cab model only)	1.5 ton plus	All years	16,000 max

Trim Levels

The Nite package, which was introduced for the 1991 model year, returned for 1992 before being replaced with the SVT Lightning for 1993. The Nite package featured an all-black exterior with either a pink or a blue/purple stripe and a Nite decal on the sides of the cargo box. The Nite package was also available on the 1992 Bronco.

The SVT Lightning

In 1993, SVT created the Lightning trim, which was introduced to compete against the Chevrolet 454 SS and GMC Syclone. The team added the following to the standard F-150 to create the Lightning version: heavy-duty suspension, upgraded brakes, a 240-hp version of the 5.8L V8, and an upgraded E4OD overdrive automatic transmission that was originally used behind the higher torque engines such as the 7.3L diesel and 460-ci V8.

Trim Level	Model Year
Custom	1992–1993
XL	1992–1997
XLT	1992–1997
Nite	1990–1992
SVT Lightning	1993–1995
Eddie Bauer	1995–1996, F-150 only
4x4 Offroad	1992–1997

Engines

The 1992 redesign carried over much of the powertrain lineup from the previous generation. The gasoline lineup of the 4.9L inline-6, 5.0L, 5.8L Windsor V8s, and 7.5L V8 were all carried over. A 1993 model year option was the 7.3L (444-ci) International Indirect Diesel Injection (IDI) V8 now turbocharged.

The 1994 model year engine lineup was re-tuned to increase output. Despite sharing identical displacement with its predecessor, the turbocharged Power Stroke/T444E was an all-new design with direct fuel injection.

When the 7.3L T444E (*T* for turbo and *E* for electronic control) Power Stroke was released, it was equipped with the hydraulically actuated electronically controlled unit injector (HEUI) system. This electronic fuel management system was jointly developed by Navistar and Caterpillar.

As before, the 5.0L V8 was not offered above the 8,500-pound GVWR, and the F-Super Duty was offered with the 7.5L gas engine and 7.3L direct-injection (DI) diesel only. The diesels and the 7.5L were offered above the 8,500-pound GVWR only (F-250 HD and heavier). The 4.9L was available in the F-350 through 1996 as a "delete" option.

The 7.3L (T444E) engine was built by Navistar (International Truck and Engine Corporation). The first version was the 6.9L. It used a Stanadyne DB2 distributor-type mechanical fuel injection pump with no electronic control. The first versions of the 7.3L also used the DB2 pump. The 1994 Power Stroke was released with a hydraulically actuated electronic unit injection (HEUI) system.

The HEUI system was jointly developed by Navistar and Caterpillar. Higher injection pressure combined with four valves per cylinder increased performance and fuel economy while lowering emissions due to more complete mixing of fuel and air for better combustion.

In the 1994 model year, Ford sold both the old IDI 7.3L and the new Power Stroke 7.3L DI engines, but after 1994, the old IDI 7.3L engine was discontinued. The key feature of the 7.3L Power Stroke DI engines is the common-rail HEUI system.

This HEUI DI direct injection system combines several technologies that permit the engine to operate with improved efficiency, reduced noise, and lower emissions. This corrected several weak points of the older IDI diesels.

DI permits ignition timing control that was not possible when fuel was injected just after the beginning of the compression stroke, as it was on the IDI 7.3L. Early injection causes the familiar diesel knock and provides time for burned fuel molecules to clump together and create visible exhaust smoke. DI systems require much higher injection pressures; up to 25,000 psi as compared to injection pressures of 15,000 psi in older IDI diesels. DI also permits multiple fuel shots for a single ignition event.

At low and middle engine speeds, there is a pilot injection stage, a small fuel shot at the beginning of the injection event that warms the cylinder and helps initiate the main combustion event. The majority of the fuel required for power production is injected in a large second "main-injection" fuel shot. This two-stage injection, introduced in the 1997 Power Stroke, reduces both exhaust soot and combustion noise.

All Power Stroke engines have a common-rail fuel supply, which is a shared fuel supply rail that feeds the fuel injectors. This permits a simpler high-pressure fuel system through elimination of the fuel distributor and the complex multiple piston high-pressure fuel pump used in the 6.9L and 7.3L IDI engines. Instead of the mechanical timing and advance systems used in older diesels, common-rail designs use a powertrain control module (PCM) controlling hydraulic electrical injectors. PCM control allows the engine designer great flexibility in managing fuel and timing for improved drivability, economy, power, noise, and exhaust emission control.

Why Use an HEUI System for a Diesel Engine?

While common-rail designs are common in gasoline EFI engines and have been around for decades, DI diesels require about 500 times the fuel pressure of a gasoline EFI engine. Opening DI fuel injectors in 1/1000 of a second against pressures up to 25,000 psi takes a great deal of energy. The transistors in high-power circuits like these have to be large, fairly expensive, and well cooled. International's solution for this problem was the HEUI injector control system.

The unique HEUI system relies on a recirculating high-pressure oil supply that drives a large upper piston in each injector. The lower portion of the injector has a small piston in a fuel-filled chamber. When the PCM commands the injector oil valve to open, the upper and lower pistons are pushed down as a unit.

Since the lower piston is very small relative to the upper piston, the pressure on the upper piston is intensified. All of its force is concentrated on the small surface area of the lower piston. The lower piston rams the fuel into the cylinder at an extremely high pressure. The difference in piston diameters allows 4,000-psi oil to produce upward of 25,000 psi in the lower fuel-filled portion of the injector. While controlling the 4,000-psi oil is not as simple as controlling 50-psi gasoline injectors, this approach does take much less electrical power than attempting to control 25,000-psi fuel directly.

1992

The 1992 F-Series received more aerodynamic styling, including new side mirrors. The Flareside design also made a return after a four-year hiatus. There were a number of other changes to the exterior and interior.

Ford celebrated its 75th anniversary of making trucks in model year 1992. To celebrate this event, a special anniversary edition was introduced that consisted of special stripes plus an argent (silver) colored step bumper and 75th anniversary logos. The Econoline was also updated for 1992. It had not had any major changes since 1975, and this update was a welcome modernization.

The 1992 Ford Ranger's STX package came with side graphics. Other changes made to the F-series in 1992 included:

- The hood and front fenders were rounded off to improve aerodynamics.
- A larger grille and headlights with the turn signals below were added.

New interior features included a redesigned dash, easier-to-use instrumentation, and new plusher seats. Extended-cab (Super Cab) models received larger rear side windows.

Instead of the previous classic-style bed, the Flareside bed was now a narrow-body version of the dual rear-wheel bed, where the rear fenders were repositioned to fit the width of the cab.

The changes matched the F-Series with the design of the newly introduced Explorer and redesigned E-Series and Ranger. Along with the exterior updates, the interior received a complete redesign.

GM pickup trucks (Chevrolet and GMC combined) outsold Ford during most of the ninth generation (1992–1996) of the F-Series pickup trucks. Finally, in the 1996 model year, the sales of the F-Series rose to almost 800,000 and exceeded the sales of the GM trucks.

1993

The model year 1993 brought the debut of a high-performance F-150 called the SVT Lightning. The Lightning replaced the short-lived Nite package from the previous generation. Ford's Special Vehicle Team built the Lightning for buyers who wanted the truck utility with the power and handling of a high-performance car. The Lightning model always stayed true to its originally stated mission.

Ford built more than 11,000 240-hp SVT Lightning trucks from 1993 to 1995. Trim level categories were also changing for the 1993 model year, where the XL trim level replaced the Custom trim level.

The Ford Ranger pickup was updated for the first time since it was introduced in 1983.

This is a 1993 F-150 equipped with side rails on the top of the bed and alloy wheels. Notice this truck has two gas tanks, which was not uncommon for trucks of this era. (Photo Courtesy Creative Commons)

1994

The 1994 models brought a slightly updated dashboard plus several safety improvements. There was the addition of a driver-side airbag on F-150s only. A center high-mount stop lamp (CHMSL) and a third brake light were added. Brake-shift interlock and CFC-free (R-134a) air-conditioning were also included.

New options for 1994 included remote keyless entry with alarm, a compact disc (CD) player fitted into the regular stereo system, and a power driver's seat.

Midway through the 1993 model year, the redesigned Ranger added a sporty Splash model to its lineup, including a Flareside bed and special trim. At first offered only as a regular cab, an extended-cab version was added for 1994. Ford-owned Mazda sold its own version of the Ranger as the B-Series, which did not come with a Flareside bed.

In 1994, a flashy Flareside design was offered. This is a 1994 F-150 with a side step. There's a special emblem that says Flareside on the quarter panel over the wheel well. (Photo Courtesy Creative Commons)

The 1994 F-150 received some significant changes to the interior. One of the major safety additions included a driver-side airbag.

The 1993 Ford F-150 Lightning model was introduced on December 15, 1992, by Ford president Ed Hagenlocker. Ford's Special Vehicle Team (SVT) developed the SVT Lightning F-150 and was part of the 1993 model year. Three-time World Champion driver Jackie Stewart was highly involved in fine-tuning the truck's handling.

Jackie Stewart was a highly paid consultant to Ford for many years and was critical of how poorly its cars and trucks handled when he first started. He had many suggestions that were incorporated into the Lightning F-150. Gale Halderman, who rode with him at the Ford test track in Dearborn, was impressed with how he could make any vehicle go fast around turns and corners. When Gale asked him how he does it, Jackie said, "You need to learn to use all four tires on the pavement at all times."

Ford introduced the Lightning to compete with the Chevrolet 454 SS. It also gave Ford skin in the game of sporty, personal-use pickups. The Lightning was built on the same basic platform with the regular F-150 with only a few changes to the vehicle systems.

The Lightning chassis used thicker frame rails from the 4WD F-250 to increase rigidity. A 351-ci (5.8L) Windsor V8 producing 240 hp and 340 ft-lbs of torque replaced the standard F-150 engine. The engine was based on an existing block, but Ford engineers fit it with high–flow rate GT40 heads and a special intake manifold with hypereutectic pistons. These changes helped increase response, output, and durability. The engine was fitted with stainless steel "shorty" headers. Other changes and features included:

- A heavy-duty version of the Ford E4OD automatic transmission was the only transmission available in the Lightning.
- An aluminum driveshaft was used to reduce rotational inertia and connected it to a 4.10:1 limited-slip rear differential.
- The suspension height was lowered 1 inch in the front and 2.5 inches in the rear compared to a stock F-150.
- The suspension also featured front and rear anti-roll bars and a special leaf in the rear, tipped with a rubber snubber that acted as a ladder bar and controlled rear wheel hop during hard acceleration.
- Special 17-inch aluminum wheels with Firestone Firehawk tires were used.
- Lightning badging, a front air dam with fog lamps, and a 120 mph (190 km/h) speedometer all differentiated the Lightning from normal F-150s.
- Bucket seats featuring adjustable side bolsters and lumbar supports were part of the Lightning package.

Ford SVT created a performance-oriented F-150 called the Lightning. The F-150 Lightning debuted in 1993. (Photo Courtesy Ford Motor Company)

The SVT Lightning had its own engine. This 1993 Lightning had a 351-ci (5.8L) Windsor V8 producing 240 hp (179 kW) and 340 ft-lbs of torque. Ford engineers fit it with high–flow rate GT40 heads and a special intake manifold with hypereutectic pistons to increase response, output, and durability. (Photo Courtesy Richard Truesdell)

The SVT Lightning was built on the same platform as the F-150 with several modifications. The badging was more vibrant and emphasized the high-performance capabilities of this truck. (Photo Courtesy Richard Truesdell)

1995

The biggest addition to the 1995 model year was the Eddie Bauer trim added to the F-Series. This was, to date, the most luxurious trim offered in an F-150. The Eddie Bauer trim had already been introduced on the Ford Explorer.

Also newly available that year was a flexible-fuel version (FFV) that could run on a mixture of gasoline and ethanol, a fuel made from corn. There was an optional 7.3L Power Stroke Turbo Diesel engine available for the F-250 Super Duty. This was the first year for this engine offering, which produced 210 hp and 425 ft-lbs of torque, making this a favorite for those who needed to haul.

Ford offered a new minivan for the 1995 model year called the Windstar. This front-wheel-drive people mover was initially intended to replace the aging Aerostar. The Aerostar's continued popularity made it the Windstar's running mate until finally being retired after 1997.

1996

For 1996, the F-150 was a complete carryover, except for engines and exhaust emission control. Ford was in the final stages of creating the next generation of F-Series, mostly in response to the growing competition, especially from Chrysler via the Dodge Ram. The 1996 model year would be the final year of the Eddie Bauer trim for the F-150.

A Mercury version of the Ford Explorer, the Mercury Mountaineer, was equipped with unique trim and only available with a V8 engine. Ford spent a lot of time, money, and effort developing these vehicles, giving them sleek styling intended to take them into the 21st century.

A beautiful two-tone 1996 F-250 with an 8-foot bed was 235 inches long and 79 inches high. The 1996 F-250 had a maximum GVW of 8,300 pounds. (Photo Courtesy Wyatt Kaenel)

The F-250s and the F-350s of this era came with several V8 and diesel engine options. Special off-road packages were also available with special skid plates. The 3/4-ton truck was available with five trim levels. (Photo Courtesy Wyatt Kaenel)

Those with towing needs often opted for the 3/4-ton F-250, which had a lot more towing capability. (Photo Courtesy Wyatt Kaenel)

This 1996 F-150 features the spare tire mounted in the bed instead of under the bed of the truck. This was the last year of the ninth generation, as Ford was preparing to launch a redesign of the F-Series. The redesign was partially due to the success of the Dodge Ram pickup truck during this time. (Photo Courtesy Creative Commons)

Conclusion

The ninth-generation F-Series would soon be replaced as the competition tightened. The pickup truck segment was now the best-selling segment in the automotive industry. It had every executive's attention. The race for SUVs to be built, as well as pickup trucks that appealed to the masses, was on.

Ford spent years trying to hold onto its best-selling crown. As important as the ninth generation was for Ford, its next move would have to be perfectly executed. The next generation of Ford's pickup truck needed to be a winner!

Year	Engine	Horsepower (hp)	Torque (ft-lbs)	VIN Code
1992	300-ci (4.9L) inline 6-cylinder	145	265 at 2,000 rpm	Y
	302-ci (5.0L) V8	185	270 at 2,400 rpm	N
	351-ci (5.8L) V8	210	315 at 2,800 rpm	H
	446-ci (7.3L) diesel V8	180	345 at 1,400 rpm	M
	460-ci (7.5L) V8	230	390 at 2,200 rpm	G
1993	300-ci (4.9L) inline 6-cylinder	145	265 at 2,000 rpm	Y
	302-ci (5.0L) V8	185	270 at 2,400 rpm	N
	351-ci (5.8L) V8	200	310 at 2,800 rpm	H
	351-ci (5.8L) V8 (Lightning)	240	310 at 2,800 rpm	R
	446-ci (7.3L) diesel V8	180	345 at 1,400 rpm	M
	460-ci (7.5L) V8	230	390 at 2,200 rpm	G
1994	300-ci (4.9L) inline 6-cylinder	150	260 at 2,000 rpm	Y
	302-ci (5.0L) V8	205	275 at 3,000 rpm	N
	351-ci (5.8L) V8	210	325 at 2,800 rpm	H
	351-ci (5.8L) V8 (Lightning)	240	310 at 2,800 rpm	R
	444/5-ci (7.3L) diesel V8 (Turbo Diesel)	190	390 rated	F
	460-ci (7.5L) V8	245	395 at 2,400 rpm	G
1995	300-ci (4.9L) inline 6-cylinder	150	260–265 at 2,000 rpm	Y
	302-ci (5.0L) V8	195–205	270–275 at 3,000 rpm	N
	351-ci (5.8L) V8	210	325 at 2,800 rpm	H
	351-ci (5.8L) V8 (Lightning)	240	310 at 2,800 rpm	R
	445-ci (7.3L) diesel V8 (Power Stroke Turbo Diesel)	210	425 at 2,000 rpm	F
	460-ci (7.5L) V8	245	395 at 2,400 rpm	G
1996	300-ci (4.9L) inline 6-cylinder	150	260–265 at 2,000 rpm	Y
	302-ci (5.0L) V8	195–205	270–275 at 3,000 rpm	N
	351-ci (5.8L) V8	210	325 at 2,800 rpm	H
	445-ci (7.3L) diesel V8 (Power Stroke Turbo Diesel)	210	425 at 2,000 rpm	F
	460-ci (7.5L) V8	245	395 at 2,400 rpm	G
1997	256-ci (4.2L) V6	205	225 at 3,000 rpm	2
	281-ci (4.6L) V8	220	290 at 3,250 rpm	W or 6
	330-ci (5.4L) V8 (Triton)	235	330 at 3,000 rpm	L
	351-ci (5.8L) V8	210	325 at 2,800 rpm	H
	445-ci (7.3L) diesel V8 (Power Stroke Turbo Diesel)	210	425 at 2,000 rpm	F
	460-ci (7.5L) V8	245	395 at 2,400 rpm	G

Note: Information included in this chart is designed to be inclusive. Dependent upon reference, year, and carryover, information may vary.

Note: From 1992 to 1997, the engine VIN is the eighth character listed.

Color	Available Year and VIN Code					
	1992	1993	1994	1995	1996	1997
Pawnee Tan	AV	AV	AV	AV	–	–
Dark Chestnut Metallic	A8	–	–	–	–	–
Light Prairie Tan Metallic	–	–	–	–	–	BA
Chrome Yellow	–	BZ	BZ	BZ	–	–
Medium Palomino Metallic	–	–	CB	CB	–	–
Dark Chestnut Metallic	CE	CE	CE	CE	–	–
Cayman Metallic	DA	DA	DA	DA	–	–
Light Mocha	DB	DB	–	–	–	–
Medium Mocha Metallic	DC or DJ	DC or DJ	DC or DJ	DJ	DJ	–
Mocha Frost Metallic	DD	DD	DD	DD	–	–
Pumice Metallic	–	–	–	–	DK	–
Dark Mocha Metallic	DW	DW	DW	DW	–	–
Light Saddle Metallic	–	–	–	–	DY or DZ	DY or
Currant Red	EC	EC	EC	EC	–	–
Electric Currant Red Metallic	EG	EG	EG	EG	–	–
Medium Cabernet	EH	EH	–	–	–	–
Wild Strawberry Metallic	EL	EL	–	–	–	–
Midnight Red Metallic	–	–	–	–	EN	–
Vermillion	EP or E4	EP or E4	EP or E4	EP or E4	EP or E4	E4
Medium Cranberry Metallic	–	–	–	EX		
Performance Red	EY	EY	EY	–	–	–
Sunrise Red Pearl Metallic	FC	FC	FC	–	–	–
Toreador Red Pearl Metallic	–	–	–	–	FL	–
Toreador Red Metallic	–	–	–	–	FN	FN
Vermont Green Metallic	–	–	–	–	F7	F7
Medium Aubergine Metallic	GA	GA	GA	GA	–	–
Iris Metallic	GC	GC	GC	GC	–	–
Bright Sapphire Metallic	–	–	–	JA	JA	–
Desert Violet Pearl	–	–	–	–	JC	–
Lapis Metallic	KE	KE	KE	KE	–	–
Medium Lapis Metallic	–	KG	KG	KG	–	KG
Indigo Blue Metallic	–	–	–	–	KK	–
Dark Lapis Metallic	–	KH or KN	KH or KN	KH or KN	–	–
Royal Blue Metallic	–	–	–	–	KM	–
Indigo Blue Metallic	–	–	–	–	KT or KU	KU
Bimini Blue Metallic	K3	K3	K3	–	–	–

...or	Available Year and VIN Code					
	1992	1993	1994	1995	1996	1997
...dium Royal Blue ...allic	LA	LA	LA	LA	–	–
...al Blue Metallic	–	–	–	–	LC or LE	LE
...t Crystal Blue ...allic	MA	MA	MA	–	–	–
...eberry Metallic	–	–	–	–	MB	–
...t Smoke Metallic	MK or ZJ	MC or ZJ	MC	MC	–	–
...ight Blue Metallic	–	MK	MK	–	–	–
...oke Metallic	MS	MS	MS	MS	–	–
...ht Regatta Blue ...allic	MW or ZK	MW	–	–	–	–
...k Shadow Blue ...allic	MX	MX	–	–	–	–
...k Tourmaline ...allic	NA	NA	NA	NA	NB or ND	NB
...el Green Metallic	PB	PB	PB	PB	–	–
...f Blue Metallic	PC	PC or PD	PC	PC	PC	–
...dium Calypso ...en Metallic	–	–	PL	PL	PL	–
...fic Green ...allic	–	–	–	–	PS	PS
...ypso Green ...allic	–	–	–	–	PT	PT
...ht Calypso ...allic	PM	PM	PM	PM	–	–
...dium Platinum ...allic	RC	RC	RC	RC	RC	RC
... Metallic	–	–	–	–	RD	RD
...ow Frost Pearl	–	–	–	–	SD	–
...t Willow Metallic	–	–	–	–	SL	–
...dium Willow ...allic	–	–	–	SH	–	–
...dium Graphite ...allic	–	–	–	TR	–	–
...er Frost Metallic	–	–	–	–	TS	TS
...k Ebony	UA	UA	UA	UA	UA	UA
...ny	–	–	–	–	–	UD
...k Toreador Red ...l	–	–	–	–	UF	JL
...dium Opal ...allic	WC	WC	WC or WM	WC or WM	WO	WO
...t Opal Metallic	–	–	–	–	WE	–

Ford Light- and Light/Medium-Duty Truck Paint Colors CONTINUED

Color	Available Year and VIN Code					
	1992	1993	1994	1995	1996	1997
Ultra-Red	WH	WH	WH or WA	WH	–	–
Performance White	–	–	–	–	WT	–
Green	W7	W7	W7	W7	–	–
Portofino Metallic	–	–	–	–	XC	XC
Light Santa Fe Metallic	–	–	XD	XD	–	–
Black	YC	YC	YC	YC	YC	–
Medium Titanium Pearl Metallic	YG	YG	YG	–	–	–
Silver Metallic	YN	YN	YN	YN	–	–
Oxford White	YO or YZ	YO or YZ	YO or YZ	YO or YZ	YO or YZ	YO or YZ
White	YY	YY	YY	YY	YY	–
Colonial White	–	–	–	–	ZM	ZT
Ultra-White	–	–	–	ZR	–	–

Note: Information included in this chart is designed to be inclusive. Dependent upon reference, year, and carryover, information may vary.

Note: For 1992 to 1997, paint color is listed on a VIN tag located on the driver-side doorjamb as "EXTERIOR PAINT."

Ford Light- and Light/Medium-Duty Truck Transmissions (1992–1997)

Year	Model	Automatic/ Manual	Number of Gears	Transmission
1992–1997	F-150	Manual	5	Standard (Overdrive)
1992–1997	F-150	Manual	5	Optional
1992	F-150	Manual	4	Optional
1992–1997	F-150	Automatic	3	Optional
1992–1997	F-150	Automatic	4	Overdrive (AOD-E)
1992–1997	F-150	Automatic	4	Overdrive (E4OD)
1992–1997	F-250	Manual	5	Standard (Overdrive)
1992–1997	F-250	Manual	5	Optional
1992	F-250	Manual	4	Optional
1992–1997	F-250	Automatic	3	Optional
1992–1997	F-250	Automatic	4	Overdrive (AOD-E)
1992–1997	F-250	Automatic	4	Overdrive (E4OD)

Note: Information included in this chart is designed to be inclusive. Dependent upon reference, year, and carryover, information may vary.

Ford Light- and Light/Medium-Duty Truck Sales and Prices (1992–1997)

Year	Model	Wheelbase (inches)	Length (inches)	Bed Length (feet)	Height (inches)	Width (inches)	Gross Vehicle Weight (pounds)	Price	Number Manufactured
1992–1997	Ford F-150 1/2 ton	117–163	197–244	6.75/8	71–74	79–80	4,800–6,250	$10,921–$27,735	2,258,984*
1992–1997	Ford F-250 3/4 ton	133–172	213–235	6.75/8	79	79–80	6,800–8,800	$14,476–$28,025	696,947**

Note: Information included in this chart is designed to be inclusive. Dependent upon reference, year, and carryover, information may vary.

Note that price is based on MSRP listing.

Note the 1994–1996 F-250 offered HDE models with GVWs of 9,000 to 10,000 pounds.

* Is a total of all F-150 1/2-ton Styleside and Flareside body, bed, engine, and cab types.

** Is a total of all F-250 3/4-ton Styleside body, bed, engine, and cab types excluding HDE models.

FORD F-SERIES TENTH GENERATION (1997–2004)

One could argue that the tenth-generation F-Series might be the most influential one in the history of the F-Series. If not, it certainly ranks in the top three. To say that the tenth generation was a hurried response to the Dodge Ram's successful new full-size pickup truck, which former Ford vice president Hal Sperlich helped launch and develop, is unfair and represents an incomplete picture of what was going on at Ford during this time.

The Ram had Ford's attention, but the tenth generation was in the works before the Ram's success, according to Jim Bulin, who was a product planner working in the Ford Truck Studio at this time. The tenth generation was known at Ford as the PN-96. This was the most ambitious and radical transformation for the F-Series, as it included changes to the exterior, interior, and chassis. Work on the tenth generation started in the late 1980s.

The timing was perfect to radically change the best-selling vehicle at Ford. Certainly, the risk was there too. The Baby Boomers, who had been consistent buyers of Ford products all along, now had children who had families and were active consumers. Ford felt confident in giving the Boomers a truck that was appealing to their work ethic and mindset. During this time, the aging Boomer market helped spur the growth of the minivan segment and the emerging SUV market. Ford did not want to forget about the Boomers, especially since many of them had a lot of disposable income.

The housing market was bustling again, along with the stock market. The Tech Boom that started early in the 1990s was still going, although the dot-com bubble would soon burst. President Bill Clinton, who was also a Baby Boomer, was in his second term. As the Boomers inched toward financial freedom and retirement, they wanted trucks to pull boats and recreational vehicles. Meanwhile, their children also found trucks appealing.

The tenth generation spanned from model year 1997 until 2004. During this time, both Flareside and Styleside bodies were offered. (Photo Courtesy Creative Commons)

The tenth-generation F-150 debuted in 1997. This 1997 F-150 pictured in this Ford advertisement focuses on the F-150 as a fleet truck to be used by businesses. (Photo Courtesy Ford Motor Company)

It was Jim Bulin, along with others at Ford, who put this knowledge to work during the development of the tenth generation. Bulin developed a strategy based around demographics to work with designers. Bulin said, "We developed a way of crawling inside the heads and hearts of tomorrow's customers." The concept was called Value Groups Strategy. At the core of this was looking at the mindset and buying habits of everyone who might buy a Ford truck. This included the Baby Boomers but also included the post Boomers who were more into SUVs and smaller cars. And of course, the Baby Boomers' children were a key cog in the Value Groups Strategy.

These Gen-Xers shared many of the Boomers' same values but also had their own independence and preferences. This market was still forming, and Bulin and the F-150 designers were able to perfectly capture them with the tenth generation. Using demographic knowledge and consumer buying habit research, Bulin was able to convince Ford executives and truck designers that the tenth generation had to be leaner and more muscular but also more luxurious than it had ever been.

Andy Jacobson was design director of trucks in 1989, when the tenth generation began development. He confirms that Bulin's approach was integral in the truck's success and that the designers used that information from the very early sketches on through the clay modeling.

"The development process we used was entirely different, as we talked a lot with the customers to find out what had set their life values per age segments and transposed that into what they would like or might use on the truck and design both interior and exterior with that knowledge in mind," Jacobson said.

"The PN-96 was virtually the first F-Series since the 1953–1956 model that customers would consider good enough in its appearance to be a personal truck. The F-Series pickup was no longer confined solely to the role of a work truck, but was seen to be worthy of becoming something you would like to show up in at a social function as a personal vehicle. The smoother shapes made that possible as well as the improved interior ergonomics," he said.

Part of this mindset change involved expanding the seating capacity to include a three-passenger bench seat with extended cab. The Super Cab, which featured a rear-hinged back door on the passenger's side, was created as part of the tenth generation, and it was very well received. The doors were hinged at the rear and could only be opened after the corresponding front door was opened.

Later in the tenth generation, the F-150 would get four doors officially. Jacobson said that the "half door" presented significant design challenges. "Access to the larger opening posed a problem. With the addition of the third door, we had no B-pillar," Jacobson recalled. "Eventually, there was a fourth door added, which helped facilitate easy ingress and egress."

All told, the tenth-generation Ford F-Series is historically significant as one of the most transformational vehicles and redesigns in Ford's history.

Changes and Features

The tenth generation of the F-Series line of pickup trucks produced by Ford was sold in model years 1997 to 2004. In a major product shift in the Ford truck lineup, the F-250 and F-350 were split off from the F-150. In Mexico, the

From 2000 to 2012, Ford partnered with motorcycle manufacturer Harley-Davidson to create a special-edition Harley-Davidson F-Series. It was available as both an F-150 and an F-250.

PN-96

In late 1989, Ford began the PN-96 Program on a new truck platform. Thomas Baughman was assigned as chief engineer. He worked closely with Jim Bulin, who had conducted extensive generation consumer-buying research as part of the PN-96 project. The PN-96 was Ford's most ambitious undertaking in years and the most radical to happen to the F-Series in decades, if not ever.

Bulin's data showed two key buying groups, both with very different wants and expectations of a pickup truck. Ford had successfully used focus groups in the past, including for the launch of the Ford Mustang. Focus groups and demographics were nothing new to Ford, but this was the first time it was ever done with pickup trucks. Prior to this, they would just make minor to semi-major changes from year to year with the F-Series. Sometimes even the new generations weren't that radical. But the PN-96 was different; it was a major undertaking.

As the PN-96 was displayed to various groups ranging in age from their early 20s to their late 60s, the drastic change in appearance received a lukewarm reception. Despite the disapproval from some of the focus groups toward softer styling, Ford management backed the more aerodynamic design philosophy that had Bulin's and Jacobson's endorsements. Bulin's research showed drastic changes were needed.

"The basic pickup truck design had not really changed for an entire generation," Bulin said. So naturally, having some pushback to such a radical change was to be expected. The end result that Bulin reached with designers in November 1992 (and was prepared for production in February 1993), took the aerodynamic styling further with a rounded nose on the new F-Series.

"The PN-96 was my favorite vehicle during my entire career at Ford," Jacobson said. "It was no longer just a work truck but was able to enter the personal use market successfully."

According to Bulin, production work began in earnest in 1995 for the 1996 model year. There would be a huge promotional push for this truck, which was all part of the product launch that Bulin and others came up with. There was even an ad placed on TV during Super Bowl XXX. Bulin said that marketing executives were concerned that it would not be well received by the traditional truck buyers. As such, the previous 1996 would be produced simultaneously for several months. Indeed, many Ford executives' jobs were on the line if the PN-96 was a failure. Bulin admitted it was a stressful time for all in the truck studio.

Sales of the F-150 surged in the tenth generation from 750,000 to more than 900,000 in 2001. Products from General Motors and Chrysler Corporation lagged behind Ford. The PN-96 saw mass appeal with both Baby Boomers, who still made up two-thirds of the truck buying segment, and the younger crowd, who found it incredibly luxurious and perfect for their young families. The new F-150 was *Motor Trend* magazine's Truck of the Year in 1997. Eventually, Ford's sales dropped for the final years of the tenth generation as the redesigned Dodge trucks were released.

tenth-generation F-150 was rebranded as the Ford *Lobo* from 2004 to 2010, until it was replaced by the twelfth-generation model. The heavy-duty pickups (Ford F-250 HD and F-350) were redesigned in the 1999 model year. Both Flareside and Styleside beds were offered.

Grilles came in either body color or chrome, depending on trim level. Power came from a trio of new engines: a 4.2L overhead-valve V6 and overhead cam V8s of 4.6 and 5.4 liters. All produced more horsepower than the larger engines they replaced. Ford entered the new F-150 in the NASCAR Craftsman Truck Series. It also partnered with motorcycle manufacturer Harley-Davidson to make a special Harley-Davidson F-150 from 2000 to 2012.

Trim

The trim levels for the tenth-generation F-Series included XL (base), XLT (mid-grade), and Lariat (highest level).

A variety of body options were available for the tenth generation: the two–three passenger regular cab and the five–six passenger Super Cab, 8- and 6.5-foot beds, and a choice of Styleside or Flareside beds on the 6.5-foot models. A new Lightning package was introduced in March 1999, and Harley-Davidson and King Ranch versions were also created for the 2000 and 2001 model years, respectively. A Sport 4WD model was introduced in 2000 and used the 5.4L Triton V8 and color-matched bumpers and mirror housings. It was available in regular cab and Super Cab in four colors: white, red, black, and silver.

In 2002, an FX4 model was introduced, which came with skid plates, a carbon steel frame, Rancho shock absorbers, and unique 17-inch aluminum wheels, along with more standard features that were optional on the XLT.

A new trim level, the STX, was introduced to appeal to younger buyers. This trim level included the following features:

- Color-keyed front and rear bumpers
- Clear lens headlights plus integrated round fog lamps
- Chrome step rails
- 17-inch chrome wheels
- A Kenwood Z828 stereo installed in place of the standard Ford radio

In 2003, a special trim package "Heritage Edition" version with special badging was produced to mark the 100th anniversary of Ford trucks, which was available only in the 139-inch wheelbase Super Cab model.

Safety Issues

This generation F-150 received an overall poor rating from the Insurance Institute for Highway Safety (IIHS) in the frontal offset test. It was ranked the Second Worst Performing Vehicle behind the 1997–2005 GM U-Platform minivans.

Ford had found that the cruise control system in many of its trucks could catch fire because the switch system would corrode over time, overheat, and ignite. This ignition was later blamed on spillage from the adjacent master cylinder. On March 5, 2007, Ford recalled 155,000 2003 full-size pickups and full-size SUVs for the defective ignition part. During the previous two years, Ford had recalled 5.8 million vehicles because of the defective cruise control systems in trucks, SUVs, and vans. That recall was one of the largest in history at the time, covering 1994–2002 model years.

Powertrain

The all-new 1997 chassis shared only the transmissions with the previous generation. A 4.2L OHV V6, based on Ford's 3.8L Essex V6, replaced the 4.9L OHV I6, while 4.6L and 5.4L SOHC V8s replaced the 5.0L and 5.8L OHV V8s. The 4.6L Modular V8 shared with the cars was optional (with a 5.4L version added in mid-1997); originally developed for use in the F-Series, the Modular/Triton V8.

Throughout the tenth generation, Ford offered several variants of the V8 Triton engine, including a 4.6L and 5.4L. (Photo Courtesy Randy Stern)

Transmissions

The transmissions offered included a 4-speed 4R70W automatic, a 4-speed E4OD automatic, a 4-speed 4R100 automatic, a 5-speed M5OD-R2 manual, and a 6-speed 6R automatic.

Engines

The 4.6L and 5.4L V8s were marketed under the name Triton, and they marked the first use of Ford's Modular Single Overhead Cam (SOHC) engines in the F-Series pickups. Ford's own 8.8:1 IFS front axle replaced the Dana 44 front end, while the Ford 8.8:1 rear remained. In 2000, the Sterling 10.25:1 axle became an option.

This is a 5.8L V8 engine. It has twin intake hoses from the air filter to the twin throttle body. Ford offered this engine throughout the tenth generation on F-250s and even F-350s. (Photo Courtesy Richard Truesdell)

Ford split the F-Series product line into two separate entities, making the F-150 more universal for a wider audience while reinventing the F-250 and F-350 for the weekend warrior and the traditional truck buyer. This 1997 F-250 maintains the original body style look of the previous generation. Ford would transition the F-250 and F-350 onto the tenth-generation platform in 1998.

DIESEL ENGINES

The 7.3L (444 ci) Power Stroke was replaced by the 6.0L (365 ci) beginning in the second quarter of the 2003 model year. The 6.0L Power Stroke was used in Ford Super Duty trucks until the 2007 model year, but they lasted until 2009 in the Ford Econoline vans (model year 2010). They were also used in the Ford Excursion SUVs until after the 2005 models, when Ford discontinued Excursion production in the US.

The 6.0L had a 3.74-inch (95-mm) bore and 4.13-inch (105-mm) stroke, creating a displacement of 365 ci (6.0L) or 5,954 cc. It used a variable geometry turbocharger and intercooler, producing 325 hp (242 kW) and 570 ft-lbs (773 Nm) of torque with an 18:1 compression ratio, with fuel cutoff at 4,200 rpm.

The key feature of the Gen II 6.0L Power Stroke injectors was that they were electrically triggered open and remained open until electrically closed. These injectors have extremely fast response time: millionths of a second. Injector response is so fast that up to seven injection stages can be timed into a single injection event. Gen II injectors are identified by a four-wire injector connector instead of the earlier two-wire design. Responding to field issues, Ford and International extensively redesigned the Gen II 6.0L fuel system halfway through model year 2004. The 6.0L was replaced by the International/Navistar 6.4L MaxxForce 7 engine in 2008.

1997

For 1997, the F-150 was completely redesigned. The traditional Twin I-Beam front suspension was replaced with a fully independent front suspension (IFS).

With this redesign, the F-Series pickup line was essentially split in two. The company decided to make the F-150 a contemporary vehicle for personal use, while the F-250 and F-350 retained the previous generation's conservative styling for work-based customers.

The F-250 increased load capability due to a heavy-duty rear axle and load-leveling rear suspension. During the second half of the 1997 model year, Ford introduced a heavier GVWR version (8,800 GVW), bearing the F-250 Heavy Duty (HD) name. It was distinguished by seven–lug nut wheels. The F-250 HD was in the same series as the F-350 (same bodystyle as the 1992 to 1997 model years) built in South America only.

Only 3,000 of these special-edition NASCAR F-150s were made in 1998. They came with special floor mats and seats. There was a special NASCAR checkered-flag emblem on the side and the truck had a lowered suspension. The owner of this truck swapped the street wheels for those from a Harley-Davidson edition. (Photo Courtesy Justin Chesnik)

1998

While this model year was nothing more than some minor changes and updates, 1998 represented Ford's 50th anniversary of the F-Series. Ford made a limited-edition 50th anniversary F-150 that is considered a collector truck. The front end of the 1998 F-150 had a slightly different appearance, and the back window of the Super Cab was slightly modified with more of a darker tint.

1999

Model year 1999 saw several changes to the F-150 but also to the F-250/350 lines. The 1999 F-150 had a new bumper and a new-look grille. While it wasn't significant, the changes were

The redesign of the tenth generation started in 1997, with the F-150 trying to get as contemporary of a look as possible. Ford wanted to shake the persona of looking too much like "old trucks" with the stylish design cues created for these trucks. (Photo Courtesy Creative Commons)

noticeable enough to garner excitement during the third year of the tenth generation. To improve rear-seat access for F-150 Super Cab models, a rear-hinged door on the passenger's side only was added to all versions.

The F-250 and F-350 pickups were introduced as the 1999 Ford F-Series Super Duty model line, completely separating these heavier trucks from the F-150 once and for all. This may not seem significant, but it showed a major pivot in Ford's mentality and production, separating the 150 from the bigger 250/350. These trucks would be treated differently from this point forward with different design details, different bodies, and different engines.

One of the designers who worked on the Super Duty, Bill Moraniec, said, "The 1999 all-new Super Duty team was energized from the beginning. The Design Studio was increased in size to allow for additional studio engineering and modeling support." Moraniec said this was a big change in the way things had been done prior. "Exterior and Interior Design and Modeling was combined in the same studio to create a more efficient means of communication, enabling the sharing of package information for design and clay modeling development."

Jacobson recalls using the same customer-based information they had from the PN-96 F-150 focus groups to improve things on the Super Duty product line. "We used everything we learned about the customer and extrapolated that information to develop the completely unique F-250/350 that was released as a 1999 model," Jacobson said. "It required minimal market research and also went on to become a very successful model."

In 1999, Ford released the second-generation SVT Lightning. It was powered by a 5.4L Triton V8 engine with forged internals and an Eaton Roots-type supercharger, making 360 hp and 440 ft-lbs of torque that was good for low-14-second quarter-mile times. The truck also featured a lowered ride height, bigger brakes, specially calibrated shocks, and a pair of beefy anti-sway bars. Special trim and instrumentation rounded out the package. More than 28,000 were produced from 1999–2004.

Also, in 1999, Lincoln-Mercury gained its first full-size pickup truck since 1968 with the introduction of the Lincoln Blackwood, the first Lincoln pickup. Due to very poor sales, the Blackwood was discontinued after 2002.

2000

The tenth generation continued its evolution toward family-friendly production. In February 2000, the Super Crew was added to the lineup early in the 2001 model year, entering production on December 13, 1999.

The Super Crew was focused on passenger comfort, with seating for six people total. It blended roomy comfort with rugged capability. The Super Crew was only available in the top-of-the-line Lariat trim.

Model year 2000 was the first year for the special-edition F-150 Harley-Davidson. The Harley-Davidson F-150 was available only in black and only on the Super Cab Flareside initially. The first year of this special truck became quite collectible. The 20-inch wheels were the first time Ford put wheels this size on a production vehicle.

2001

In 2001, the F-150 became the first pickup truck in its size segment to become available with four full-size doors. The four-door pickup truck was an instant success with sales jumping more than 50 percent. Many customers wanted to trade in their late-model F-150 just to get the four doors.

Sharing the length of a standard-bed Super Cab, the F-150 Super Crew was produced with a slightly shortened bed. The Super Crew with four doors became the most popular version of the 2001 F-150.

Model year 2001 saw the launch of a new trim. The super-luxurious King Ranch trim was initially only offered on the Super Crew. Some of the features of the King Ranch included:

- Front and rear leather captain-style seats
- King Ranch logo embossed in leather on the headrests and center console
- King Ranch–exclusive painted aluminum wheels
- Two-tone paint schemes that are exclusive to the King Ranch trim
- Special King Ranch fenders

2002

Ford launched an off-road-ready package called the FX4. This package was geared toward a younger buyer, whereas the King Ranch was geared toward a more mature consumer.

This is a beautiful 2002 F-150 that is all stock except for the fiberglass bed cover, dual exhaust, and lowered height. This truck has the 4.6L V8 engine. One of the most attractive design features on the 2002 F-150 is the side step notch behind the passenger's door of this two-door truck. The rounded taillights are quite attractive on this sport trim. (Photo Courtesy Mike Redkey)

SECOND-GENERATION LIGHTNING (1999–2004)

The performance-based SVT Lightning received a redesign, and a second generation was released and revised for production from 1999 to 2004. In 1999, after a three-year hiatus, Ford SVT released a new Ford Lightning powered by a modular SOHC 16-valve 5.4L Triton V8 engine, producing 360 hp at 4,750 rpm and 440 ft-lbs of torque at 3,250 rpm using a factory-installed Eaton supercharger. Other features included:

- 4R100 automatic transmission
- Rear gear ratio of 3.55:1
- 18-inch wheels and Goodyear Eagle F1 295/45ZR-18 tires

The suspension system was modified from the standard F-150 to lower the truck 1 inch in the front and 2 inches in the rear. It retained the front short- and long-arm system with coil springs and a 31-mm solid stabilizer bar along with the rear solid axle with five-leaf springs and a 2-mm (1-inch) solid stabilizer bar. Monroe shocks were used from 1999 to 2001 and then replaced with Bilstein shocks from 2002 to 2004.

For the 2001 model year, the engine design was slightly altered to produce 380 hp at 4,750 rpm and 450 ft-lbs at 3,250 rpm. The intercooler was redesigned to reduce leaking problems. There was a federal recall for earlier models to address this problem. The SOHC 16-valve 5.4L Triton engine used a cast-iron block instead of aluminum. These upgrades were critical in order to support the 8 psi (0.55 bar) of boost delivered from the stock Eaton M112 roots supercharger.

Later in the 2003 model year, the engine was modified again to resolve a lack of sufficient threads in the cylinder heads for spark plugs. The engine still had some cold-morning piston slap (mild knocking noise while the engine is cold).

At the other end of the drivetrain, the final drive ratio was reduced to 3.73:1 with a 9.75-inch rear end in 2001. The specially developed 295/45ZR-18 Goodyear Eagle F1-GS unidirectional tires were upgraded using a new-generation F1 GS rubber compound. For 2003, the Lightning's cargo capacity was raised from 800 pounds (360 kg) to 1,350 pounds (610 kg).

The second-generation Lightning was initially offered in just bright red, black, and white. In 2002, True Blue, a very dark blue, was offered but replaced with a lighter Sonic Blue in 2003. The 2003 model year also saw the introduction of the Dark Shadow Gray color. For 2002, the second-generation Lightning was manufactured at Ford's Canada Truck Facility in Oakville, Ontario, until its closure.

Lightning Specs				
Year	Engine	Power	Torque	Production
1999		360 hp at	440 ft-lbs at	4,000
2000	5.4L	4,750 rpm	3,250 rpm	4,966
2001	Super-			6,381
2002	charged	380 hp at	450 ft-lbs at	4,726
2003	Triton V8	4,750 rpm	3,250 rpm	4,270
2004				3,781

Following the success of the first generation, Ford's SVT released a second generation of the F-150 Lightning. Initially, the Lightning was only offered in black, white, or red exterior paint. (Photo Courtesy Richard Truesdell)

SVT Lightnings had 18-inch performance wheels. The F-150 Lightning was also lowered by 1 inch in the front and 2 inches in the back. (Photo Courtesy Richard Truesdell)

Ford sold about 4,000 special edition SVT Lightning F-150s per year during the performance truck's second generation. (Photo Courtesy Richard Truesdell)

The F-150 Lightning had a modular SOHC 16-valve 5.4L Triton V8 engine. It produced 360 hp and 440 ft-lbs of torque. (Photo Courtesy Richard Truesdell)

The interior of a 2002 F-150 two-door Sport trim is stock except for the added black rubber floor mat. The interior is basic, as this truck was more about rugged abilities than top-of-the-line luxury like other trucks in this generation and model year. (Photo Courtesy Mike Redkey)

This shows how the tenth generation tried to be everything to everyone. This model year really did represent the vast range and appeal of the F-Series. The King Ranch trim was offered for Super Cab as well as the Super Crew lines.

2003

The 2003 F-150 was a carryover F-Series from 2002. Ford also built a limited run of Heritage F-150s of the 2003 bodystyle in late 2003 as 2004 models to finish out production. This generation of F-150 was sold in Mexico until the twelfth-generation 2010 model was released there.

The Heritage trim was an homage to the F-150's success as the best-selling truck for 25 years straight. Following government safety regulations and also showing its focus on families, the 2003 F-150 came standard with child LATCH car seat attachment.

Conclusion

The late 1990s represented one of the most exciting times in Ford truck history. The 50th anniversary of the F-Series happened, and the 25th anniversary of Ford's truck being the top-selling pickup in the market occurred. Ford was living up to the Built Ford Tough marketing slogan.

The F-Series was a brand and a recognized name; almost as much as Ford's blue oval logo. Ford capitalized on all this with a successful rebuild/rebrand of the F-Series. The F-150 split apart from the bigger F-250/350 permanently. The new-look F-Series had mass appeal.

According to Andrew Jacobson, this was as intended. With market research in hand, the designers of the tenth generation were able to build a truck that was more streamlined, modern, family-friendly, and car-like, all while appealing to the old-school truck buyers too. That's some accomplishment!

Jacobson said, "We had tremendous support from the vice president of All Trucks, Ed Hagenlocker, who believed in what we were doing and the approach we took to develop the truck. The very top of the house did get a little nervous when the New Dodge Ram took off and became so well received," Jacobson recalls. "Those concerns were quickly put aside when the F-Series was released in the third quarter of 1995 and turned out to be the most successful vehicle ever introduced by Ford."

The 2003 F-150 was mostly a carryover from the 2002 model year. This was the last model year before the eleventh generation launched. (Photo Courtesy Creative Commons)

Year	Engine	Horsepower (hp)	Torque (ft-lbs)	VIN Code
1997	256-ci (4.2L) V6	205	225 at 3,000 rpm	2
	281-ci (4.6L) V8	220	290 at 3,250 rpm	W or 6
	330-ci (5.4L) V8 (Triton)	235	330 at 3,000 rpm	L
	351-ci (5.8L) V8	210	325 at 2,800 rpm	H
	445-ci (7.3L) diesel V8 (Power Stroke Turbo Diesel)	210	425 at 2,000 rpm	F
	460-ci (7.5L) V8	245	395 at 2,400 rpm	G
1998	256-ci (4.2L) V6	205	255 at 3,000 rpm	2
	281-ci (4.6L) V8 (Triton)	220	290 at 3,250 rpm	W or 6
	330-ci (5.4L) V8 (Triton)	235	330 at 3,000 rpm	L
	351-ci (5.8L) V8	210	325 at 2,800 rpm	H
	445-ci (7.3L) diesel V8 (Power Stroke Turbo Diesel)	210	425 at 2,000 rpm	F
1999	256-ci (4.2L) V6	205	255 at 3,000 rpm	2
	281-ci (4.6L) V8 (Triton)	220	290 at 3,250 rpm	W or 6
	330-ci (5.4L) V8 (Triton)	260	345 at 2,300 rpm	L
	330-ci (5.4L) V8 (Lightning, Supercharged)	360	440 at 3,000 rpm	3
	415-ci (6.8L) V10	310	425 max	S
	444-ci (7.3L) diesel V8 (Power Stroke Turbocharged)	235	500 at 2,000 rpm	F
2000	256-ci (4.2L) V6	205	250 at 3,000 rpm	2
	281-ci (4.6L) V8 (Triton)	220	290 at 3,250 rpm	W or 6
	330-ci (5.4L) V8 (Triton)	260	345 at 2,300 rpm	L
	330-ci (5.4L) V8 (Lightning, Supercharged)	360	440 at 3,000 rpm	3
	415-ci (6.8L) V10	310	425 max	S
	444-ci (7.3L) diesel V8 (Power Stroke Turbocharged)	235	500 at 2,000 rpm	F
2001	256-ci (4.2L) V6	205	250 at 3,000 rpm	2
	281-ci (4.6L) V8 (Triton)	220	290 at 3,250 rpm	W
	330-ci (5.4L) V8 (Triton)	260	345 at 2,300 rpm	L
	330-ci (5.4L) V8 (Lightning, Supercharged)	380	450 at 3,250 rpm	3
	415-ci (6.8L) V10	310	425 max	S
	444-ci (7.3L) diesel V8 (Power Stroke Turbocharged)	215–235	500 at 2,000 rpm	F
2002	256-ci (4.2L) V6	205	250 at 3,000 rpm	2
	281-ci (4.6L) V8 (Triton)	220	290 at 3,250 rpm,	W or 6
	330-ci (5.4L) V8 (Triton)	260	345 at 2,300 rpm	L
	330-ci (5.4L) V8 (Lightning, Supercharged)	380	450 at 3,250 rpm	3
	415-ci (6.8L) V10	310	425 max	S
	444-ci (7.3L) diesel V8 (Power Stroke Turbocharged)	250	525 at 1,600 rpm	F
2003	256-ci (4.2L) V6	202	252 at 3,400 rpm	2
	281-ci (4.6L) V8 (Triton)	231	293 at 3,500 rpm	W
	330-ci (5.4L) V8 (Triton)	260	350 at 2,500 rpm	L
	330-ci (5.4L) V8 (Lightning, Supercharged)	380	450 at 3,250 rpm	3
	355-ci (6.0L) diesel (Power Stroke Turbocharged)	325	560 at 2,000 rpm	P
	415-ci (6.8L) V10	310	425 max	5 or 6
	444-ci (7.3L) diesel V8 (Power Stroke Turbocharged)	250/275	525 at 1,600 rpm	F

Note: Information included in this chart is designed to be inclusive. Dependent upon reference, year, and carryover, information may vary.

Note: From 1997 to 2004, the engine VIN is the eighth character listed.

Color	Available Year and VIN Code						
	1997	1998	1999	2000	2001	2002	2003
Arizona Beige Metallic	–	–	–	–	AQ	AQ	AQ
Light Prairie Tan Metallic	BA	BA or BM	BM	–	–	–	–
Bright Amber Metallic	–	BN	BN	BN	BN	–	–
School Bus Yellow	–	–	–	BY	BY	BY	–
Chrome Yellow	–	BZ	–	–	–	BZ	–
Harvest Gold Metallic	–	–	B2	B2 or B5	B2 or B5	–	–
Chestnut Metallic	–	–	–	B4	B4	B4	B4
Dark Shadow Gray Pearl	–	–	–	–	–	CX	CX
Medium Sonora Metallic	–	–	–	–	DN	–	–
Light Saddle Metallic	DY or DZ	–	–	–	–	–	–
Vermillion	E4	E4 or F1	E4, EP, or F1	E4, EP, or F1	E4, EP, or F1	E4 or F1	E4 or F1
Toreador Red Pearl Metallic	–	–	FL	FL	FL	FL	FL
Toreador Red Metallic	FN	–	–	–	FN	FN	FN
Woodland Green Metallic	–	FV	FV	FV	–	–	–
Vermont Green Metallic	F7	–	–	–	–	–	–
Merlot Pearl	–	–	–	–	–	–	FX
Deep Toreador Red	–	–	–	GX	GX	–	–
Dark Toreador Red Pearl	JL	JL	JL or JM	JM	–	–	–
Thistle Pearl		JS	JS	–	–	–	–
Medium Lapis Metallic	KG	–	–	–	–	–	–
Royal Blue Metallic	–	KM	–	–	–	–	–
Deep Wedgewood Blue Metallic	–	–	KQ or LL	KQ or LL	LL	–	–
Indigo Blue Metallic	KU	–	–	–	–	–	–
Charcoal Blue Metallic	–	–	–	–	KW	KW	KW
Light Denim Blue Metallic	–	K1	–	–	–	–	–
Medium Melina Blue Metallic	–	–	–	–	K9	–	–
Royal Blue Metallic	LE	LE	–	–	–	–	–
Sapphire Blue Pearl Metallic	–	–	–	–	–	LR	–
True Blue Metallic	–	–	–	–	L2	L2	L2
Dark Tourmaline Metallic	NB	NB	NB	–	–	–	–

Color	Available Year and VIN Code						
	1997	1998	1999	2000	2001	2002	2003
Jewel Green Metallic	–	–	PB	PB	PB	–	–
Chesapeake Blue Metallic	–	–	PK	PK	PK	–	–
Pacific Green Metallic	PS	PS	–	–	–	–	–
Calypso Green Metallic	PT	–	–	–	–	–	–
Dark Highland Green Metallic	–	–	–	–	PX	PX	PX
Dark Highland Green Waterborne Metallic	–	–	–	–	PY	PY	PY
Medium Platinum Metallic	RC	–	–	–	–	–	–
Teal Metallic	RD	RD	RD	–	–	–	–
Dark Teal Metallic	–	–	–	R1 or R2	R1 or R2	R2	–
Sonic Blue Pearl Metallic	–	–	–	–	–	–	SN
Estate Green Metallic	–	–	–	–	ST	ST	ST
Amazon Green Metallic	–	–	SU	SU	–	–	–
Silver Frost Metallic	TS	–	–	–	–	–	–
Bright Silver Metallic	–	–	–	TX	TX	–	–
Black Ebony	UA	UA	UA	UA	UA	UA	UA
Ebony	UD	UD	UD	UD	UD	UD	UD
Performance White	–	–	–	WB	WB	WB	WB
Light Opal Metallic	WO	–	–	–	–	–	–
Hugger Orange	–	–	–	–	–	–	W5
Portofino Metallic	XC	–	–	–	–	–	–
Silver Metallic	–	YN or Z3	YN or Z3	YN or Z3	YN or Z3	YN or Z3	YN or Z3
Oxford White	YZ or Z1	YZ or Z1	YO, YZ, or Z1	YO, YZ, or Z1	YO, YZ, or Z1	YZ or Z1	YZ or Z1
Ultra-White	–	–	–	–	ZR	–	–
Colonial White	ZT	–	–	–	–	–	–

Note: Information included in this chart is designed to be inclusive. Dependent upon reference, year, and carryover, information may vary.

Note: For 1997–2003, paint color is listed on a VIN tag located on the driver-side doorjamb as "EXTERIOR PAINT."

Year	Model	Automatic/ Manual	Number of Gears	Transmission
1997–2003	F-150	Manual	5	Standard (OD)
1997–2003	F-150	Automatic	4	Optional (OD)
1997–2003	F-150	Automatic	4	Optional (HD Package)
1997–1998	F-250	Manual	5	Standard (OD)
1997–1998	F-250	Automatic	4	Optional (OD)
1999	F-250	Manual	6	Standard
1999	F-250	Manual	5	Optional
1999	F-250	Automatic	4	Optional
2000–2001	F-250	Manual	6	Overdrive
2000–2001	F-250	Manual	5	Overdrive
2000–2001	F-250	Automatic	4	Overdrive
2002	F-250	Manual	6	Overdrive
2002	F-250	Automatic	4	Overdrive
2003	F-250	Manual	5	Overdrive
2003	F-250	Automatic	2	Overdrive
2003	F-250	Automatic	5	Overdrive

Note: Information included in this chart is designed to be inclusive. Dependent upon reference, year, and carryover, information may vary.

Year	Model	Wheelbase (inches)	Length (inches)	Bed Length (feet)	Height (inches)	Width (inches)	Gross Vehicle Weight (pounds)	Price
1997–2003	Ford F-150 1/2 ton	120–163	202–248	5.5/8	71–76	78–80	5,450–8,200	$15,145–$37,830
1997–2003	Ford F-250 3/4 ton	133–172	213–258	6.4/8.2	70–80	78–80	6,800–8,800	$17,070–$37,195

Note: Information included in this chart is designed to be inclusive. Dependent upon reference, year, and carryover, information may vary.

Note that price is based on MSRP listing.

FORD F-SERIES ELEVENTH GENERATION (2004–2008)

Halfway through the first decade of the new millennium, America was in an unusual place. Bruised but united after the attacks on America on September 11, 2001, there was a sense of patriotism still permeating the country. What was more symbolic of America than a pickup truck? Ford was basking in the sales success of the tenth generation, perhaps capitalizing on America's new-found patriotism. However, there was a split at Ford and within the truck-buying community about the tenth generation.

Some at the Blue Oval felt that the tenth generation had gone too far and lost its tough look and was too "family looking." It is only logical to assume that the eleventh generation, which started in the 2004 model year and continued through the 2008 model year, was a correction of sorts. Trying to bring the truck back from suburbia and give it a tougher appearance was a challenge for the design team. Yet, this

The eleventh-generation F-150 boasted a new appearance. Ford's design team wanted to add an element of ruggedness. This is a 2004 Ford F-150. (Photo Courtesy Ford Motor Company)

Ed Golden was one of the designers of the eleventh-generation F-Series trucks. This is a 2004 Ford F-150. (Photo Courtesy Ford Motor Company)

Each generation of Ford trucks got significantly better when it came to the interior. Each generation, and seemingly each year, offered more and more creature comforts and added luxury. This 2004 F-150 is the Lariat trim and has leather seats and faux wood grain. (Photo Courtesy Creative Commons)

new F-Series had to also maintain its family-friendly appearance too. This was a tough challenge for all those involved with the eleventh generation.

Ed Golden came to Ford in 1998 as chief designer for all trucks, including the F-Series and all the SUVs. Golden went on to succeed Gary Haas as design director of trucks by 1999. Golden and his team were tasked with designing the eleventh-generation F-Series. Golden said, "I loved Ford truck design history, and I loved that it had a long line of clear evolutionary steps in each generation."

With that history in mind, and knowing the divided opinion on the tenth generation, Golden and his team went to work on a new design strategy. But he knew to tread carefully, as the sales numbers supported the changes made to the previous generation. "The fact that Ford trucks were loved by customers told me that our strategy was correct and didn't need to be randomly changed by some newcomer."

Golden recalls the ambitious plans for the eleventh generation, known internally as the P-221. There would be an entirely new engineering platform to build this truck from. The product planners and engineers had come up with the plan for the next-generation F-Series.

The P-221 included the greatest number of new parts in F-Series history. "There was so much more to design, so much more to model in clay," Golden said. "The complexity of this project was huge. It was a financial cornerstone for the company and there were so many decisions and so many design elements that had to be reviewed."

Golden said one of his key designers on the project was Tyler Blake, who "effortlessly and naturally delivered the right answers on the P-221 program." Additionally, Ford continued to use focus groups as a way to get feedback. This practice had been used successfully by Ford for several decades but was more important than ever for the F-Series.

With several truck concepts as well as models from General Motors and the Dodge Ram, Golden recalled being nervous about the response. He knew what was intended for the eleventh generation and what direction he felt it needed to go. The focus group feedback on the P-221 was strong. "It felt very good to have the research conclude that we had a strong family look and, for the majority of the participants invited, also the most attractive and most exciting."

It was full-speed ahead in the Design Studio on the eleventh generation and the end result was a truck that had sharper-edged styling. Another major change was the adoption of the stepped driver's window from the Super Duty trucks. All F-150s, regardless of cab type, were given four doors with the rear doors on the regular cab providing access to behind-the-seat storage. From 2005 to 2008, Lincoln-Mercury dealers sold this version of the F-150 as the Lincoln Mark LT, replacing the Blackwood.

There were other changes in the eleventh generation. The Super Duty used a new platform starting in late 2008. While using the same bed and cabin as before, these are distinguished from their predecessors by an all-new interior and a much

PERFORMANCE VERSIONS OF THE F-150

There were several performance versions of the F-150 available.

Roush Performance Vehicles F-150

Roush Performance vehicles offered an aftermarket version beginning with the second half of the 2007 model year. The Roush Performance F-150 vehicles were assembled at Roush Performance's Plymouth Township, Michigan, facility, adding performance upgrades that you could buy through a select number of Ford dealers, as well as aftermarket parts and accessories that could be installed on a vehicle.

This package also included the styling and body kit enhancements of the Stage 1 version and the suspension upgrades that were incorporated into the Stage 2 version of the truck. The tuned sport suspension system under the Stage 3 offered a balance between comfort and handling capability without significant reduction in payload capacity. The enhancements to the suspension included:

- Specially valved front and rear shock absorbers
- Increased rate rear leaf springs and front coil springs
- A large-diameter, solid front sway bar

Saleen F-150

The Saleen forced-induction package was available from Ford on the Harley-Davidson edition as an OEM option. Saleen is headquartered in Corona, California. Saleen made its reputation by building high-performance Mustangs dating back to the 1980s. Saleen's flagship car was the Saleen S7, which was introduced in 2000. The S7 was wholly built by Saleen and featured a mid-engine design in a high-performance supercar package. Saleen offered its own OEM version of the F-150, which was badged as the S331.

Foose Edition of the F-150

In 2008, Ford introduced the Foose edition of the F-150. It was named after Chip Foose, a well-known designer of hot rods. It was based on an F-150 FX2 Sport with a Roush-developed powertrain. The supercharged 5.4L V8 put out 450 hp (340 kW) and 500 ft-lbs of torque.

This truck engine is equipped with an aftermarket air induction system. Most of these systems are designed to bring outside air into the engine instead of under-the-hood air. Outside air is always cooler than under-the-hood air, even on hot summer days. Using outside air results in greater horsepower output by 1 percent for each 10 degrees cooler the air is. (Photo Courtesy Richard Truesdell)

Saleen is a performance-based automotive company that is known for adding power and performance to cars and trucks. Pictured here is a 2021 Saleen F-150. Saleen has been modifying cars and trucks since 2000, and it offers its own OEM version of the F-150. (Photo Courtesy Marcus Cervantes)

High performance is not just for cars! The trend of performance pickup trucks started in the 1990s and really took grip in the 2000s. Between lift kits, tuned sport suspensions, and horsepower that can exceed 500 hp, the Ford F-150 performance market is strong. (Photo Courtesy Richard Truesdell)

larger grille and headlamps. The F-450, which was previously available only as a chassis-cab model, was now available as a pickup directly from Ford.

F-Series Awards and Accolades

The Ford F-Series won several awards and was recognized with several industry accolades. The 2012 F-Series won *Motor Trend*'s Truck of the Year award. In 2006, the F-150 was recognized by *Automotive Fleet* and *Business Fleet* magazines as Fleet Truck of the Year. The next year, all three variants (F-150, F-250, and F-350) were chosen Best Fleet Vehicle by the automotive data-analysis firm, Vincentric. Lastly, the eleventh generation received the Golden Icon Award in 2006 for Best Truck.

Eleventh Generation Dimensions		
Wheelbase Length (inches)	Cab	Bed (feet)
126	Regular cab	6.5
133	Super Cab	5.5
139	Super Crew	5.5
145	Super Cab/Regular Cab	6.5/8
151	Super Crew	6.5
163	Super Cab	8
211.8	Regular cab	6.5
217.8	Super Cab	5.5
223.8	Super Crew	5.5
229.8	Super Cab/Regular	6.5/8
235.8	Super Crew	6.5
247.8	Super Cab	8 bed

Safety

The eleventh-generation F-150 received the top safety ratings (5 stars) from the US National Highway Traffic Safety Administration (NHTSA) in frontal collisions. It not only got a "Good" rating from the Insurance Institute for Highway Safety's frontal offset test, but also a *Best Pick*. The sensors in the test dummies recorded no injuries to any area of the human body.

Engines

Initially for the eleventh generation, Ford offered the F-150 with only two Triton V8 engines: a base 231-hp 4.6L and an optional 300-hp 5.4L unit. The V8s were paired with a 4-speed automatic transmission, and for the first time Ford mounted the shift lever on the floor. A 4.2L Essex V6 option (210 hp) was also offered.

The Modular engine used in Ford trucks and passenger cars is an overhead camshaft (OHC) V8 gasoline-powered small-block engine family. The name *modular* was derived from a manufacturing plant protocol where the plant and its tooling could be changed in a few hours to manufacture different versions of the engine family. Modular engines in Ford trucks were marketed under the Triton name from 1997 to 2010. The transmissions available for the gas engines were a 4-speed automatic, a 5-speed manual, and a 6-speed automatic.

Diesel Engines

The MaxxForce 7 Ford Power Stroke engine built on International's new 6.4L V8 platform featured a high-pressure common-rail fuel injection system. This engine used electronically actuated piezo-electric injectors and an advanced air management system for fuel economy, power, performance, reliability, and durability. This engine was fully compliant with EPA emissions standards.

The Ford Power stroke application introduced in 2008 used a sequential twin-turbo intercooled forced induction system. The engine also used a high-pressure common-rail (HPCR) electronically controlled fuel injection system. The Ford Power stroke version produced 350 hp (260 kW) at 3,000 rpm and 650 ft-lbs of torque at 2,000 rpm.

A Siemens high-pressure common-rail fuel system used piezo-actuated fuel injectors to deliver as many as five fuel injection events during each cycle. This reduced emissions and noise along with fuel economy improvements and after-treatment control. The piezoelectric linear actuator was a solid-state ceramic actuator that converted electric energy into linear motion, precisely controlling the needle's opening and closing through the hydraulic circuit. The system could deliver injection pressures up to 23,250 psi.

Diesel Exhaust After Treatment

Before the 2007 model year, most light diesel engines needed two exhaust emission-control devices to meet the exhaust emissions standards. These devices included:
- A diesel oxidation catalyst (DOC) to help reduce the hydrocarbons (HC) and carbon monoxide (CO) created during the combustion process.

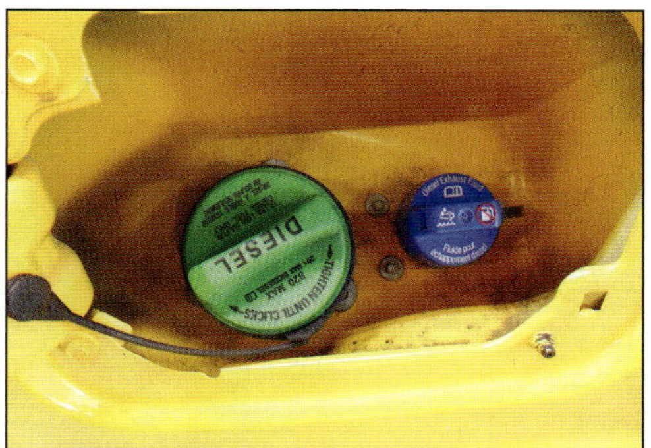

Behind the fuel fill door on a Ford F-250 or F-350 equipped with a diesel engine are two fill caps. The green fill cap on the left is for adding diesel fuel and has an opening that is larger than the fuel opening on a vehicle equipped with a gasoline-powered engine. This allows the vehicle to be filled at truck stops that use a nozzle size that varies from 15/16 inch (24 mm) to 1.5 inches (38 mm). The blue cap on the right is where the diesel exhaust fluid (DEF) is added.

- A diesel particulate filter (DPF) designed to trap and hold particulate matter that would otherwise contribute to unwanted tailpipe emissions and smoke

Starting with the 2007 model year, the emissions standards for oxides of nitrogen (NOx) were reduced, and as a result, most manufacturers of light diesel engine vehicles started to use a system called selective catalyst reduction (SCR). The SCR catalyst required the use of diesel exhaust fluid (DEF) to reduce the NOx exhaust emissions. The DEF was stored in a separate reservoir. The reservoir was equipped with a pump and a heater. The pump was used to transfer the fluid from the reservoir to the dosing module, where it was sprayed into the exhaust stream from the SCR catalyst.

DEF is a mixture of 32.5-percent laboratory-grade urea and 67.5-percent deionized water. DEF will freeze at about 12°F (-11°C). The concentration of urea and water ensures that both elements will freeze at the same temperature. The heater element in the reservoir was designed to thaw the DEF before it was injected.

NOTE: No antifreeze needed to be added to the DEF because the reservoir and the DEF system were designed to withstand the freezing without harm to the system. Adding anything except DEF to the reservoir could result in failure of the system and may require replacing all of the components in the system.

According to Ford, the size of the DEF reservoir meant that the diesel exhaust fluid should, under normal operating conditions, need to be refilled at about the same time as when the engine oil is replaced, usually every 7,500 miles. This makes it convenient for the truck owner by reducing the number of services that need to be performed. The DEF reservoir was equipped with a system that would detect the level of the fluid and turn on a dash warning when the DEF level needed to be refilled.

The driver information display showed a series of messages regarding the amount of DEF available.

- As the DEF level neared empty, the DEF warning symbol displayed and a series of tones sounded with the messages starting at 500 miles remaining before DEF is depleted.
- Within a certain number of miles to empty, vehicle speed would be limited upon vehicle restart.
- Further vehicle operation without refilling the DEF tank would cause the engine to enter an "idle-only" condition.

- A minimum of 0.5 gallon (1.9L) of DEF needed to be added to the tank to exit the idle-only condition, but the vehicle would still be in the speed-limiting mode until the DEF tank was refilled completely.
- For either vehicle speed limiting or idle-only condition, normal vehicle operation resumed when the DEF tank was refilled.

2004–2005

Model year 2004 represented the first time in Ford's truck history that all cab configurations came with four-door options. The drastic new look of the F-Series displayed well with an attractive new front fascia, modern-looking automatic headlamps, and a front bumper with integrated fog lights and tow hooks.

Continuing the redesign, there was a higher belt line, which meant improved posture for driver and passengers. The interior featured more luxury than ever before with a focus on reducing road noise. Each trim level had a different instrument panel. The most drastic addition to the interior was the brushed aluminum overhead rail system. This look was some of what would come in future generations of F-Series, but for this generation it represented an exciting, fresh, and universally appealing interior.

A top-of-the-line King Ranch trim was added in 2005, and a basic work truck trim was added. This small but significant change for 2005 showed that Ford had not abandoned the commercial industry or the small-business owner who relied on a truck for work.

Ford catered to all truck owners, including diehard sports fans. In 2004, the automaker produced only 400 limited-edition Steelers Special Edition F-150s. They were available in black as XLT or Super Crew or as an FX4 model in Steelers gold (pictured here). (Photo Courtesy Dave Wagner)

This Steelers Special Edition F-150 had custom badging on the front fenders and tailgate. It showcased the official NFL-licensed logo of the Pittsburgh Steelers. (Photo Courtesy Dave Wagner)

The 2004 Steelers Special Edition F-150 had Pittsburgh Steelers emblems on the interior, including floor mats and the dashboard. (Photo Courtesy Dave Wagner)

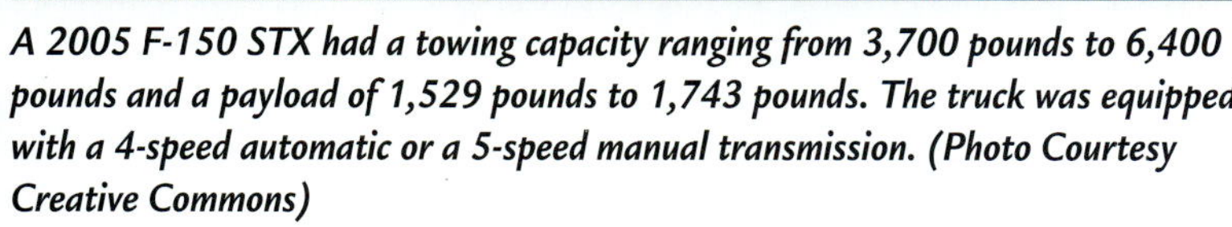

A 2005 F-150 STX had a towing capacity ranging from 3,700 pounds to 6,400 pounds and a payload of 1,529 pounds to 1,743 pounds. The truck was equipped with a 4-speed automatic or a 5-speed manual transmission. (Photo Courtesy Creative Commons)

F-150 Heritage

There are some within Ford who will say that the tenth generation was so good that many executives didn't want to stop producing it. That's an unconfirmed rumor, but it has merit. In 2004, Ford continued to make the older version of the F-150 based on the previous platform and badged it as the F-150 Heritage.

This was mostly a financial decision. There were multiple assembly plants for the F-150. Rather than do a complete shutdown, Ford slowly switched over from the old platform to the new P2 platform. Meanwhile, the plants continued producing tenth-generation-style F-150s as to never have to shut down production and ensure a seamless (and financially lucrative) transition. The F-150 was manufactured at plants in Brazil and Mexico but also in Dearborn, Michigan; Claycomo, Virginia; Norfolk, Virginia; and Oakville, Ontario (until that plant was shuttered in 2004).

The 2004 F-150 Heritage was available on XL and XLT trims only. The 2004 F-150 Heritage looked similar to the 2003 F-150, which was the last of the tenth generation. It was available as a regular cab and a Super Cab. As such, 2004 F-150 Heritage trucks remain highly collectible due to their limited availability for the 2004 model year only.

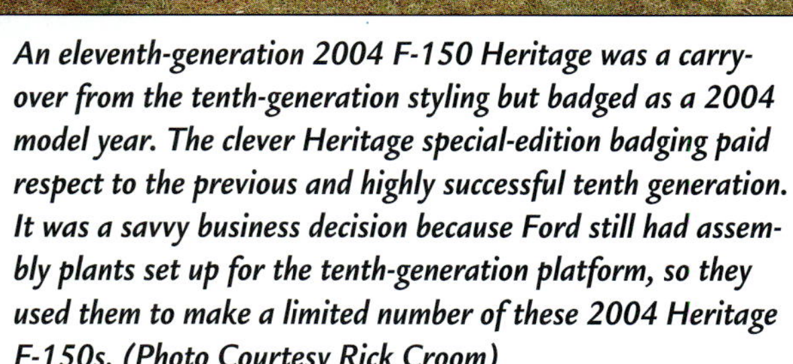

An eleventh-generation 2004 F-150 Heritage was a carry-over from the tenth-generation styling but badged as a 2004 model year. The clever Heritage special-edition badging paid respect to the previous and highly successful tenth generation. It was a savvy business decision because Ford still had assembly plants set up for the tenth-generation platform, so they used them to make a limited number of these 2004 Heritage F-150s. (Photo Courtesy Rick Croom)

2006

For the 2006 model year, new features and accessories were available on the F-150 including:

- A flex-fuel version of the 3-valve 5.4L Triton V8 allowed this engine to operate on ethanol enhanced fuel such as E-85 (85 percent ethanol; 15 percent gasoline).
- The Super Crew model was now available with a 6.5-foot bed.
- A new front bumper with round fog lamps and a smaller bumper vent made the front of the truck appear different from previous models.
- Improved front seat gave improved support.
- New 20-inch wheels were available for FX4, Lariat, and King Ranch trim level trucks. The King Ranch was founded in 1853 by Richard King in what is now Kingsville, Texas. The King Ranch consumes 825,000 acres (1,289 square miles) or in other words, is slightly larger than the state of Rhode Island. The first King Ranch F-150 was offered in 2001 and this trim level is still available today.
- SIRIUS satellite radio became available during the 2006 model year on all trims except the XL.
- A Harley-Davidson special edition was offered for 2006. This unique trim level truck was a cooperative effort with Harley-Davidson Motorcycle company and was available in two- or four-wheel drive, but only in a Super Cab.

This great-looking bright silver 2006 F-250 Super Duty has a 5.4L V8 Triton engine in it. It had 300 hp and 365 ft-lbs of torque. This model year, a flex fuel version of this engine became available that allowed the owner to use E-85. (Photo Courtesy Sami Lynn Mentzer)

2007

The 2007 model year saw very few changes except for color and trim changes and options. A Harley-Davidson edition was offered as a Super Crew version as well as the original Super Cab version. The FX4 4WD model was also made available in two-wheel drive, called the FX2 sport package.

2008

The 2008 F-Series was a carryover truck with only minor cosmetic changes. A new diesel engine from International was added for 2008: the MaxxForce 7 Ford Power Stroke engine featuring a high-pressure common-rail fuel injection system.

This 2006 Ford F-150 is hauling farm materials in the bed and towing them as well. Although modern amenities have been added to each generation, the F-150 has never lost focus on its agricultural roots and overall appeal to farmers and ranchers. (Photo Courtesy Ford Motor Company)

This is an almost-stock 2008 F-350 4x4 that features aftermarket dark tinted windows. Notice the trailer mirrors and chrome side step that is a huge help to get into this high truck. The automotive data-analysis firm Vincentric named this vehicle the best fleet vehicle for 2008. (Photo Courtesy Carole Dubé)

Conclusion

When Ed Golden took over duties as director of Truck Design for Ford, he knew he had a big task ahead. The success and momentum of the tenth generation was on his side, but that same success was part of his challenge. How do you take something that was already incredibly successful and make it more popular?

"I was more excited than scared," Golden said. "I knew I had a great team and our truck was moving in the right direction. We didn't need a new course, we just needed to keep feeding the success machine."

With the eleventh generation, Golden and everyone involved with this new truck fed the success machine indeed. They capitalized on the country's enthusiasm for pickup trucks. Ford was the leader in the truck segment again. In 2005, Ford sold more than 939,000 F-150s, smashing its record from the previous generation. Golden mentioned advancing the momentum of the tenth generation. Ford certainly gained even more momentum within the truck segment and won over even more truck consumers with the eleventh-generation F-Series.

Ford Light-Duty Truck Engines (2004–2008)

Year	Engine	Horse-power (hp)	Torque (ft-lbs)	VIN Code
2004	256-ci (4.2L) V6	205	250 at 3,000 rpm	2
	281-ci (4.6L) V8 (Triton)	220	290 at 3,250 rpm	W
	330-ci (5.4L) V8 (Triton)	260	345 at 2,300 rpm	L
	330-ci (5.4L) V8 (Lightning)	380	450 at 3,250 rpm	3
	365-ci (6.0L) diesel (Power Stroke Turbocharged)	325	560 at 2,000 rpm	P
	415-ci (6.8L) V10	310	425 max	S
2005	256-ci (4.2L) V6	210	260 at 3,000 rpm	2
	281-ci (4.6L) V8 (Triton)	231	290 at 3,500 rpm	W
	330-ci (5.4L) V8 (Triton)	300	365 at 3,750 rpm	5
	365-ci (6.0L) diesel (Power Stroke Turbocharged)	325	570 at 2,000 rpm	P
	415-ci (6.8L) V10	305	455 at 3,000 rpm	S
2006	256-ci (4.2L) V6	210	260 at 3,000 rpm	2
	281-ci (4.6L) V8 (Triton)	231	290 at 3,500 rpm	W
	330-ci (5.4L) V8 (Triton)	300	365 at 3,750 rpm	5
	365-ci (6.0L) diesel (Power Stroke Turbocharged)	325	570 at 2,000 rpm	P
	415-ci (6.8L) V10	305	420 at 3,250 rpm	S
2007	256-ci (4.2L) V6	210	260 at 3,000 rpm	2
	281-ci (4.6L) V8 (Triton)	248	294 at 4,000 rpm	W
	330-ci (5.4L) V8 (Triton)	300	365 at 3,750 rpm	5
	365-ci (6.0L) diesel (Power Stroke Turbocharged)	325	570 at 2,000 rpm	P
	415-ci (6.8L) V10	362	455 at 3,000 rpm	Y or S
2008	256-ci (4.2L) V6	202	260 at 3,750 rpm	2
	281-ci (4.6L) V8 (Triton)	248	294 at 4,750 rpm	W
	330-ci (5.4L) V8 (Triton)	300	365 at 3,750 rpm	5
	390-ci (6.4L) V8 (Power Stroke Turbodiesel)	350	650 at 2,000 rpm	R
	415-ci (6.8) V10	305	457 at 3,250 rpm	Y or S

Note: Information included in this chart is designed to be inclusive. Dependent upon reference, year, and carryover, information may vary.

Note: From 2004 to 2008, the engine VIN is the eighth character listed.

Ford Light- and Light/Medium-Duty Trucks (2004–2008)

Color	Available Year and VIN Code				
	2004	2005	2006	2007	2008
Arizona Beige Metallic	AQ	AQ	AQ	AQ	–
Chestnut Metallic	B4	–	–	–	–
Dark Shadow Gray Pearl	CX	CX	CX	CX	–
Dark Shadow Gunmetal Gray Effect	–	–	–	–	CX
Competition Orange	CY	–	–	–	–
Dark Blue Effect	–	–	–	DX	DX
Screaming Yellow	D6	–	–	–	–
Vermillion	E4 or F1	E4 or F1	E4 or F1	E4	E4
Toreador Red Pearl Metallic	FL	FL	FL	–	–
Toreador Red Effect	–	–	–	–	FL
Dark Satin Green Metallic	FU	FU	FU	–	–

Ford Light- and Light/Medium-Duty Trucks (2004–2008) *CONTINUED*

Color	Available Year and VIN Code				
	2004	2005	2006	2007	2008
Dark Green Satin Metallic	FW	–	–	–	–
Dark Satin Green Effect	–	–	FW	–	–
Merlot Pearl	FX	–	–	–	–
Forest Green Effect	–	–	–	GG	GG
Amber Gold Metallic	–	–	–	–	GQ
Redfire Pearl Effect	–	–	–	G2	G2
Pueblo Gold Metallic	–	–	G3	G3	G3
Smokestone Metallic	HG	–	HG	HG	–
Vintage Copper Pearl	–	–	–	–	HR
Earth Metallic	–	–	–	–	HS
Cinnamon Metallic	–	–	–	–	HT
Dark Toreador Red Pearl	JL or JM	JL or JM	JL or JM	JL	JM
Dark Toreador Red Effect	–	–	–	–	JL
Medium Wedgewood Metallic	LD	LD	LD	LD	–
True Blue Metallic	L2	L2	L2	L2	L2
Dark Amethyst Effect	–	–	–	PG	–
White Chocolate Tricoat	–	–	–	PV	PV
Dark Highland Green Metallic	PX	–	–	–	–
Aspen Green Pearl Metallic	P5	P5	P5	P5	P5
Medium Platinum Metallic	–	RC	–	–	–
Sonic Blue Pearl Metallic	SN	–	–	–	–
Blue Flame Metallic	–	–	–	–	SZ
Mineral Gray Effect	–	TK	–	–	–
Dark Copper Metallic	–	–	T5	T5	T5
Charcoal Beige Metallic	–	T7	T7	T7	T7
Tungsten Gray Effect	–	–	–	T8	–
Estate Green Metallic	ST	–	–	–	–
Black Ebony	UA	–	UA	UA	UA or UD
Ebony	UD	UD	UD	–	–
White Platinum Tricoat	–	–	–	–	UG
Tuxedo Black	–	–	–	–	UH
Brilliant Silver Metallic Cladding	–	–	–	–	UI

Ford Light- and Light/Medium-Duty Trucks (2004–2008) *CONTINUED*

Color	Available Year and VIN Code				
	2004	2005	2006	2007	2008
Sterling Gray Metallic Cladding	–	–	–	–	UJ
Royal Red Metallic Cladding	–	–	–	–	UK
Ingot Silver Metallic	–	–	–	–	UX
Performance White	–	–	WB	WB	WB
Medium Opal Metallic	WD	–	–	–	–
Hugger Orange	W5	–	–	–	–
Light Brown	–	–	–	XO	–
Silver Metallic	YN or Z3	YN or Z3	YN or Z3	–	Z3
Silver Effect	–	–	–	YN	YN
Oxford White	YZ or Z1	YZ or Z1	YZ or Z1	YZ	YZ or Z1

Note: Information included in this chart is designed to be inclusive. Dependent upon reference, year, and carryover, information may vary.

Note: The 2004–2008 paint color is listed on a VIN tag located on the driver-side doorjamb as "EXTERIOR PAINT."

Ford Light- and Light/Medium-Duty Trucks Transmissions (2004–2008)

Year	Model	Automatic/Manual	Number of Gears	Transmission
2004	F-150	Automatic	4	Overdrive
2005–2008	F-150	Manual	5	Standard
2005–2008	F-150	Automatic	4	Overdrive
2004	F-250	Manual	6	Overdrive
2004	F-250	Automatic	5	Overdrive (Diesel Only)
2004	F-250	Automatic	4	Overdrive
2005–2008	F-250	Manual	6	Overdrive
2005–2008	F-250	Automatic	5	TorqShift Overdrive

Note: Information included in this chart is designed to be inclusive. Dependent upon reference, year, and carryover, information may vary.

Ford Light- and Light/Medium-Duty Trucks Sales and Prices (2004–2008)

Year	Model	Wheelbase (inches)	Length (inches)	Bed Length (feet)	Height (inches)	Width (inches)	Gross Vehicle Weight (pounds)	Price
2004–2008	Ford F-150 1/2 ton	126–163	211–248	5.5/8	73–76	79	6,650–8,200	$20,100–$40,940
2004–2008	Ford F-250 3/4 ton	137–172	227–262	6.75/8.2	76–80	80	8,800–9,600	$23,185–$38,560

Note: Information included in this chart is designed to be inclusive. Dependent upon reference, year, and carryover, information may vary.

Note that price is based on MSRP listing.

FORD F-SERIES TWELFTH GENERATION (2009–2014)

"Ford was hopeful that truck sales would return on the other side of a recession after seeing a 59-percent drop in sales from earlier in the decade."

In America during the late 2000s and middle part of the 2010s, hope and optmism returned after some tough economic times. Barack Obama swept into the White House on this concept of hope. But in the truck world, that hope and optimism was a slow build. Truck sales were greatly impacted by the recession of 2008 and the government bailouts of General Motors and Chrysler.

Ford, through some savvy leadership, only required a government loan to stay afloat. All told, the entire automotive industry was bruised and battered, and the F-150 was not immune. Yet, through this time, the F-150 continued to be the best-selling vehicle in America. Ford was hopeful that truck sales would return on the other side of a recession after seeing a 59-percent drop in sales from earlier in the decade.

Needing to see an increase in truck sales, the F-Series underwent another redesign. Ford hoped that the twelfth generation, from the 2009 model year to the 2014 model year, would be as successful as the other trucks produced during the last two decades. F-150 sales in 2009 were only 413,625, but by the time the twelfth generation was finished in 2014, the sales had rebounded to more than 780,000. These numbers still trailed those of the previous generation's peak of more than 900,000.

Ford's plan was to make the F-150 something for a mass consumer base. This meant affordable base trims still aimed at the working class but also to bolster the

The old days where trucks were just work trucks were a thing of the past. In the twelfth generation, the F-Series was boldly designed. Both the exterior and interior had mass appeal. It was a truck for everyone; one that was comfortable on the farm or on the highways as a daily commuter. (Photo Courtesy Randy Stern)

Inside the Truck Design Studio at Ford, a switch in mentality meant higher-end materials and luxurious cabins for even the basic trim levels of F-150s. As Ford truck designer Ed Golden said, "We couldn't over appoint them." This is a 2014 F-150 Lariat trim, which is a middle-of-the-line trim, and you can see such comforts as a leather steering wheel, soft materials on the dashboard, and a big center console for storage. All this was par for the course when it came to the interiors of the twelfth generation. (Photo Courtesy Randy Stern)

F-150's interior with luxurious amenities. Ford was aiming the F-150 at a higher class that had disposable income and recreational vehicles.

Ed Golden said Ford had its finger on the pulse of the consumer when it came to trucks. The automaker seemed to understand what the American consumer wanted with trucks, and it was luxury.

"Luxury in trucks was gaining a lot of momentum in the early 2000s," Golden said. "It made a lot of sense to focus on that. Of all the Lincoln- and Ford-branded products, our most expensive (and therefore most profitable) were high-end trucks." Golden went on to say, "We just couldn't charge too much for them. There were many wealthy customers glad to drive them off the dealers' lots."

By the end of the twelfth generation, Ford was knee-deep in the luxury truck market and didn't even need to slap a Lincoln badge on the front to convince the consumer. The rebounding sales numbers showed that Ford had the right plan for the truck market.

Twelfth Generation Highlights

The twelfth generation saw both a new appearance and new engines. It was a big fundamental shift at the Blue Oval, focusing on luxury, looks, and fuel efficiency. That was a challenge for all involved from the design team to product planning and engineers.

The exterior design included evolutionary styling upgrades such as a larger grille and headlights, aligning it with the styling of the Super Duty trucks. Ed Golden said one of the big ideas at Ford for this generation was to bring the F-150 more in line with the look of the Super Duty trucks while also maintaining a separate appeal.

The interior saw the introduction of higher-quality materials in all but the most basic trim levels in a similar fashion as the Ford cars. Attention to detail on the inside showcased the importance of touch points to the F-150 buyer.

The basic F-150 again had two doors instead of four. The Flareside bed was continued until 2010 and was dropped along with the manual transmission, making the automatic transmission the only transmission available. Also new for 2009 was the electric power steering (EPS) system on most models.

The twelfth-generation F-150 was produced at the Dearborn Truck Plant in Dearborn, Michigan, and the Kansas City Assembly Plant in Claycomo, Missouri.

The 2009 F-150 was revealed during the 2008 North American International Auto Show in Detroit. Matt O'Leary was the chief engineer, and the process for redesigning this truck started in November 2003. The code name at Ford was P-415. Once approved, production of the 2009 F-150 began in October 2008 at Ford's Kansas City Assembly Plant.

The truck, especially the F-Series, seemed like an invincible force. It survived through a major economic downturn and recession. It even overcame the federal government cracking down on vehicles that were not very fuel efficient, such as pickup trucks.

In 2011, the Obama administration announced a change to the Corporate Average Fuel Economy (CAFE), a law that was first enacted in 1975, where automakers agreed to have their fuel economy average hit 54.5 miles per gallon. These new restrictive CAFE standards only applied to cars. Light-duty trucks had much lower standards during this time, but CAFE forced the hand of truck makers too. The change in environmental standards would impact the truck market and the F-150, but not by much.

The CAFE standards certainly played a role in the development of a more fuel-efficient powertrain for the F-150. The turbocharged V6 EcoBoost engine was created during this era and was truly a game changer for Ford. It helped improve the F-150's EPA fuel economy numbers. It helped Ford's overall image and resonated with a consumer that was still thirsty for trucks but wanted one that was more fuel efficient. Ford still offered V8 engines and diesel powertrains for the consumer who still was not on board with a more fuel-efficient pickup truck as well.

The EcoBoost combined gasoline direct injection and turbocharging to create an incredibly efficient amount of power. Here are the benefits:

Turbocharging

A turbocharger is used to pack a denser air-fuel charge into the cylinders. The turbine wheel of a turbocharger is powered primarily by exhaust gases. Because the density of the air-fuel charge is greater, the power is increased. This added pressure allows more air to enter the intake port before the intake valve closes. By increasing the airflow into the intake, more fuel can be mixed with the air while still maintaining the same air-fuel ratio.

If a turbocharger develops 12 psi (83 kPa) boost at sea level, it will develop the same amount at a 5,000-foot altitude because boost pressure is measured inside the intake manifold. A turbocharger uses the heat of the exhaust to power a turbine wheel and does not directly reduce engine power.

In a naturally aspirated engine, about a third of the heat energy contained in the fuel goes out the exhaust system. Hot exhaust gases flow from the combustion chamber to the turbine wheel. The gases are heated and expanded as they leave the engine. It is not the speed or force of the exhaust gases that forces the turbine wheel to turn, as is commonly thought, but the expansion of hot gases against the turbine wheel's blades.

A turbocharger consists of two chambers connected with a center housing. When the engine is started and runs at low speed, both exhaust heat and pressure are low and the turbine runs at a low speed (approximately 1,000 rpm). As the engine runs faster or load increases, both exhaust heat and flow increase, causing the

This 3.5L V6 had two features that together formed what Ford designated as EcoBoost. The two technical features were gasoline direct injection (GDI) combined with turbocharging. Each of them increases engine torque and horsepower, but together the combination works so well that Ford was able to provide V8 performance in a full-size pickup truck that also provides improved fuel economy with lower exhaust emissions. (Photo Courtesy Randy Stern)

turbine and compressor wheels to rotate faster. Since there is no brake and very little rotating resistance on the turbocharger shaft, the turbine and compressor wheels accelerate as the exhaust heat energy increases.

The typical turbocharger normally rotates at speeds between 100,000 and 150,000 rpm, so proper engine oil and oil change intervals are a must. The turbocharger is lubricated by engine oil through an oil line to the center bearing assembly. The amount of boost (or pressure in the intake manifold) is measured in PSI, inches of mercury (inch Hg), bars, or atmospheres.

Gasoline Direct Injection (GDI)

A gasoline direct-injection system sprays high-pressure fuel, up to 2,900 psi, into the combustion chamber as the piston approaches the top of the compression stroke.

With the combination of high-pressure swirl injectors and a modified combustion chamber, almost instantaneous vaporization occurs. This, combined with a higher compression ratio, allows a direct-injected engine to operate using a leaner-than-normal air–fuel ratio, which results in improved fuel economy with higher power output and reduced exhaust emissions.

EcoBoost combines turbocharging and gasoline direct injection in one integrated system. The combination of these two technologies results in improved fuel economy, increased engine power, as well as reduced exhaust emissions.

	Port Fuel Injection (PFI)	Gasoline Direct Injection (GDI)
Fuel pressure	35–60 psi	Lift pump—50 to 60 psi
High-pressure pump	500 to 2,900 psi	
Injection pulse width at idle	1.5–3.5 ms	About 0.4 ms (400 μs)
Injector resistance	12–16 ohms	1–3 ohms
Injector voltage	6V for low resistance	
Injectors, 12V for most injectors	50–90 V	
Number of injections per event	One	1–3
Engine compression ratio	8:1–11:1	11:1–13:1

2009

The 2009 model year F-150 included the following:

- Updated interior
- A new three-bar grille
- More high-strength steel used in the chassis to improve payload and towing capacity
- Quiet Steel was used on the cab floor, bulkhead (firewall), and other parts of the cab to help reduce noise, vibration, and harshness (NVH). Quiet Steel uses a polymer between two layers of steel to reduce the road noise from entering the cabin.
- A V8 engine was the standard engine in all 2009 models (no 6-cylinder engine was available).

A new Platinum trim level for the F-150 replaced the poor-selling Lincoln Mark LT pickup truck. Other changes included a factory-installed trailer brake controller with trailer sway control. Side steps were added for easier access to the pickup bed. A rear camera was part of the tailgate along with the trailer controls for people who had to hitch up a recreational vehicle. The standard wheel of FX4 models was enlarged to 18 inches, up from 17-inch wheels used previously.

2010

Very little changed from 2009 to the 2010 model year. There was a change in the brake system, which included larger rotors and bigger calipers. A new electric cooling fan replaced an engine-driven fan. This was a minor but important change for more fuel efficiency. Ford introduced MyKey, which was a programmable key fob that could work as a nanny system for new drivers that controlled radio volume and could even put speed limit alerts in. This was an attractive safety feature for families.

A new 6.2L (379-ci) V8 was also introduced for the 2010 model year. This new OHV engine was designed for use in the F-150 and featured a cast-iron block and aluminum cylinder heads. It was first used in the Ford F-150 Raptor, where it produced 411 hp at 5,500 rpm and 434 ft-lbs of torque at 4,500 rpm.

2011

The 2011 model year featured many engine changes used in the F-150. Both versions of the modular 4.6L V8 and the 5.4L V8 were discontinued. The new 3.7L V6 and the 5.0L V8 were introduced for use in the F-150. While the new 5.0L V8 shared the same basic architecture as the 4.6L, it was totally redesigned for improved power and fuel economy. In fact, the 5.0L V8 was used in the Mustang for the 2011+ model years.

Also, for the 2011 model year was an all-new 3.5L twin-turbocharged V6, called the EcoBoost, which produced 365 hp. The new 6.2L OHV V8 replaced the 6.8L V10 in the Ford Super Duty trucks (F-250 and F-350).

Other changes for the standard F-150 included the availability of a four-door Super Crew cab as well as a new color option: Ingot Silver Metallic. The new 6.7L Power Stroke diesel engine was used by Ford in pickup trucks and vans for the 2011+ model years. The 6.7L was the first medium-duty diesel designed and built by Ford.

This 2011 Ford F-150 XL trim shows that this was a truck that was popular in the suburbs as well as in the country. This model year, Ford introduced two new engines that focused even more on fuel economy to appeal to drivers who used the F-150 as their daily driver. (Photo Courtesy Jeremy Fischer)

The 2010 F-Series had few changes from the previous model year. Mechanically, there was a new electric cooling fan and upgraded brake components. (Photo Courtesy Creative Commons)

Raptor Takes Flight

The Raptor was the creation of Ford's Special Vehicle Team (SVT). It was intended to appeal to a different type of consumer: the youthful, "Jeep type" of consumer who likes performance and also off-road ability.

The Raptor was unveiled in 2009 for the 2010 model year. The performance was something the average truck consumer was not used to from a pickup. The 5.4L (330-ci) engine was standard. There was also a 6.2L option. The 5.4L made 310 hp and 365 ft-lbs of torque. The big 6.2L blew everyone away with 411 hp and 434 ft-lbs of torque. But beyond that, the Raptor's ability to go off-road was what caught the attention of the truck community.

The Fox Racing Shox were a new introduction for Ford trucks. The internal bypass shocks allowed for 11 inches of suspension travel in the front and 12 inches in the rear. The ground clearance was a great feature for the off-road enthusiast. The 35-inch BFGoodrich All-Terrain tires made it confident over rocky terrain and creek beds. The rear locking differential had a 4.10:1 gear ratio.

The 6-speed automatic transmission was met with a little disappointment from the enthusiasts who like manual transmissions. Upon its introduction, sales were brisk. In the first month of its release, Ford sold 1,186 Raptors. The Raptor was also known for its bolder color palette. In addition to the standard black, white, and red, there were Blue Flame and Molten Orange. In fact, the very first production Raptor was Molten Orange. It recently sold at an auction for $130,000.

By model year 2011, Ford eliminated the 5.4L engine and offered the Raptor only with the 6.2L V8. For this model year, the suspension was tweaked and ride height increased.

Design of the Raptor was handled by the SVT studio so it would truly have a different look from the rest of the F-150 family. The composite hood and fenders immediately had a unique look, especially since the blue oval badge was not integrated into the new grille design. The Raptor had a 5.5-foot bed with a wider stance (by almost 7 inches) than the F-150. Plus, the Raptor was lifted 2 inches higher than even the biggest F-150.

The Raptor borrowed a lot of existing technology to give it credibility with off-road enthusiasts. The Raptor was the first Ford with hill-descent control and electronic locking differential. This allowed the Raptor to crawl down rugged terrain or climb up a slope. The Raptor came with a push-button Off-Road Mode, which turned on Ford's AdvanceTrac RSC (roll stability control). Traction control could be disengaged as well. This really excited off-road enthusiasts. The Raptor's Off-Road Mode was cutting edge; it changed the throttle sensitivity and transmission shift points causing a more linear power and torque curve for low-traction situations.

The Ford F-150 Lightning was replaced by the Raptor, a performance-oriented but also off-road-ready truck. This is a 2010 SVT F-150 Raptor. (Photo Courtesy Ford Motor Company)

As a niche vehicle, pricing for the Raptor was a concern. There was a lot of expensive technology found on the performance, off-road truck. Ford initially intended to keep the price in the mid-$30,000 range, but the Raptor was released with a price of more than $42,000.

The first generation of the Raptor ran from model year 2010 until the 2014 model year. It returned to a bolder design with a high-performance engine in the 2017 model year.

The Raptor featured Fox Racing Shox internal bypass shocks with external reservoirs, which allows for 11 inches of suspension travel in the front and 12 inches in the rear. It also features a skid plate to protect the under-vehicle components. (Photo Courtesy Tracy Dinsmore)

The liner in the bed of this 2017 Ford Raptor is prepared to take a little beating and get some mud sprayed on it. The Raptor was based on the F-150 but had more off-road features than a standard F-150. (Photo Courtesy Tracy Dinsmore)

Safety Features

The 2009 F-150 came with the following standard safety features:

- AdvanceTrac Electronic Stability Control (ESP)
- Front and rear row side curtain airbags
- Front row torso side airbags

As a result of these enhancements and the built-in strength of the chassis, the F-150 received the Good overall score in both front and side impact tests and was given the Top Safety Pick award by IIHS. The US National Highway Traffic Safety Administration (NHTSA) F-150 crash test results included:

- Frontal driver: 5/5 stars
- Frontal passenger: 5/5 stars
- Side driver: 5/5 stars
- Side rear passenger: 5/5 stars
- 2WD rollover: 4/5 stars
- 4WD rollover: 3/5 stars

Engines

Three engines were offered with the 2009 redesign:

- A revised 5.4L 3-valve Triton V8 with an output rating of 320 hp (240 kW) and 395 ft-lbs of torque
- A 292-hp 4.6L 3-valve V8
- A 248-hp 4.6L 2-valve V8

The 3-valve 5.4L and 4.6L V8s used Ford's new 6R80E 6-speed automatic transmission, whereas the 4R75E 4-speed automatic transmission was carried over for the 2-valve 4.6L V8.

Two of the new engines included a 3.7L V6 and a 5.0L V8. The carryover engines included:

- The 6.2L gasoline V8 used in the 2011 Ford Super Duty was made available with the F-150 Platinum, Lariat, SVT Raptor, and Harley-Davidson editions.
- The new 3.5L direct-injected twin-turbo EcoBoost V6 was offered in the F-150 starting in early 2011.

3.7L Tri-VCT 4V V6

The Duratec 3.7L engine has a bore diameter of 95.5 mm (3.76 inches) and a stroke of 86.7 mm (3.41 inches). The first Ford application of the 3.7L V6 was the 2009 Lincoln MKS and the F-150.

Ford uses variable valve timing on both the intake and exhaust camshafts, which it calls Tri-VCT. Variable-camshaft timing (VCT) allows the valves to be operated at different points in the combustion cycle to improve performance. The Ford truck EcoBoost engines use variable camshaft timing on both intake and exhaust cams or both at the same time.

6.7L Ford Built Power Stroke Diesel Engine

The 6.7L was the first medium-duty diesel designed and built by Ford. It was designed in conjunction with AVL of Austria. During design, Ford engineers gave this engine the code name *Scorpion* due to the exhaust manifold and turbo being mounted in the valley between the cylinder bores, making it look like a scorpion.

The engine used a compacted graphite iron (CGI) block for greater strength while reducing weight. The reverse-flow aluminum cylinder heads (exhaust ports were located in the lifter valley) with dual water jackets were equipped with six head bolts per cylinder and a 29,000-psi (1,999 bar) HPCR Bosch electronic fuel injection system. The HPCR system delivered up to five injection events per cylinder per cycle, using eight-hole piezo injectors spraying fuel into the piston bowl.

This engine also supported B20 biodiesel, allowing fueling options of up to 20-percent biodiesel and 80-percent diesel fuel. It used Garrett's single-sequential turbocharger with a double-sided compressor wheel mounted on a single shaft. The connecting rods were made by Mahle.

Emissions controls included: exhaust gas recirculation (EGR), a selective catalytic reduction (SCR) converter, and a diesel particulate filter (DPF). The engine at first release produced 400 hp (298 kW) at 2,800 rpm and 800 ft-lbs at 1,600 rpm.

The 2015 engines were rated at 440 hp and 860 ft-lbs. The 2017 engines saw an increase in torque, while horsepower remained unchanged. The engine still produced 440 hp at 2,800 rpm, but torque jumped up to 925 ft-lbs and peaked at 1,800 rpm instead of 1,600 rpm like previous model years.

6.7L Power Stroke Specs	
Type	**4-cycle Turbocharged and Intercooled**
Configuration	90-degree V8 cam-in-block OHV, four valves per cylinder
Displacement	6.7L (409 ci)
Bore and stroke	3.90 x 4.25 inches (99x108 mm)
Block/heads	Compacted graphite iron block/aluminum
Compression ratio	16.2:1
Fuel injection system	High-pressure common rail (HPCR)
Starting heat method	Glow plugs
Horsepower	400 hp at 2,800 rpm (2010–2014) 440 hp at 2,800 rpm (2015+)
Torque	800 ft-lbs at 1,600 rpm (2010–2014) 860 ft-lbs at 1,600 rpm (2015–2016) 925 ft-lbs at 1,800 rpm (2017+)
Oil capacity with filter	13 quarts for 2011–2016 model years 15 quarts for 2017+ model years

2012

For 2012, the F-150 was a complete carryover truck. It had the following trim levels in order from the basic truck to the fully loaded: XL, STX, XLT, FX2, FX4, Lariat, King Ranch, Platinum, Harley-Davidson, and SVT Raptor.

The 2012 F-350 was quite capable and a favorite for people with large boats and recreational vehicles. This truck could tow up to 12,500 pounds and had a payload of more than 4,500 pounds. (Photo Courtesy Martha Davis)

The Ford F-150 has been assembled at the Kansas City Assembly Plant since 1957. This is a 2013 Ford F-150. (Photo Courtesy Ford Motor Company)

This beautiful 2014 F-150 Super Crew has chrome on the grille and the front end. The big headlights take on a more obtuse shape than trucks of the previous generation. The front end, specifically the light shapes, was an area where designers could focus their attention and give trucks a modern, unique appearance. (Photo Courtesy Randy Stern)

2013

For the 2013 model year, the F-150 received minor changes, such as three new grilles (replacing all four previous grilles) and new optional 18-, 20-, or 22-inch wheels. Other options included:

- MyFord Touch navigation system
- Power-folding and telescoping trailer tow mirrors
- High-intensity discharge headlamps
- Three new color options (Blue Jeans Metallic, Kodiak Brown Metallic, and Ruby Red Clearcoat Metallic)

The 2013 model year also saw the return of the Limited model and the 6.2L V8 being made available in XLT, FX2, and FX4 (Super Cab and Super Crew only).

2014

The 2014 F-150 was another carryover truck with some trim exceptions. The STX trim level also became available on Super Crew models with the 5.5-foot bed. The STX Sport package was added for 2014, which included 20-inch wheels, black cloth seats, and black exterior accents.

For 2014, a special truck called the "Tremor" was released. It was essentially an EcoBoost-equipped FX2 or FX4 truck in a regular cab model, a 6.5-foot bed, and a special FX Appearance Package.

Conclusion

The twelfth generation was just the beginning of Ford putting fuel economy into the discussion of how it could evolve the F-Series. The next generation expanded on the EcoBoost technology and even offered a 4-cylinder truck as well as an aluminum-based pickup. Ford felt as if it had the consumer capital with the success of the EcoBoost. It was a popular option during the time that saw a 40-percent increase in the cost of fuel.

Ford invested a lot of money into the F-Series program. The company also financially reaped the benefits of the popularity of this truck. Throughout the entire twelfth generation, the F-150 continued to be the best-selling vehicle in America. Ford had, once again, managed to redesign the truck and nail the design and engineering. Even with prices exceeding $40,000 for an F-150 for the first time, there seemed to be no ceiling for this truck.

This is a 2014 F-150 Platinum trim. The 2014 model year represented a carryover in styling and design from the 2013 model year. (Photo Courtesy Creative Commons)

The Ford F-Series truck has undergone an incredible transformation over the years. This is a visual representation of that transformation taken in front of Ford's world headquarters. (Photo Courtesy Ford Motor Company)

Year	Engine	Horsepower (hp)	Torque (ft-lbs)	VIN Code
2009	281-ci (4.6L) V8 (Modular, 2V)	248	294 at 4,000 rpm	W
	281-ci (4.6L) V8 (Modular, 3V)	292	320 at 4,000 rpm	8
	330-ci (5.4L) V8 (Modular)	320	390 at 3,500 rpm	V
	390-ci (6.4L) V8 (Power Stroke Turbo Diesel)	350	650 at 2,000 rpm	R
	415-ci (6.8L) V10	362	457 at 3,250 rpm	Y
2010	281-ci (4.6L) V8 (Modular, 2V)	248	294 at 4,000 rpm	W
	281-ci (4.6L) V8 (Modular, 3V)	292	320 at 4,000 rpm	8
	330-ci (5.4L) V8 (Modular)	320	390 at 3,500 rpm	V
	390-ci (6.4L) V8 (Power Stroke Turbo Diesel)	350	650 at 2,000 rpm	R
	415-ci (6.8L) V10	362	457 at 3,250 rpm	Y
2011	213-ci (3.5L) V6 (EcoBoost)	365	420 at 2,500 rpm	C
	225-ci (3.7L) V6 (Tri-VCT)	302	278 at 4,000 rpm	M
	302-ci (5.0L) V8	360	380 at 4,250 rpm	F
	379-ci (6.2L) V8	383	405 at 4,500 rpm	6
	406-ci (6.7L) V8 (Power Stroke Turbo Diesel)	390	735 at 1,600 rpm	T
2012	213-ci (3.5L) V6 (EcoBoost)	365	420 at 2,500 rpm	T
	225-ci (3.7L) V6 (Tri-VCT)	302	278 at 4,000 rpm	M
	302-ci (5.0L) V8	360	380 at 4,250 rpm	F
	379-ci (6.2L) V8	383	405 at 4,500 rpm	6
	406-ci (6.7L) V8 (Power Stroke Turbo Diesel)	400	800 at 1,600 rpm	T
2013	213-ci (3.5L) V6 (EcoBoost)	365	420 at 2,500 rpm	T
	225-ci (3.7L) V6 (Tri-VCT)	302	278 at 4,000 rpm	M
	302-ci (5.0L) V8	360	380 at 4,250 rpm	F
	379-ci (6.2L) V8	383	405 at 4,500 rpm	6
	406-ci (6.7L) V8 (Power Stroke Turbo Diesel)	400	800 at 1,600 rpm	T
2014	213-ci (3.5L) V6 (EcoBoost)	365	420 at 2,500 rpm	T
	225-ci (3.7L) V6 (Tri-VCT)	302	278 at 4,000 rpm	M
	302-ci (5.0L) V8	360	380 at 4,250 rpm	F
	379-ci (6.2L) V8	411	434 at 4,500 rpm	6
	406-ci (6.7L) V8 (Power Stroke Turbo Diesel)	400	800 at 1,600 rpm	T

Note: Information included in this chart is designed to be inclusive. Dependent on reference, year, and carryover, information may vary.

Note: From 2009 to 2014, the engine VIN is the eighth character listed.

Year	Model	Automatic/ Manual	Number of Gears	Transmission
2009–2010	F-150	Automatic	4	Overdrive
2009–2010	F-150	Automatic	6	Overdrive
2011–2014	F-150	Automatic	6	Standard
2009	F-250	Automatic	5	TorqShift
2009	F-250	Manual	6	Standard
2010	F-250	Automatic	5	Overdrive
2011–2014	F-250	Automatic	6	SelectShift

Note: Information included in this chart is designed to be inclusive. Dependent upon reference, year, and carryover, information may vary.

Color	Available Year and VIN Code					
	2009	2010	2011	2012	2013	2014
Dark Shadow Gun Metal Gray	CX	–	–	–	–	–
Dark Blue Effect	DX	DX	DX	DX	–	–
Sunset	–	–	–	–	–	D7
Vermillion	E4	E4 or F1	E4 or F1	E4	E4 or F1	E4 or F1
Tornado Red Effect	FL	–	–	–	–	–
Pueblo Gold Effect	G3	G3	–	–	–	–
Vista Blue Effect	G9	–	–	–	–	–
Forrest Green Effect	GG	GG	GG	GG	–	–
Amber Gold Metallic	GQ	–	–	–	–	–
Autumn Red Pearl	–	–	–	GT	GT	–
Earth Metallic	HS	–	–	–	–	–
Kodiak Brown Metallic	–	–	–	–	J1	J1
Golden Bronze	–	–	JQ	JQ	–	–
Pale Adobe	–	–	LQ	LQ	LQ	LQ
True Blue Effect	L2	–	–	–	–	–
Blue Jean Metallic	–	–	–	–	N1	N1
Race Red	–	–	PQ	PQ	PQ	PQ
White Chocolate Tricoat	PV	UG	–	–	–	–
Aspen Green Effect	P5	–	–	–	–	–
Ruby Red Tricoat	–	–	–	–	RR	RR
Red Candy Pearl Tricoat	–	–	RZ	RZ	–	–
Blue Flame Metallic	SZ	SZ	SZ	SZ	SZ	SZ
Charcoal Beige Metallic	T7	–	–	–	–	–
Black Ebony	UA or UD	UD	–	UA or UD	–	–
White Platinum Tricoat	–	UG	UG	UG	UG	UG
Tuxedo Black	–	UH	UH	UH	UH	UH
Brilliant Silver Metallic Cladding	UI	–	–	–	–	–
Sterling Gray Metallic Cladding	UJ	UJ	UJ	UJ	UJ	UJ
Royal Red Metallic	UK	UK	UK	–	–	–
Steel Blue Metallic	–	UN	–	–	–	–
Ingot Silver Metallic	–	UX	UX	UX	UX	UX
Molten Orange Tricoat	–	UY	UY	–	–	–
Lava Red Metallic	–	UZ	–	–	–	–
Sport Blue Metallic	–	–	–	–	–	U1
Red Candy Tricoat	U6	U6	U6	–	–	–
Terrain	–	–	–	–	VA	VA
Bronze Metallic	–	–	V7	V7	–	–
Performance White	WB	WB	WB	WB	–	–
Green Gem Pearl Metallic	–	–	–	W6	W6	W6
Bright Red	–	–	–	W8	–	–
Silver Effect	YN	–	–	–	–	–
Oxford White	YZ or Z1	YZ or Z1	YZ or Z1	YZ or Z1	YZ or Z1	YZ or Z1

Note: Information included in this chart is designed to be inclusive. Dependent upon reference, year, and carryover, information may vary.

Note: For 2009 to 2014, paint color is listed on a VIN tag located on the driver-side doorjamb as "EXTERIOR PAINT,"

Year	Model	Wheelbase (inches)	Length (inches)	Bed Length (feet)	Height (inches)	Width (inches)	Gross Vehicle Weight (pounds)	Price
2009–2014	Ford F-150 1/2 ton	126–163	211–248	5.5/8	73–76	79	6,650–8,200	$20,100–$40,940
2009–2014	Ford F-250 3/4 ton	137–172	227–262	6.75/8.2	76–80	80	8,800–9,600	$23,185–$38,560

Note: Information included in this chart is designed to be inclusive. Dependent upon reference, year, and carryover, information may vary.

Note that price is based on MSRP listing.

FORD F-SERIES THIRTEENTH GENERATION (2015–2020)

On and off the farm, the F-150 was America's best-selling vehicle year after year. Trucks and their SUV offshoots were the money makers at the Blue Oval. Excluding the big cities, pickup trucks, and more specifically the Ford F-Series, were everywhere. The profit margins were huge on trucks (and SUVs) compared to the smaller margins on cars. For this reason, in 2018, Ford announced it was eliminating its entire car line with the exception of the iconic Ford Mustang. The automaker would focus solely on trucks, crossovers, and SUVs. Some analysts questioned whether the SUV fad was here to stay and if Ford was making an error in jumping out of the car business.

For the thirteenth generation, Ford made a bold move with the truck, moving it to a new platform based on aluminum. It was the first of the truck makers to make such a move. Its competitors, General Motors and Toyota, pounced on this opportunity to demonstrate how the aluminum body was weaker and that Ford trucks were no longer "Built Ford Tough." However, the durability of the aluminum bed is fine aside from extreme cases that would damage a steel bed as well.

To demonstrate this, YouTube videos were posted of cargo being dropped into the bed and denting an aluminum-based F-150; some trucks even had holes ripped into it. But the move to aluminum served its purpose. Still under the watchful eye of the government, the weight dropped 700 pounds. In doing so, the thirteenth generation was the most fuel-efficient F-Series ever built.

Trucks have become the biggest money maker for Ford. This is why Ford has begun to move out of the car-making business and focus on pickup trucks and SUVs. What started out as a rural, farmer-focused pickup truck has grown into a profitable, popular market for Ford. In the thirteenth generation, Ford spared no expense in the materials used for the interior and on the styling and design of the exterior. (Photo Courtesy Randy Stern)

The top-of-the-line F-150 King Ranch trim looks like a luxury SUV inside. The price points have grown exponentially with every new feature and creature comfort added. (Photo Courtesy Randy Stern)

The 2019 version continues to look current and modern. Even in the middle of the F-150's life cycle, Ford invested money in keeping its best-selling vehicle current and updated. (Photo Courtesy Tracy Dinsmore)

The technological advances in Ford's EcoBoost system further improved fuel economy. For all the marketing campaigns against Ford's "aluminum truck," it didn't hinder sales. In fact, during this generation, Ford surpassed the 800,000 and even the 900,000 sales volume level, a mark it had not been to since the early part of the century.

The thirteenth-generation Ford F-Series was unveiled at the North American International Auto Show on January 13, 2014. This generation was based on an all-new platform and marked the implementation of an aluminum body construction for the F-Series for the first time with the 2015 models.

The 2015 F-150 introduced a number of advanced driver assistance systems, including a 360-degree camera, adaptive cruise control, collision warning with brake support, blind spot information system, cross-traffic alert, and lane-keeping system.

A handsome 2019 F-150 Super Crew with a 145-inch wheelbase is shown. This 4x4 truck has a beautiful Race Red exterior. (Photo Courtesy Tracy Dinsmore)

Body Features

The LED headlights were originally planned to use glass for the optics to focus the beam, but it could not achieve the needed clarity. Ford designers instead used polycarbonate

Within the truck industry, a lot of attention is paid to the tailgate. General Motors debuted a multifaceted tailgate on its GMC Sierra. Ford added this step-up attachment on the tailgate to assist with getting in and out of the back of the truck. (Photo Courtesy Tracy Dinsmore)

For 2019, rear legroom continued to increase. In this 2019 F-150, three passengers can sit comfortably in the back seat. The back window slides open, and there's also a sunroof. (Photo Courtesy Tracy Dinsmore)

thermoplastic. Each lamp used one LED for the high beam, a second one for the low beam, and one for the orange thermoplastic light pipe. The two beams, along with the light pipe, are housed within one module.

On the tailgate, the area between the taillamps became partially recessed with the option of chrome trim. The taillamp assembly also houses the blind spot monitor.

Trim Levels

In an effort to consolidate models, the STX and FX2/FX4 trims were discontinued. The Tremor and Harley-Davidson special editions were not included in the 2015 redesign.

Under-seat storage is available on this 2019 F-150. With the pull of one lever, you can access more area to store items. This once again shows the family emphasis of the F-150. (Photo Courtesy Tracy Dinsmore)

This is a 2019 F-150 with leather-trimmed seats and a leather-wrapped steering wheel. There is ambient lighting and an 8-inch touchscreen as well as a telescoping steering wheel. (Photo Courtesy Tracy Dinsmore)

To complete engineering work on the 2015 model, the SVT Raptor sub-model went out of production but returned for the 2017 model year. The thirteenth-generation F-Series used the traditional Ford truck nomenclature with XL, XLT, and Lariat trims, as well as the King Ranch and Platinum trims (shared with the Super Duty line). The trim levels included:

- XLT (2015+)
- Lariat (2015+)
- King Ranch (2015+)
- Platinum (2015+)
- Limited (2016+)
- Raptor (2017+)

Chassis

Almost all of the body panels of the F-150 were changed from steel to aluminum construction. The only significant sheet metal component constructed of steel is the firewall plus the frame, which was constructed from high-strength steel. To demonstrate the durability of the aluminum-intensive design, Ford entered prototypes of the model disguised as twelfth-generation F150s in the Baja 1000 endurance race.

Powertrain

Ford also introduced its first diesel engine in the F-150, which was also called the Power Stroke engine, like all previous Ford Diesel light-duty applications. This diesel engine

This F-150 is equipped with a 6.7L Turbo Diesel engine. Notice the two batteries located side by side in this truck. Other Ford diesel pickups have the two batteries separated with one on the driver's side and the other on the passenger's side. Whenever testing a vehicle with two batteries, they must be disconnected and tested separately. If one is bad, both should be replaced to help ensure that they are matched. Otherwise, the weaker battery will cause the better battery to become weaker as a result. (Photo Courtesy Tracy Dinsmore)

was a twin turbo 3.0L V6 from the Lion lineup of engines shared by PSA (Peugeot Citroën) and Jaguar Land Rover. The engine produced 440 ft-lbs of torque and was mated to the new 10-speed transmission. It also featured hybrid-style stop/start technology.

Ford offered a wider range of fuel-efficient engines for the F-150. A 3.5L version of the Tri-VCT V6 replaced the 3.7L version as the entry-level engine. The 3.7L V6 was replaced by a new 2.7L EcoBoost V6 with the 3.5L EcoBoost continuing.

With the 6.2L V8 again exclusive to the Super Duty line, the 5.0L V8 was retuned for additional horsepower and torque output. No manual transmission was available with a 6-speed automatic paired with all drivelines except the 3.0L V6 diesel.

The Duratec 33 (3.3L) is a downgraded version of the Duratec 35 with direct injection starting in the 2018 model year for the Ford F-150. It served as the new base engine.

RETRO CHIC

There's a trend with today's modern truck-buying market. While today's truck buyer wants big, modern trucks loaded with amenities, they also want to be able to customize the truck to their liking. Most dealers are more than happy to accommodate, and many dealerships have specialized the customization process to cater to the high-end truck buyer with specific, niche demands and even have sales staff dedicated to these buyers. One such trend takes customization to a whole new level.

An example of retrofitting is when a car dealer takes a modern truck and adds throwback styling. These retro kits contain such things as two-tone vinyl covering, KC HiLiTes light bars, chrome accents, and fat tires with thicker white walls. Any or all of these retro options can really change the look of a modern F-150 and give it a late 1970s or early 1980s vibe. Of course, the interior remains mostly unchanged and has all the luxury of today's trucks. There is also modern power and efficiency under the hood. Look on the lots of specialist Ford dealers, and you might see some of these retro-looking trucks.

One option within this trend is to add power and performance to these throwback trucks. It's not uncommon for a truck buyer to drop an additional $10,000 for these retro kits and then add another couple thousand dollars by adding a Roush or a Whipple supercharger to increase the horsepower or Roush exhausts to tune up a bigger growl. Some of these retro trucks may look old school, but they're modern pieces of machinery with horsepower that can exceed 600 hp. This shows where the F-150 has evolved after all these years. What's old is new again. Ford makes so many different trucks with several engine options. It's not enough for the discerning truck buyer who wants what they want, how they want it. And Ford and its dealers are happy to accommodate and customize.

Retrofitting has become a popular trend among some truck enthusiasts. This process involves buying any trim truck then having a dealer install a retro package, which could include chrome highlights, a KC light bar, vinyl covering to represent the two-tone paint schemes that were popular in the late 1970s and early 1980s, and throwback tires.

One facet of the retrofit trend is adding power and performance or at least tuned-up growl to the F-150. This is done by adding a Roush exhaust. This Ford F-150 XLT trim was customized with a retro vinyl covering and a 3-inch lift kit, as well as the Roush exhaust.

2015

Model year 2015 was the first for the redesigned look and was the new platform for the thirteenth-generation F-Series. For the 2015 model year, Ford reduced curb weight by nearly 750 pounds by switching most of the

In addition to a lavish interior, the top-of-the-line King Ranch trim had special badging on the tailgate for this 2015 F-150. (Photo Courtesy Randy Stern)

This is a nice example of a 2015 F-150 Lariat Super Crew. Model year 2015 was the first year for the new design of the thirteenth generation. (Photo Courtesy Randy Stern)

For the 2015 model year, there were two EcoBoost V6 engine options: a 2.7L and a 3.5L. EcoBoost combines gasoline direct injection and turbocharging to make a more fuel-efficient engine. (Photo Courtesy Randy Stern)

The back seat of this 2015 F-150 was the largest back seat area in terms of leg room that Ford had produced. It's why the thirteenth generation was an immediate success as families found the space and interior very friendly. This F-150 has room for three passengers in the back. (Photo Courtesy Randy Stern)

The 2015 Ford F-150 was the first full-production vehicle made from aluminum to be the best-selling vehicle in North America. As of 2016, 85 percent of the F-150 is made in the United States. There was concern by the collision repair shops about the 2015 Ford F-150 being largely made of aluminum. Yet, this is not brand-new technology. There have been a lot of aluminum car parts over the years. General Motors used aluminum rear decklids in the 1990s, and certain models of the Land Rover used aluminum body panels.

Aluminum makes the truck lighter, which helps Ford meet the Corporate Average Fuel Economy (CAFE) standards. It is also the most common metal on the planet. In fact, it is the third most abundant element. There is a lot of new, approved repair equipment on the market to deal with the repair and painting of aluminum panels. There will be less to remove and replace for body repair. Repairing aluminum uses a different process compared to steel.

Painting an aluminum panel also requires a slightly different process than steel or fiberglass. For aluminum and steel, the refinish process is somewhat the same, which includes the following procedures:

- Clean
- Abrade
- Clean
- Condition
- Etch
- Prime
- Seal
- Paint

However, there are substrate-specific products that must be used to ensure success. The process includes preparing the part to the specific paint line and then sealing it while being careful not to cut through the E-coat and expose the aluminum. In most cases, minor cut-throughs on steel panels can be safely sealed over. However, you will need to apply an etch primer to cut-throughs on aluminum panels prior to sealing.

Larger areas of bare aluminum require a different cleaning approach. Use a wax and grease remover to remove any surface contaminants. Keep the scratch patterns to a 240 or finer grit on your sander. Next, use an aluminum-specific metal conditioner/cleaner according to the manufacturer's specifications. When rinsing off the conditioner with water, look for the water to sheet off as opposed to beading. Beading indicates a presence of wax or grease.

After the surface has dried thoroughly, an aluminum-specific metal conversion coating is applied. This coating stabilizes and modifies the surface while offering a layer of corrosion protection. Do this immediately after drying, as aluminum will oxidize/corrode very quickly. The conversion coating will have good corrosion resistance and adhesion properties. In most cases, it can be directly sealed or primed.

This is a section of an aluminum Ford F-150 door on display during the 2014 North American International Auto Show (NAIAS). Ford was about to introduce the aluminum body to its iconic pickup truck.

A closer inspection shows a section of the aluminum body where the front doors mount to the cowl. Note the use of rivets to hold the two layers of the aluminum body together as well as the bolts used to attach the door hinge to the body.

Here is a cross sectional view of part of the body structure of the aluminum F-150, showing that it uses many components all fastened together to help create a very strong yet lightweight structure. The center part appears to be a hydroformed aluminum tube that was changed from a round extruded tube to the complex shape shown. It is then fastened to several other parts to create the finished body section.

In 2016, Ford debuted the Pro Trailer Backup Assist system. This enables people to make maneuvering easier when backing up their truck with a trailer attached. This feature creates more appeal to the weekend warrior who may be apprehensive about towing. (Photo Courtesy Tracy Dinsmore)

Even lower-level trims like this Lariat had incredibly nice interiors. Notice the faux wood accents and the leather seats in this 2015 F-150. (Photo Courtesy Randy Stern)

This alloy wheel features six lugs, which is one more than commonly used on passenger vehicles. (Photo Courtesy Randy Stern)

body panels to military-grade aluminum. The majority of the frame itself remained high-strength steel. Except for the firewall, all sheet metal used for the F-150 body is aluminum.

Technologically, there were some firsts for the F-Series. The 2015 F-150 was the first truck to have adaptive cruise control. Of the four available engines for the 2015 F-150, only one was a V8. The new 2.7L EcoBoost engine was met with some pushback from traditional truck buyers, but it proved to be quite popular with the daily commuter. Ford no longer offered the 6.2L V8 in the F-150 V8.

Outside of new engine features, Ford stopped offering the Sony stereo system as an option and replaced it with B&O PLAY, a sound system designed by Danish audio system manufacturer Bang & Olufsen. The thirteenth generation was American built at both the Dearborn Truck Plant in Michigan and the Kansas City Assembly Plant in Claycomo, Missouri. The F-150 is built at the rate of one truck per minute.

2016

From its outward appearance, the F-Series was a carry-over for 2016 from the 2015 models. However, the 2016 model featured an improved infotainment system. Ford launched its Sync3 system in the 2016 F-150. This system improved the interaction of the driver with various aspects of the infotainment system significantly. It had improved voice commands—something that users criticized about the previous Sync and MyFord Touch systems.

Aesthetically, the 2016 F-150 looked like the previous model year. For this year, however, Ford updated its infotainment system to the new Ford Sync3 system. (Photo Courtesy Tracy Caulfield)

The Ford Raptor returned in the 2017 model year after a two-year hiatus. The 2017 version had a fresh new appearance, including a 5.5-foot bed. (Photo Courtesy Tracy Dinsmore)

There is no blue oval Ford logo on the front of the 2017 Ford Raptor. Only "FORD" is spelled out in special big letters on the dominant grille of this off-road truck. (Photo Courtesy Randy Stern)

Additionally, the 2016 F-Series featured Ford's Pro Trailer Backup Assist feature. This catered to the more casual truck owner who owned a boat or a camper but might not have been as confident or comfortable backing up. While this feature did not impress the old-school truck owners, it did help win over some of the more casual truck enthusiasts.

2017

For the 2017 model year, the Ford Super Duty truck line was completely redesigned for the first time since the 1999 model year. All models of the F-Series from the F-150 through the F-550 used a common cab design. The Super Duty had its own front bodywork and unique bed, as well as two separate platforms (depending on GVWR).

Mechanically, the 2017 F-150 received a significant upgrade to the transmission, introducing a 10-speed automatic that greatly improved fuel economy. Ford continued to tweak and improve the Sync3 system by adding smartphone integration with Apple CarPlay and Android Auto for the first time.

Following a two-year hiatus, the F-150 Raptor returned for the 2017 model year without the SVT prefix. Ford absorbed SVT into the global "Ford Performance" family/branding. The 2017 Raptor was an off-road vehicle produced in Super Cab and Super Crew configurations with a model-exclusive 5.5-foot bed. The model does not use a Ford blue oval grille badge, but does use "F-O-R-D" spelled across the center of the grille.

As with a standard Ford F-150, the Raptor was an aluminum-paneled vehicle built on a steel frame, and nearly all its body panels are built using aluminum. The new 2017 replaced the previously used 6.2L V8 with a 3.5L twin-turbo EcoBoost V6 paired with a 10-speed automatic transmission. The new engine improves the horsepower by 39 hp to an overall 450, and increases the torque substantially from the old engine to 510 ft-lbs.

To improve its off-road ability over a standard F-150, the Raptor is fitted with a torque-on-demand transfer case, 13-inch travel front, and 13.9-inch travel rear Fox Racing suspension, and all-terrain 35-inch tires and wheels.

F-150 is spelled predominantly on the tailgate of the 2018 Ford F-150. This is an easy way to spot trucks from this model year. (Photo Courtesy Beth Fitzgibbons)

The 2018 F-150 received a new grille that features LED headlights. Model year 2018 had the most drastic changes to occur for this generation of the F-Series. (Photo Courtesy Beth Fitzgibbons)

The interior of the F-150 Platinum shows how luxurious the modern truck had become. Additionally for 2018, several key safety features debuted including pre-collision assistance and pedestrian detection. (Photo Courtesy Randy Stern)

2018

In 2018, the Ford F-150 received a new grille, new LED headlights and taillights, and F-150 stamped in the tailgate. The new F-150 introduced an all-new standard turbocharged 3.3L V6 engine with direct injection for increased fuel efficiency without a decrease in power. An all-new second-generation 2.7L EcoBoost engine featured advanced dual port and direct injection technology, reduced internal friction, and improved robustness. All this is for improved levels of output, efficiency, quality, and durability.

Like the 3.5L EcoBoost, the 2.7L EcoBoost was paired to the segment-exclusive 10-speed automatic transmission for 2018. The 5.0L V8 was also improved; the naturally aspirated engine featured significant upgrades for increased power and torque. It was paired with the 10-speed automatic transmission for the first time. Also, the truck had new and advanced safety features, such as new automatic emergency braking, pre-collision assist with pedestrian detection, and adaptive cruise control with stop-and-go (stop-start) technology.

Ford relaunched the Ranger as a stand-alone truck nameplate in 2019. The Ranger was categorized as a smaller truck than the F-150. This is a preproduction version of the Ranger, as seen in the fall of 2018. The styling and even the size was quite similar to the F-150. Notice the protective cover over the front end, which was something manufacturers do in the preproduction process.

This preproduction Ford Ranger shows how close in style the Ranger will be to the F-150, although the Ranger is smaller. Similar to the thirteenth-generation F-150, the Ranger has its name stamped into the tailgate.

Ford Light-Duty Truck Engines (2015–2019)				
Year	Engine	Horsepower (hp)	Torque (ft-lbs)	VIN Code
2015	165-ci (2.7L) (EcoBoost)	325	375 at 3,000 rpm	P
	213-ci (3.5L) V6 (EcoBoost)	365	420 at 2,500 rpm	G
	213-ci (3.5L) V6 (Tri-VCT)	282	253 at 4,000 rpm	8
	302-ci (5.0L) V8 (Tri-VCT)	385	387 at 3,850 rpm	F
	379-ci (6.2L) V8	385	405 at 4,500 rpm	6
	406-ci (6.7L) V8 (Power Stroke Turbo Diesel)	440	860 at 1,600 rpm	T
2016	165-ci (2.7L) (EcoBoost)	325	375 at 3,000 rpm	P
	213-ci (3.5L) V6 (EcoBoost)	365	420 at 2,500 rpm	G
	213-ci (3.5L) V6 (Tri-VCT)	282	253 at 4,000 rpm	8
	302-ci (5.0L) V8 (Tri-VCT)	385	387 at 3,850 rpm	F
	379-ci (6.2L) V8	385	405 at 4,500 rpm	6
	406-ci (6.7L) V8 (Power Stroke Turbo Diesel)	440	860 at 1,600 rpm	T
2017	165-ci (2.7L) (EcoBoost)	325	375 at 3,000 rpm	P
	213-ci (3.5L) V6 (EcoBoost)	375	470 at 3,500 rpm	G
	213-ci (3.5L) V6 (Tri-VCT)	282	253 at 4,000 rpm	G
	302-ci (5.0L) V8 (Tri-VCT)	385	387 at 3,850 rpm	F
	379-ci (6.2L) V8	385	430 at 3,800 rpm	6
	406-ci (6.7L) V8 (Power Stroke Turbo Diesel)	440	925 at 1,800 rpm	T
2018	165-ci (2.7L) (EcoBoost)	325	400 at 2,750 rpm	P
	183-ci (3.0L) (Power Stroke Turbo Diesel)	250	440 at 1,750 rpm	1
	202-ci (3.3L) V6 (Tri-VCT)	290	265 at 4,000 rpm	B
	213-ci (3.5L) V6 (EcoBoost)	375	470 at 3,500 rpm	G
	213-ci (3.5L) V6 (H.O. EcoBoost)	450	510 at 3,500 rpm	G
	302-ci (5.0L) V8 (Tri-VCT)	395	400 at 4,500 rpm	F
	379-ci (6.2L) V8	385	430 at 3,800 rpm	6
	406-ci (6.7L) V8 (Power Stroke Turbo Diesel)	450	935 at 1,800 rpm	T
2019	165-ci (2.7L) V6 (EcoBoost)	325	400 at 2,750 rpm	P
	183-ci (3.0L) (Power Stroke Turbo Diesel)	250	440 at 1,750 rpm	1
	202-ci (3.3L) V6 (Tri-VCT)	290	265 at 4,000 rpm	B
	213-ci (3.5L) V6 (EcoBoost)	375	470 at 3,500 rpm	G
	213-ci (3.5L) V6 (H.O. EcoBoost)	450	510 at 3,500 rpm	G
	302-ci (5.0L) V8 (Tri-VCT)	395	400 at 4,500 rpm	F
	379-ci (6.2L) V8	385	430 at 3,800 rpm	6
	406-ci (6.7L) V8 (Power Stroke Turbo Diesel)	450	935 at 1,800 rpm	T

Note: Information included in this chart is designed to be inclusive. Dependent upon reference, year, and carryover, information may vary.

Note: From 2015 to 2019, the engine VIN is the eighth character listed.

Ford Light- and Light/Medium-Duty Trucks Transmissions (2015–2019)

Year	Model	Automatic/ Manual	Number of Gears	Transmission
2015–2016	F-150	Automatic	6	SelectShift Automatic
2015–2016	F-150	Automatic	6	Automatic
2017	F-150	Automatic	6	Electronic Automatic
2017	F-150	Automatic	10	Electronic Automatic
2018–2019	F-150	Automatic	6	SelectShift Automatic
2018–2019	F-150	Automatic	10	SelectShift Automatic
2015–2016	F-250	Automatic	6	SelectShift Automatic
2015–2016	F-250	Automatic	6	Overdrive
2017–2019	F-250	Automatic	6	TorqShift-G (SelectShift) Automatic
2017–2019	F-250	Automatic	6	TorqShift (SelectShift) Automatic

Note: Information included in this chart is designed to be inclusive. Dependent upon reference, year, and carryover, information may vary.

Ford Light- and Light/Medium-Duty Trucks Paint Colors (2015–2019)

Color	Available Year and VIN Code				
	2015	2016	2017	2018	2019
School Bus Yellow	–	BY	BY	BY	BY
Avalanche	–	–	DR	–	–
Stone Gray Metallic	–	–	–	D1	D1
Magma Red	–	–	–	E2	E2
Vermillion	E4	–	–	–	–
Blue Diamond Metallic	–	–	–	FT	FT
Absolute Back Pearl	–	G1	G1	G1	G1
Palladium White Gold	–	–	GN	GN	GN
Guard Metallic	HN	–	–	HN	HN
Caribou Metallic	H5	H5	H5	–	–
Bronze Fire Pearl	H7	H7	H7	–	–
Lead Foot Gray	–	–	–	JX	JX
Magnetic Metallic	J7	J7	J7	J7	J7
Tangier Orange	–	J8	J8	J8	J8
Bold Yellow	–	LE	LE	LE	LE
Abyss Gray	–	–	–	ME	–
Blue Jeans Metallic	N1	N1	N1	N1	N1
Blue Lightening Pearl	–	–	N6	N6	N6
Race Red	PQ	PQ	PQ	PQ	PQ
Ruby Red Tricoat	RR	–	–	–	–
Ruby Red Pearl Tricoat	–	RR	RR	RR	RR
Burgundy Velvet Tricoat	–	–	–	R3	R3
Blue Flame Metallic	SZ	SZ	–	–	–
Real Steel		TB	TB	–	–
White Platinum Tricoat	UG	UG	UG	UG	UG
Tuxedo Black	UH	–	–	–	–
Ingot Silver Metallic	UX	UX	UX	UX	UX
Performance White	WB	–	–	–	–
Green Gem Pearl Metallic	–	W6	W6	W6	W6
Dark Titanium Metallic	YU	–	–	–	–
Oxford White	YZ	YZ	YZ or Z1	YZ or Z1	YZ or Z1

Note: Information included in this chart is designed to be inclusive. Dependent upon reference, year, and carryover, information may vary.

Note: For 2015–2019, paint color is listed on a VIN tag located on the driver-side doorjamb as "EXTERIOR PAINT."

Ford Light- and Light/Medium-Duty Truck Sales and Prices (2015–2019)

Year	Model	Wheelbase (inches)	Length (inches)	Bed Length (feet)	Height (inches)	Width (inches)	Gross Vehicle Weight (pounds)	Price
2015–2019	Ford F-150 1/2 ton	122–164	209–250	6.5/8	75–78	80	6,010–7,850	$25,800–$67,135
2015–2019	Ford F-250 3/4 ton	137–176	227–266	6.7/8	77–81	80	10,000	$31,045–$86,505

Note: Information included in this chart is designed to be inclusive. Dependent upon reference, year, and carryover, information may vary. Note that price is based on MSRP listing.

FORD F-SERIES FOURTEENTH GENERATION (2021+)

Ford put a lot of planning into the fourteenth-generation F-150. With this latest generation, many aspects changed. Ford added its first-ever hybrid powertrain to the F-150 and announced its first-ever all-electric pickup truck. The F-150 electric vehicle (EV) dons a familiar name: Lightning. While some enthusiasts balked at Ford's reuse of the Lightning name that was previously used for a high-performance model from more than a decade ago, it was appropriate for the electrified F-150.

This generation and era is incredibly important for Ford Motor Company. Jim Farley took over as CEO of Ford Motor Company and took the Blue Oval in a new direction. Beyond a push toward fuel efficiency, Farley pushed the envelope, and Ford Motor Company made bold moves. Farley outlined goals for improving product quality, eliminating unnecessary complexity, reducing costs, improving brand image, and driving toward modern technology across the entire Ford line. Even the best-selling vehicle in America was not immune from Farley's vision.

The fourteenth-generation F-150 has a new appearance and new technology, and it provides a glimpse into the future. The F-150 did not lose what made it so successful, as the V8 and the V6 EcoBoost engines are both available. Ford included over-the-air updates, hands-free driving technology, and an upgraded infotainment system. Plus, Ford added an off-road Tremor trim package and launched the third generation of the F-150 Raptor.

In 2021, the Ford truck lineup underwent a transformation that included the addition of new trucks, such as the Ford Maverick as well as the addition of the hybrid F-150, Tremor trim, and the first-ever all-electric pickup truck. (Photo Courtesy Ford Motor Company)

Debuting at the launch of the fourteenth-generation F-150 was the PowerBoost hybrid F-150, which is pictured here. The PowerBoost F-150 makes 430 hp and 570 ft-lbs of torque.

The 2021 F-150 features new aesthetics and a new exterior, including LED lighting in the box and zone lighting. The grille pictured here has a new design that separates it from the previous generation.

"F-150" is imprinted large on the tailgate of the 2021 Ford F-150 with a new taillight configuration.

In summation, the fourteenth generation of the F-150 represents the most ambitious and radical change in Ford's modern history. Consider that Ford did this while coming out of a global pandemic that saw challenging production shutdowns and supply-chain shortages.

Body Features

Ford continued the high-strength aluminum body from the previous generation, which was a radical change. Ford didn't take a hit to its reputation because there were no recalls related to the body or aluminum frame. Despite some advertisements and crazy videos on the internet showing the bed taking damage when pelted with heavy load, the move to an aluminum body paid off for Ford.

The fourteenth generation had new features, including LED lighting in the box as well as zone lighting as part of the 85P configuration. The zone lighting was optional for the XLT Mid and was standard on the XLT High (302A), Lariat, King Ranch, and Platinum trims. A new power tailgate included a step and work

One of the most noticeable differences on the back side of the fourteenth-generation F-150 is the work surface area on the tailgate that includes space for a laptop and pencil along with a measuring area. Ford modified the step so that it now disappears into the tailgate. A yellow assist handle retracts in and out, as does a non-slip extra step that folds down.

surface. This type of focus on work surfaces was a highlight of the fourteenth generation, and it is a common theme throughout the interior and exterior.

Some colors were added for 2021, and some were removed. New colors were Antimatter Blue, Carbonized Gray, Guard, Kodiak Brown, Smoked Quartz Tinted Clearcoat, and Space White. Colors no longer available for this generation were Abyss Gray, Blue Jean, Magma Red, Magnetic, and Silver Spruce.

Trim Levels

Ford continued all of the previous trim levels except for the XL Sport Appearance package. After the initial launch, a Tremor package was added, which was more rugged than the

There are six trims available for the 2021 Ford F-150. This is the Lariat trim in Iconic Silver paint.

Ford launched the Tremor package for the Super Duty line and Ranger. Ford also announced a mid-cycle addition of the Tremor to the F-150 line, which is expected around the 2023 model year. This is the 2021 Ford F-250 Tremor.

This 2021 Ford Ranger Tremor has special tires, ground clearance, exterior configurations, and features on the interior.

FX4 package. The Tremor was essentially a sub-brand across other models, including the Super Duty and Ranger. Ford also did this with the Raptor, adding it to the Bronco and the Ranger overseas. The Tremor has a special appearance, featuring a unique hood and grille with Active Orange highlights.

Powertrain

The most significant change for the 2021 Ford F-150 is the addition of a full hybrid powertrain called the PowerBoost. This V6 3.5L engine is combined with a 40-plus-hp electric motor. The PowerBoost also has its own hybrid electronic 10-speed automatic transmission.

Ford continued its other engine options but discontinued the 6-speed automatic transmission and made a 10-speed automatic with progressive range selection standard.

Available Engines

Type	Displacement	Power
V-6	3.3L	290 hp, 265 ft-lbs of torque
V-6 (EcoBoost)	2.7L	325 hp, 400 ft-lbs of torque
V-8	5.0L	400 hp, 410 ft-lbs of torque
V-6 (Power Stroke turbo diesel)*	3.0L	250 hp, 440 ft-lbs of torque
V-6 (EcoBoost)	3.5L	400 hp, 500 ft-lbs of torque
V-6 (PowerBoost hybrid)	3.5L	430 hp, 570 ft-lbs of torque

*discontinued halfway through 2021

Interior

The improvements continue on the interior with several new items, including new interior color choices. Ford added the Max Recline Driver and Passenger Seat (91S) option midway through the model year for the King Ranch, Platinum, and Limited trims only. These seats recline back and lift up in the lumbar area to provide a flat surface that is perfect for napping or resting.

There is a fold-flat interior workspace that is optional for all trims. In this optional setup, the gear shifter folds flat while a flat work surface folds over the top of the center

The interior of this 2021 Ford F-150 Lariat has black leather bucket seats and Equipment Package 502A. It also has 10-way power adjustable seats along with heated and cooled front seats.

One of the new features of the fourteenth-generation F-150 is a foldable gear shift knob. With the push of a button, the shifter folds flat to make room for a flat work surface.

As the gear-shift area folds down, the flat work surface flips over the top of the gear-shift area to make a usable flat surface. This is an update for the 2021 F-150. It has an additional cost of $650 and is available on all trims.

console, creating an ideal flat surface for a laptop or writing work orders with a pen and paper. This configuration is part of Ford's decision to make the F-150 more geared to the working class.

A 12-inch touchscreen is standard on Lariat, King Ranch, Platinum, and Limited trims and runs the new Sync4 infotainment system. Ford discontinued the Sync3 system for all F-150 trucks for the fourteenth generation.

A Bang & Olufsen HD radio with eight speakers is new for the model year and is optional on the XLT 302A and Lariat 500A. It is included on the Lariat 502A, King Ranch 600A, and Platinum 700A.

F-150 HYBRID ELECTRICAL OUTLETS

The PowerBoost hybrid uses Ford's twin-turbocharged 3.5L V6 combined with a 40-plus-hp electric motor. The electric motor is located between the engine and the standard 10-speed automatic transmission. A 450-volt liquid-cooled 1.5-kilowatt-hour (kWh) lithium-ion battery is located under the bed of the truck. It is mounted between the frame rails below the load floor, which allows the hybrid to have the same amount of space in the cargo and passenger areas as the non-hybrid version.

The combined output of both the V6 and the electric motor is 430 hp and 570 ft-lbs of torque. The electric motor is not designed to propel the truck by itself. Instead, it allows for short periods of electric cruising at low speeds similar to many other hybrid electric vehicles. The PowerBoost hybrid needs to be plugged in to charge the high-voltage battery because the system self-charges through regenerative braking and engine power. Two versions are available: one with a 2.4 kW output and another with a 7.2 kW output.

2.4 kW

This version includes four 110-volt outlets in the bed of the truck as well as several in-cabin outlets.

The PowerBoost in-bed outlets should not be confused with the outlets that are available on non-PowerBoost trucks that provide just 2.0 kW output and do not include the electric motor that is mounted between the engine and the transmission. The 2.0-kW system is an option that is available with any F-150 equipped with the 2.7L V6, 3.5L V6, or 5.0L V8.

7.2 kW

The optional 7.2kW output version includes a 220-volt outlet that is suitable for a welder as well as the 4 120-volt/20-amp plug outlets in the rear bed. Like the 2.4-kW version, it draws first from the battery before the engine is started.

The 220-volt, 30-ampere outlet can provide up to 7,200 watts of electricity and uses a three-terminal (two power terminals and one ground terminal) twist-lock National Electrical Manufacturers Association (NEMA) L6-20 outlet. NEMA defines the terminology, construction, and dimensions of electrical outlets and related components.

The 220-volt NEMA L6-20 outlet can be used to power a welder on the jobsite. The power available from this outlet is 30 amperes (7.2 kW). This electrical power can also be used to power a high-capacity air compressor for pneumatic tools.

This is the bed of the F-150 PowerBoost with the 7.2 kW on-board generator. The bed includes a 220-volt outlet that is suitable for a welder, as the 4 120-volt/20-amp plug outlets are easily accessible in the bed of the truck.

THE FOURTEENTH-GENERATION F-150 IS FULL OF TECHNOLOGY

With the fourteenth-generation F-150, Ford moved its pickup truck closer toward autonomous driving but also packed it full of other technological updates and upgrades. The Sync4 system replaced the Sync3, and Sync4 has many noticeable improvements. Sync 4 has more natural voice commands (and comprehension), real-time mapping on the navigation system, and seamless user-friendly integration with smartphones both wirelessly and through USB connections. Ford even partnered with Amazon Alexa and the popular Waze navigation smartphone application.

Ford's new advanced driver-assist features made advancements in 2021 with Co-Pilot Assist, which is a series of driver-assist technologies that include emergency braking, adaptive steering, and pedestrian detection.

Active Drive Assist is part of the Ford Co-Pilot 360 Active 2.0 package, which costs $1,595. This package is standard on the F-150 Limited model and is available as an option on Lariat, King Ranch, and Platinum models.

Some F-150s that are equipped with the Co-Pilot 360 Active 2.0 package can upgrade to Ford's BlueCruise, which will be a driver-assisted, hands-free technology. BlueCruise will use camera and radar sensors to allow a driver to operate the vehicle hands-free on prequalified sections of divided highways that are called Hands-Free Blue Zones. A driver-facing camera in the instrument cluster monitors eye gaze and head position to help ensure the driver's eyes remain on the road.

According to Ford, there are currently more than 100,000 miles of highways across North America that are dedicated Hands-Free Blue Zones in the Ford global positioning system (GPS).

Another piece of new technology for the fourteenth-generation F-150 is called PowerUp. It involves software updates that are done over the air (OTA). Vehicle enhancements, software updates, and some minor repairs can be done through Power Up. Using Ford's new second-generation electrical architecture allows for many of these OTA updates. Ford said that many updates will be made without alerting customers.

Considering a much-improved Sync system, hands-free driving, and OTA updates, the fourteenth-generation F-150 is arguably the most advanced truck that Ford has ever produced.

Adaptive cruise control is not new technology, but Ford plans to bring hands-free driving technology to future versions of the Ford F-150 through a technology called BlueCruise.

With the addition of Ford's new electric platform came the ability to significantly update Ford's infotainment system. For the fourteenth generation, the F-150 received Ford's newest Sync4 system with a standard 12-inch touchscreen. Apple CarPlay and Android Auto are available, and the truck has its own WiFi.

Honors

The 2021 Ford F-150 has won several national awards and received many accolades, especially the hybrid F-150. Most prestigious of them all, the 2021 Ford F-150 was named the North American Car, Truck, and Utility of the Year (NACTOY). It also was named the Green Truck of the Year by *Ron Cogan's Green Car Journal*. Kelley Blue Book awarded the F-150 its "Best Buy Award," which is an honor the truck has won for seven straight years. Edmunds, a consumer website, named the F-150 its Top-Rated Truck of 2021.

The 2021 Ford F-150 won the 2021 North American Car, Truck, and Utility of the Year award. The media members who voted for the truck via secret ballot said it was the addition of the hybrid powertrain that worked in the truck's favor, plus the new appearance and new features of the fourteenth generation. Winning this award is one of the highest honors a vehicle can receive.

F-150 Raptor

The Raptor received a redesigned appearance as part of the fourteenth generation, which is now the third iteration of Ford's off-road performance Raptor. The 2021 Ford F-150 Raptor launched with a high-output V6 engine. A V8 engine for the Raptor R will come in a future model year.

In addition to new exterior styling, the 2021 Raptor has a new five-link rear suspension and brand-new Fox shocks with Live Valve technology. It sports 37-inch tires. The high-output 3.5L EcoBoost engine is rated at 450 hp at 5,850 rpm and 510 ft-lbs at 3,000 rpm with a maximum towing capacity of 8,200 pounds.

F-150 Lightning

For the 2022 model year, Ford launched its first-ever fully-electric truck. The F-150 Lightning has 563 hp and 775 ft-lbs of torque, according to Ford. It has a maximum 2,000-pound payload and up to 10,000-pounds of towing capacity.

The all-electric F-150 has two battery options. The standard-range battery has an estimated range of 230 miles, and the extended-range battery has an estimated range of 300 miles.

Ford offers the Lightning in three trims: XLT, Lariat, and

The third-generation Ford F-150 Raptor has a high-output V6 engine. In July 2022, Ford introduced the Raptor R, which brought back a V8 engine to the Raptor. (Photo Courtesy Ford Motor Company)

Platinum. All three trims are available as Super Crew four-door trucks with a 5.5-foot bed only.

Ford Maverick

Ford entered a revived segment in the automotive industry with a small pickup truck that had yet another familiar name.

The Maverick is 199.7 inches long and 68.7 inches tall. This makes the Maverick nearly 11 inches shorter than the Ranger and nearly 32 inches shorter than the Ford F-150. What may be the most interesting regarding the Maverick is that the hybrid powertrain, which comes standard.

The standard Maverick is available as a five-passenger, four-door pickup with a full-hybrid powertrain and a projected

Ford brought back a familiar name, Lightning, for the 2022 all-electric pickup truck. (Photo Courtesy Ford Motor Company)

One of the biggest perks of the F-150 Lightning is the large front trunk (frunk). The Lightning's frunk has 14 cubic feet of cargo room, which is comparable in size to the trunk of many midsize sedans. The Lightning has a 5.5-foot bed. (Photo Courtesy Ford Motor Company)

The F-150 Lightning can be charged at home or at a work site. According to Ford, the truck's intelligent range system reduces range anxiety through an adaptive monitoring system that calculates battery range needed to complete a trip, factoring in terrain, weather, cargo and trailer load, and distance to the destination. (Photo Courtesy Ford Motor Company)

For the 2022 model year, Ford launched a small unibody hybrid pickup truck called the Maverick. It is offered in three trim levels: XL, XLT, and Lariat and comes with an available 2.0L EcoBoost gas engine instead of the standard 2.5L Atkinson-cycle hybrid engine. (Photo Courtesy Ford Motor Company)

EPA-estimated fuel-economy rating of 40 mpg (city). The unibody Maverick is offered at three trim levels: XL, XLT and Lariat.

The 2.5L Atkinson-cycle 4-cylinder hybrid powertrain delivers 191 hp when combined with the electric motor and 155 ft-lbs of torque mated to a continuously variable transmission (CVT) driving the front wheels. It features an in-house-designed and manufactured electric traction motor that is light and powerful.

The Maverick has a standard payload of 1,500 pounds and a towing capacity of 2,000 pounds. A 2.0L EcoBoost gas engine is available with 250 hp and 277 ft-lbs of torque with an 8-speed automatic transmission and standard front-wheel drive or available all-wheel drive. Equipped with the optional 4K towing package, conventional towing doubles to 4,000 pounds.

A New Generation and Direction

It's fitting to conclude the book with this chapter, as the fourteenth-generation Ford F-150 is full of game-changing technology that includes hybrid technology, autonomous technology, and electrification.

Ford introduced the F-Series in 1948, and it's come a long way. The evolution of the Ford F-Series has not concluded with this latest generation, and one could argue that the future of the F-Series is quite bright, as the truck continues to evolve.

Conclusion

For more than 100 years, Ford has made a pickup truck. The F-Series evolved over the years from a crude farmer's truck with a cab over an engine or a raw empty chassis to the fuel-efficient, capable, luxurious towing machines they are

The 2021 Ford F-150 has much more than merely a new appearance. It represents how the truck has fully evolved with society, as buyers want more power, better fuel economy, and even a way to power their home.

today. The fourteenth generation is the most evolved, but Ford works to continue the evolution. What will the future hold? It's difficult to say.

However, one thing is unquestionable: whatever the future holds for the Ford F-Series, the truck is not going anywhere. It is here to stay as a financial juggernaut for Ford and is ingrained in the everyday lives of many people throughout North America. Every year, hundreds of thousands of people buy a new Ford pickup truck. Henry Ford would certainly be smiling if he could see what that old farmer-based Model T has become.

The 2021 F-150's new tailgate is aimed at the workforce, featuring electrical outlets in the bed to run power equipment and a measuring device built into the bed of the tailgate.

Built-in cleats on the 2021 F-150 can be used to strap down items and attach clamps for using a saw on the tailgate.

Puddle lights not only are a neat add-on but they also serve a function for farmers in the field. The light illuminates the side of the truck to allow for farming during pre-dawn and dusk hours.

Regenerative brakes use a brake pedal position sensor and a unique master cylinder that includes pressure sensors to operate the base brakes as well as turning the electric drive motor(s) into generators. This electricity, which is generated during braking, recharges the high-voltage battery.

CHARGING THE F150 LIGHTNING

The Ford F-150 Lightning is a battery electric vehicle that uses a high-voltage battery pack to propel the vehicle. The capacity of the battery pack, which is measured in kilowatt hours (kWh), determines the range of the vehicle.

Batteries work best when they are kept within a temperature range between 68°F and 78°F (20°C and 26°C).

The distance an electric vehicle can travel on a full battery charge is called range, and many factors impact it, including:

- Battery energy storage capacity
- Vehicle weight
- Outside temperature
- Terrain (driving in hilly or mountainous areas requires more energy from the battery)
- Use of heating or air-conditioning systems and other electrical devices
- Driving style or habits

Level 1 charging uses a household 110/120-volt outlet. While it takes many hours to charge the high-voltage battery, charging at a lower rate is good for battery life. The circuit should be a 20-ampere dedicated outlet with no other circuit or electric load on the circuit. Never use an extension cord because the current draw can often cause it to overheat.

The cost of electricity varies by location, service provider, and sometimes the time of day. Many service providers offer a lower rate at night called time of use (TOU). If the rate is $0.11 per kWh, charging an electric vehicle that has a 96-kWh battery with a 250-mile range would cost about $11. This

Level 2 charging requires an installed NEMA 14–50 4-terminal outlet, which is the type of outlet that Ford recommends be used to charge the F-150 Lightning at home. The circuit breaker used should be 60 ampere, and the wire gauge should be 6 gauge. The 4 wires include 2 power wires, plus a neutral and a ground.

This is a Charge Point level 2 charging station plugged into a NEMA 14–50 outlet. Being plugged in means that the charger should be set to limit the charging rate to 40 amperes. If the charging station was hard wired, then the charging rate could be increased to 48 amperes. The charging station is equipped with the SAE J1772 plug, which is the standard in the industry for Level 1 and Level 2 charging.

cost is about the same as operating the average home's central air-conditioner for about 6 hours.

The EPA expresses an electric vehicle's energy consumption in terms of the number of kilowatts per hour needed to run the vehicle for 100 miles (kWh/100 mi.). For example, in typical ranges, many electric vehicles use 28 to 35 kW per 100 miles.

Range anxiety is a feeling that many drivers experience when driving an electric vehicle because they fear running out of electric battery energy before they reach their destination. Although range anxiety is common, it generally subsides.

Level 1 charging uses a 110/120-volt standard electric outlet (20-ampere circuit). The maximum power with a Level 1 charging is 1.9 kW. This low rate of charging means that it is best to charge the vehicle overnight so that it is ready to go the next morning. The advantage is that there is little, if any, installation cost because many homes are equipped with 110/120-volt outlets and can supply up to 16 amperes protected by a 20-ampere circuit breaker.

Level 2 chargers use 220/240 volts, and they charge the same vehicle in about 4 hours. Level 2 chargers can be added to most houses, making recharging faster (up to 80 amperes) and are the most commonly used charging stations available at stores and colleges. Level 2 charging adds about 25 miles of range per hour (RPH).

Level 3 charging stations use 440/480 volts (AC input

A Level 2 SAE combined charging system (CCS) connector is used to supply high-voltage DC power to the high-voltage vehicle battery, which allows for much faster charging. Using a DC fast-charging stations allows the truck to be charged in minutes instead of hours. While not as accessible as Level 2 charging stations, the truck display (or a smartphone application) can help the driver locate most charging stations.

and DC output) to charge most electric vehicles to 80 percent in less than 30 minutes. This high-charge rate may be harmful to battery life. Level 3 chargers are often called DC Fast Charge (DCFC).

Ford uses the SAE combined charging system (CCS) connector for high-speed charging.

Charging Summary

Level (Voltage)	Rate	Time to Fully Charge	Miles of Range Added per Hour of Charging (MPH)
Level 1 (110/120 volts)	16 amperes (1.4 to 1.7 kW)	16 hours for 32-kWh battery; 40 hours for 80-kWh battery	5 mph
Level 2 (208/210/220 volts)	32 to 48 amperes (7 to 13 kW)	3.5 hours for 32-kWh battery; 8 hours for 80-kWh battery	12 mph with 3.7-kW on-board charger; 25 mph with 6.6-kW on-board charger
Level 3 (440/480 volts DC)	24 kW to 250 kW	Generally 80-percent charge in 30 minutes (varies)	Up to 200 mph

The charge time and range per mile depend upon the voltage and current available during charging.